Too Tired to *Fight*

T0322059

Too Tired to *Fight*

13 Conflicts Parents Must Have To Keep Their Relationship Strong

ERIN MITCHELL
DR STEPHEN MITCHELL

Vermilion
LONDON

Vermilion, an imprint of Ebury Publishing
20 Vauxhall Bridge Road
London SW1V 2SA

Vermilion is part of the Penguin Random House group of companies whose
addresses can be found at global.penguinrandomhouse.com

First published in Great Britain by Vermilion in 2024
First published in the United States by G.P.PUTNAM'S SONS New York
in 2024, an imprint of Penguin Random House LLC

www.penguin.co.uk

A CIP catalogue record for this book is available from the British Library

ISBN: 9781785044717

Printed and bound in Great Britain by Clays Ltd, Elcograf S.p.A.

The authorised representative in the EEA is Penguin Random House Ireland,
Morrison Chambers, 32 Nassau Street, Dublin D02 YH68

To our kids:
It is our privilege to get to know and love you.
To the moon, buddies.

Mom, our Ahma forever:
You taught us the super power of repair.

Stephen, you make everything better.

Erin Anne, it has always been you.

Contents

Before You Read
This Book ...

W E ASK YOU to consider the words *fight* and *conflict*.

As you consider these words, remember they are just words, though they can be very powerful. As you consider them, notice what happens to you, for you, in you, and around you. What does *fight* mean to you? What image comes to mind? What is your knee-jerk reaction to being invited into a conflict? How do you perceive these words? Your experience matters and will inevitably shape how you approach conflict and the content in this book.

In this book, there is no room for anything that remotely looks or feels like abuse—physical, verbal, or otherwise. This book does not address abusive relationships. If you and your partner are currently engaging in fights of that kind, you should seek professional help immediately. Everyone deserves safety. Everyone.

Finally, all the following case examples are fictional couples and are not based on any specific couple we have worked with. They are compilations of themes we have heard from the hundreds of thousands of couples we've had the privilege of interacting with over the years.

PART I

Why Conflict
Is Good for Your Relationship,
and How to Do It the Right Way

What Kind of Couple Relationship Do We Want to Have?

IMAGINE A SITUATION where you find yourself pushed to the breaking point. Maybe it's first thing in the morning. You were up with your child several times during the night. Now you're exhausted, getting breakfast ready for everyone, when your partner comes into the room and casually says on the way out the door, "Hey, I think I forgot to tell you, but I have a work trip the last two days of this week."

Can you feel your body tense just imagining this scenario? You feel your insides turn, your blood boil, and a deep feeling of loneliness wash over you. Over the course of your parenting journey, you've felt more and more disconnected from your partner, and this is just one example of many in which you feel unseen and unknown by them.

How did you get here? You set out to be a harmonious family—happy, unified, and strong. You want your kids to learn what a healthy relationship looks like by observing the two of you together. You don't want to fight! Yet as time passes, you find more than anything that you are just trying to make it to bedtime without irritating the other too much.

Now imagine that instead of absorbing this surprising news into your body and getting hot with rage at your partner—instead of erupting in anger—you choose a different path. You use this difficult, challenging, and yes, irritating moment to instead find connection. You work through this difficult situation together—and in so doing, model conflict that leads to connection for your kids.

Seems impossible, right? It doesn't have to be.

We are Erin and Stephen Mitchell—partners in life as well as in our business, Couples Counseling for Parents. Parenting changes even a strong relationship in all sorts of ways, and even couples who are on solid ground before the kids arrive can feel absolutely rocked and unsteady afterward. This isn't easy, but it is normal.

We have talked with thousands of couples over the years, and all of them have experienced this disconnected feeling at one point or another. When they share their hopes and dreams for their family with us, we hear over and over some variation of these two statements: 1) We know our couple relationship is the foundation of a healthy family, and 2) it's harder than ever to make each other laugh and enjoy each other's company now that we're dealing with the day-to-day drudgery of parenting.

You are not alone! Parenting can be messy and unpredictable. It can also bring you closer together as a couple . . . if you let it. What these couples are really saying to us is: "In the midst of all this stress, we are struggling to remember we like each other. Can you help us?"

We have three kids of our own. We know these struggles first-hand. We know the amazing upsides of parenting: the quiet moments of sitting down together and reveling in the beauty and wonder of the children we are raising. We also know what it's like to lose our patience with our kids—and with each other! We know what it's like to look at each other and say, "Really?! You're tired? Well, let me tell you about *my* night . . ." We know what it is like to feel like the person you want more than anyone in the world to understand and empathize with what you're going through for some reason just doesn't. But thankfully, we also know what it is like to regroup as a family and a couple after these moments and talk about what it means to repair.

Take a moment and reflect on the following:

- What do I want for my family?
- What kind of relationship do I want to model for my kids?
- What kind of relationship do I want to have along the bumpy, beautiful road of parenting?
- When my kids are grown and out of our home, what kind of relationship do I want to have with my partner?

If you're like us, you want to show your kids how to support and love one another on the good, bad, and truly awful days. You want to show them their parents can have a conflict with each other, but that the partnership can still remain strong even amid disagreement. And you want to remain close with your partner even in the midst of those chaotic parenting moments, knowing the two of you are ultimately on the same team.

This is why we wrote *Too Tired to Fight*: to help parenting partners transform these messy moments of conflict into experiences of healthy resolution and repair, and to give couples the skills to turn conflict into connection.

WHO IS THIS BOOK FOR?

Too Tired to Fight is for all parents in romantic relationships looking for health and connection.

Maybe you bought this book in the middle of the night when you were the only one awake feeding your baby, feeling alone and unsupported. Maybe you are a couple with older kids, and you realize you have been waiting and hoping your communication would get better once they got a little more mature—but the problems remain. Maybe you bought this book because the resentment you feel toward your partner is eating away at you, and you worry that your marriage is going to crumble under the weight of it.

This book is designed as a tool for you to work through conflicts with your partner and come out on the other side feeling connected and stronger than ever.

HOW DO I USE THIS BOOK?

In part 1, we are going to talk about fighting once kids enter the picture: why it seems to happen more, and why it feels so different. We will also enable you to view conflict as a signal that you and your partner are trying to connect. Then we are going to give you our tried and true equation for engaging in healthy conflict: the conflict-to-connection equation. This will be your guide to resolve conflicts in the moment as you're experiencing them.

Then in part 2, we'll walk you through the thirteen most common conflicts we've helped countless parenting couples through—hot-button situations that turn so many couples sideways, like the "stop micromanaging my parenting" conflict, the "I'm more tired than you" conflict, the "Sex life? What sex life?" conflict, and the "I am carrying the mental load" conflict. In each chapter we'll introduce you to a couple and their experience with this conflict—what the trigger to the conflict is, why it's important to engage in it, and how this fight often goes wrong. These case studies are based on compilations of stories we have heard from the hundreds of thousands of couples we have had the privilege of interacting with. Then we'll take you directly into a counseling session between us and the couple in trouble to show how the conflict-to-connection equation can transform these fights into healthy conflicts that lead to lasting connection. At the end of each chapter, we offer sample scripts to give you a handle on the "But how can I actually say that?!" question that inevitably arises when we consider having an old conversation in a new way. We will also provide questions to get you reflecting and connecting to yourself and your partner.

Finally, at the end of this book, we have "A Quick Guide to How to Engage in Conflict in Front of Our Kids," "Sample Scripts for Addressing the Conflict with Our Kids," and "Sample Scripts to Address the Repair with Our Kids."

THE ULTIMATE GOAL:
NOT BEING TOO TIRED TO FIGHT

We want you to come away from *Too Tired to Fight* knowing you are not alone when seemingly small things can turn into stuck communication patterns, resulting in dead-end dialogues. The solutions we present in this book will allow you and your partner a better option than just trying to "make it until bedtime."

We are sure that you can find connection through the conflicts you will inevitably face as parenting couples. We also know that after you practice these communication skills with your partner, you'll have a better sense of how to know and love your partner and, in return, be known and loved by your partner. You'll also get to model healthy communication for your kids and enjoy laughter with your partner again.

CHAPTER 1

Why We Fight More—and Differently—After Kids

PARENTING CHANGES *EVERYTHING*. Let that sit for a moment.

Becoming a parent has changed your life in beautiful and wonderful ways, as well as in ways that are just plain hard.

Change brings stress, but stress does not have to mean something negative. Stress simply is the heightened energy that comes with going from something that is routine, expected, and practiced to something new. Having kids and parenting, whether it is your first kid, second, third, etc., is a monumental change that means your routine, what you have come to expect, and what you know how to do is challenged. With this challenge comes a heightened energy that courses through our brains, bodies, emotions, and thoughts in an effort to "get back to" the routine and practiced place. Not to mention, we all handle stress differently.

If we default to our stress response in a situation, it's almost impossible to connect with our partner to resolve the issue together and stop the cycle of stuck communication. In this way, conflict that could typically be resolved with relative ease before kids turns into stuck fighting.

WHY DO WE FIGHT MORE NOW THAT WE'RE PARENTS?

Conflict is a natural part of any human interaction. Whenever you have two people with different lived experiences and ways to respond to stress, you will have conflict. While there will be misalignment, conflict can be resolved in a good way that leads to connection (what we are going to help you with in this book), or conflict can be resolved in an unhealthy way that leads to two dysregulated people, lost in their stress response, endlessly fighting with each other. This type of conflict is not productive and an indication that neither partner is in the right nervous system state to connect. The context of parenting often throws partners into this unproductive state, and this leads to an increase in the number of negative fights couples experience.

Here's an example. Sasha and Alex turned to us for help, using words similar to those we have heard from so many couples: "Before we had kids, we got along great. Of course we were not perfect communicators. We had some difficulty at times, but mostly we were able to work through conflicts without too much effort. But now, since we've had kids, it's like we can't communicate. Most of our conversations end up in some kind of fight."

Sasha and Alex had been together for five years and had always talked about having kids. When they finally decided to have kids Sasha said, "We never felt so close." Alex agreed: "Yeah, here we were working through some really tough conversations about what we wanted and what was the best option for us, and it just felt like we were a team." Sasha added that she felt like Alex understood her anxieties and knew just how to make her feel supported.

Then their daughter, Sofia, was born, and everything changed. Alex said, "Things were still pretty good the first couple of weeks. In truth we were starstruck with Sofia. But then we just started bickering more and more and picking at each other, and now all productive communication seems to have just gone out the window."

Each began to feel as if the other was not supportive; each thought they were doing more than the other. Sasha works from home as a graphic designer, and by default, she found herself taking care of Sofia, keeping the house, and making dinner. Alex works out of the house as an investment banker and resented that on top of his demanding fifty-hour-a-week job, he came home and went right to work parenting.

So, when Sasha expressed feeling like she was doing all the work, Alex wanted to try to hear where Sasha was coming from but also resented feeling like there was more he could actually be doing. He feels like Sasha paints a picture of him sitting around on the couch while she makes him dinner. Which of course makes Sasha feel like what she is trying to say is not being heard at all. Now they feel like they are in a constant standoff fighting about every "little thing" and feeling miles and miles apart.

The couple came to us feeling discouraged, surprised by how bad their relationship felt, and frightened by a feeling of "If this is the way it's going to be, I'm not sure we should stay together."

Sasha and Alex's session exemplifies two key reasons couples fight more when their parenting journey begins.

The Stakes Feel Higher Now

We have counseled many couples like Sasha and Alex. They have a good relationship, they want to have kids, they have kids, and then seemingly out of nowhere everything starts to feel like it is falling apart. This is a frightening experience, one you may be going through as you're reading this book. The long nights of waking up with an infant while your partner sleeps or the many times you are told that "you never do anything to help" no matter how much you are helping, begin to fracture the foundations of your relationship and your sense of hope and connection. Over time, as these resentments and hurts build up, deep cracks can develop.

This is where Sasha and Alex find themselves. Before having Sofia, they never imagined that they were not right for each other. In fact, they believed that having Sofia would bring them closer together. Initially it did, but the feeling didn't last. At this point they feel like strangers to each other. The intensity of their conflict and their inability to have what they think of as a normal conversation make them both feel like maybe the other has changed or maybe they just didn't know each other as well as they thought they did.

We Are Stretched Too Thin Already

The introduction of kids into a couple system is indeed stressful. It is important to understand what stress does to couples in a parenting partner relationship. It results in a loss of capacity.

Every human being has a stress response system that is meant to help us manage and navigate times of uncertainty, danger, chaos, and instability. Our sympathetic nervous system is activated in these moments to help us survive; our fight-flight-freeze-fawn response kicks into gear. Now granted, parenting is not the same as being chased by a lion, but in our day-to-day life as parents, this stress response system is still activated. We feel the weight of the world on our shoulders, and our body activates to try and figure out how to mitigate the stress.

So when Sasha snaps at Alex for once again coming home late and leaving her to deal with making dinner, cleaning up, and getting Sofia ready for bed, she is experiencing the stress response of fight.

She feels overwhelmed, so she makes a snarky comment and attacks the perceived threat, which is Alex and his tardiness. In turn, Alex feels surprised, scared, and destabilized by Sasha's anger and elevated tone, and his stress response system kicks into gear as well. He goes silent and walks out of the room. In his efforts to reduce the sense of overwhelm he feels, Alex takes flight and tries to get away from the stressor, Sasha.

The basic idea behind this stress response system is, "I need whatever is happening to stop, because it is so scary or feels so bad and my best options for that are to fight/flee/freeze/fawn." Keep in mind that when the stress response system is turned on, other biopsychosocial-spiritual systems must shut down. For example, our metabolic system stops functioning because in stress we don't need to devote any energy to metabolizing food—we can worry about food later. The focus is on getting through the threat. Our prefrontal cortex, the part of the brain that helps with rational thought, goes offline; after all, in this situation we don't need to spend time pondering the meaning of life. During periods of stress, our social and spiritual connection to others becomes limited, if not nonexistent, because we don't have time to be empathetic or in sync with the transcendent when we are trying to survive.

When our stress response system is on and our other systems are off, we are not functioning at our best.

Ideally, once the threatening moment is over, the parasympathetic nervous system steps in to help turn on the systems that have been shut down and return us to a regulated and balanced state. For example, Sasha might continue fuming when Alex walks out of the room, but instead of resorting to more sarcastic comments, she might step outside for a breath of fresh air. As she stands outside, her breathing may slow and the physical movement of walking around their patio may soothe her a bit. Her mind may clear a little. By the time she steps back inside, she might be able to reevaluate her response to Alex and say to herself: "I am still angry, but that was not how I wanted to communicate with Alex. I need to go talk to him and sort this out."

Meanwhile, Alex walked out of the room buzzing. Sasha's anger felt scary and it left his brain feeling blank, like he couldn't find any words to say. He had to get out of the room because he didn't know what else to do. As he walks up the stairs to change out of his work clothes, he begins to get his bearings. His heart rate evens out and the jumble in his brain begins to feel less messy. At this point, he can say to himself, "I don't like it when Sasha comes at me like that. It just feels scary. At the same time, I know I did come home late, and it is really overwhelming to have to deal with everything all by herself. I'll check back in with her after I change."

This is a brief glimpse into how the stress response system works in a parenting partner relationship. Parenting partners fight more because they are experiencing the state of lost capacity more frequently and many times not recovering. Yes, the ideal is that Sasha finds herself in a regulated place and can talk more calmly and that Alex is able to check in with Sasha in a balanced manner. Often this repair does not happen for parenting partners. Rather, the stressful moment happens, capacity is lost, and then couples don't resolve the problem. It would look like Sasha and Alex not finding any regulation in their nervous systems, not talking it out, then going to bed, waking up, and doing it all over again the next day.

This pattern results in couples who remain in a perpetual state of stress and lost capacity, which is exhausting. Two stressed partners result in a couple who has stressed and unhealthy communication.

Now the couple relationship becomes a source of stress, and interactions between partners or even the thought of interactions with each other instantly activates the stress response system. In this way couples move from circumstances and situations causing stress to seeing each other as the threat, the stress, and the problem; this couple is too tired to fight.

WHY DO OUR FIGHTS FEEL SO INTENSE?

Sasha and Alex didn't only want to talk with us about the frequency of their fights—there was a level of intensity in their conflict that made them both feel more resistant and deeply hurt by each other. Alex said, "It's almost like I don't even know Sasha anymore. I look at her when I am angry, and I have this feeling that she is cruel and uncaring. At times I feel like I don't want to be around her." Sasha put it this way: "Alex used to be thoughtful and considerate, but now he just seems checked out and disinterested in our life. I hate to say it, but sometimes things are easier when he's not around."

Alex and Sasha feel so deeply hurt and let down by their partner that their anger with each other is significantly greater than it was before kids. They act and behave in ways they don't like. They sometimes even question if they will make it as a couple and family unit. These changes blindside them and make them unsure about how to get back to the safer, healthier place they were in before having kids. They really don't know how to get out of this stuck place.

There is a reason behind this heightened emotion, though. The fights between couples feel more intense after kids enter the picture because the couple's attachment systems are impacted differently. Attachment theory, which has been widely supported through modern-day research in neuroscience, is based on the idea that we as human beings seek out, establish, and maintain bonds of closeness. These bonds of closeness allow us to feel safe (physically, emotionally, psychologically), which ultimately allow us to love and be loved.

All human beings have an attachment system, the development of which begins in utero and continues throughout their life. Some key developmental periods during which our attachment system is imprinted in the neurology of our brains are our original experience of caregiving (that is to say, our relationship with our own parents), our romantic relationships (our history of partnering), and our experience as parents.

Attachment Theory and Parenting

The basic premise of attachment theory is that human beings want and need to feel safe physically, emotionally, and psychologically. When we feel safe in these areas, we are free to explore and learn things about ourselves, others, and the world around us and we can trust others. Attachment theory goes on to say that a feeling of safety is established through proximity and responsiveness. The simplest example of this is when a baby cries. When babies cry, they are soothed by someone physically coming close and touching, holding, or rocking them (proximity), and by someone acknowledging their distress (responsiveness) by saying, "I see you. I hear you. You seem upset; I'll hold you." In this way babies learn that they can have a need and express it, and someone will come close and respond.

When someone has had the experience of consistent (notice we did not say *perfect*) proximity and responsiveness, they are able to offer others the same kind of relationship. This allows them to build strong interpersonal connections. Those who do not have a consistent experience of proximity and responsiveness will be insecure in their relationships and struggle to build healthy interpersonal connections. This insecurity is expressed in the form of anxiety and impacts how individuals view themselves (an overinflated or diminished sense of self).

How you were parented sets up a basic, fundamental attachment strategy that affects the rest of your life. This in turn can impact how you choose your romantic partner and ultimately how you show up as a parent. But what about how you show up as a parent *alongside* your partner, and how the two of you work through conflict as parents together? That's at the heart of what we'll explore in this book.

Parenting triggers a desire to correct
or continue your attachment experience.

Parenting takes us into our past and causes us to wonder about our future. Sasha and Alex both wanted to be parents. Sasha put it this way: "You know I didn't really have the best relationship with my parents, and I always dreamed of things being different between me and my kid. I just always thought I could be a good parent." Alex's story was different: "I loved my experience growing up. My parents were really loving and warm and I got along well with my siblings. I think I just expected to have a similar feel in my family."

Notice that Sasha and Alex are both talking about attachment: how being a parent causes them to think about their past experiences but also enables them to express a positive view about what their future will be like. They both recognize that the responsibility associated with being a parent is great. They know that how they interact with Sofia and each other will influence how Sofia feels about her life and relationships in a powerful way. Because of this, the stakes are high, which in turn raises the intensity surrounding parenting.

Sasha and Alex both have ideas about what parenting should look like. Alex is determined that Sofia should never see him and Sasha fight. "I didn't see my parents fight. They were supportive of each other, and if there were problems, they talked about them somewhere else. What do you think it makes Sofia feel like to be in all that bad energy and noise when we fight?" Sasha disagrees. "I didn't see my parents fight, either, and they ended up getting divorced. Maybe if they had actually cared enough to have some conflict, they would have been better off. Or maybe if I had seen them disagree, then I would know what to do with you when we are disagreeing. Sofia needs to see us work through this stuff."

In this exchange, Sasha and Alex are fighting for something that feels more important because they are parents and they have a future that they want to create for Sofia. This future is based on their own attachment experiences and their desire to either correct or continue these. Inevitably, parenting partners will not agree on all things, but when it feels like the disagreements will shape the attachment experience of your kid, partners dig in and things get heated very quickly.

Parenting activates your attachment needs.

As we mentioned previously one of the key developmental periods for our attachment systems is during romantic relationships. So not only is Sofia developing as a kid, but Sasha and Alex are in a developmental period of their couple relationship. Of course the increased stress of parenting can result in an unavailability to each other as partners. In stressful times, one of the deepest needs we have is to feel that we are going to make it, that someone is with us and we are not alone. In essence, we want to feel safe.

Sasha and Alex are overwhelmed and trying to survive. They are looking to each other for a sense of hope, support, and belonging so that they can feel safe and cope with their stress. This is a natural and healthy thing to do. As Sasha puts it, "Sometimes at the end of the day I just want Alex to ask me how I have been. I just want him to load the dishwasher because he knows I have been stuck doing all the other household things. I just want to feel like I'm not all by myself in this." Alex responds: "I want the same thing. I want to come home and maybe have you say, 'Hey, thanks for going to work and doing a job you hate because you know it gives us the most financial security.' Or have you realized that I also never get a break in during the day and it might be nice for me to come home and not feel like you're immediately telling me I am not doing enough? I feel like you don't understand me at all."

Sasha and Alex are expressing attachment needs; the fact that these needs are not being met with proximity and responsiveness is leading to hurt and relational isolation. These experiences of not feeling safe together as a couple and relational isolation break bonds of attachment and heightens the intensity of conflict in parenting partner relationships.

HOW DO WE DISRUPT AN UNHEALTHY CONFLICT CYCLE?

You might be reading this and saying, "I don't see our stress levels changing any time soon. In fact, I just see them increasing. So are we doomed to keep fighting, hurting each other, and failing at meeting each other's needs? Is all lost?" In short, no, all is not lost. Parenting partners have to learn a new way to engage conflict. Notice we didn't say parenting partners need to learn *not* to have conflict. Conflict itself is not bad. How you engage in conflict is what matters.

Attachment-Making vs. Attachment-Breaking Interactions

Couples must begin to engage conflict with the perspective that they want to create attachment-making interactions instead of attachment-breaking interactions. Sasha and Alex are coming to us because they are swimming in attachment-breaking interactions. Their conflicts are characterized by withdrawal and attack rather than by safe proximity and responsiveness. In this way, their conflict turns into an unhealthy fight.

Each feels the other is the problem, but really the problem is they are both frightened that the other can't, won't, or doesn't want to meet their attachment need. The moment they feel this need might not be met (or it is not met) is the moment they begin to protect themselves.

Sasha hears Alex walk in the door and sigh in exasperation. Instantly she thinks, *Alex is in a bad mood, he's not going to be available to me. He isn't going to be able to help me with my feelings of being overwhelmed by my day.* She gets scared, and rather than approach Alex gently, she amps up to try and get what she needs. Alex hears the tone of Sasha's voice and thinks, *I was just sighing because I'm tired. Sasha is so uptight and is always monitoring my mood. She can't let anyone have a bad day.* He gets scared that Sasha will never allow him to be less than perfect, so he withdraws.

These are attachment-breaking interactions, and all these little micro-moments add up. Attachment-breaking interactions always leave partners feeling scared, defensive, and alone.

Sasha and Alex do not have to stay stuck in these attachment-breaking interactions, and neither do you. You can have the trend of your relationship be attachment-making interactions. You can have disagreements and conflicts and still feel like your partner is close and responsive. You can learn how to turn conflict into connection through the tools we present throughout *Too Tired to Fight.*

CHAPTER 2

How to Turn Conflict into Connection

L ONELY. TIRED. DISCOURAGED. *Defeated.* These are some of the more common words we hear from parenting partners when they describe how they feel about their relationship. They ask how they can repair what seems broken in their partnership. Rarely do they expect our proposed solution to be *engage* the conflict—not run away from it.

Engaging conflict typically sounds exhausting to couples, and we understand why. If your conflicts right now are fairly predictable or you're at the point of begging for connection and some engagement, hearing that you need to have conflict may feel counterintuitive. We all want to fight less and enjoy life more. We don't want to spend our days doing an internal quiet scream, hoping against hope our partner hears us, sees us, and moves toward us with engagement and intentionality. Unhealthy fighting is maddeningly pointless—it can feel like swimming upstream all day long only to get too little sleep, then wake up and do it all over again the next day. But fighting does not have to be this way. True healthy conflict, the kind you should participate in with your partner, is about working toward understanding your partner when he or she is signaling to you something is wrong, and vice versa. It's about connecting in a way that leads to growth, a new shared experience, that can make your relationship and family unit stronger than ever.

Conflict arises when one partner tries to communicate something about themselves to the other and doesn't feel like the partner is getting it. Being understood is so important to creating bonds of attachment that one partner can't just let it go or move on without the other understanding. Behind every conflict is a desire to connect; this is why conflict is a "good" thing, but when conflict turns unhealthy the couple has lost the ability to connect.

The bottom line is that parenting will change your couple relationship, and those changes can be for the better. You and your partner can enjoy your family right in the parenting season you are in. You do not have to numb out what you are feeling only to later find that resentment is eating away at you. You can learn to share your truest self, even in the most vulnerable of moments. You can have conflict in a way that leads to connection.

WHY WE SHOULD ENGAGE IN CONFLICT

It's not that we love conflict. If we lived in a perfect world, we wouldn't have conflict. But we don't. We live in a world where there is brokenness and hurt, where unfortunately at times we anger and hurt the people we love. When engaging in conflict, we must keep two goals in mind in order to open ourselves up to seeing the process differently.

Goal 1: Connection

The first goal of engaging conflict is connection: building bonds of attachment through the process of creating safety (proximity and responsiveness) for each other as partners. We fight because something in the relationship feels unsafe, unsupportive, so we feel disconnected. Simply put, something feels off. We want you and your partner to notice when this "off" feeling is happening and learn how to say it in a way that your partner can hear. But that's not usually what we are cued into first, especially in these hot-topic parenting conflicts we are about to get into. Quite often, what happens is we notice something feels off, we identify it as the thing our partner said or did that didn't feel good, and we say, "You did this thing. Stop doing it."

That would seem to be simple enough, except that many times what we are trying to say comes out in a way we didn't mean and with a tone we didn't intend. This is a direct result of a stress response. We want our partner to hear and respond to the deeper meanings we are trying to communicate through our stress, but very often we don't even know what that is ourselves. Often the simple fact that we seem stressed activates our partner's stress response and they fight, flight, freeze, or fawn before anyone even knows exactly what happened. This is how conflict can feel triggering.

Connection does not mean that our stress response is never activated. Connection means we are attuned to when our stress response has been activated and how we typically respond (fight, flight, freeze, fawn) when activated. It means when we are triggered, we can pause and describe what is happening to us (not simply blame our partner), and we can be curious about what our partner is experiencing without becoming defensive. Finally, it means we can take accountability when appropriate, forgive, and move toward change. This process is what creates a consistent sense of safety in a couple relationship and builds lasting bonds of attachment and feelings of love.

Goal 2: Resolution (Repair)

The second goal of engaging conflict is everyone's favorite—to bring an end to the conflict and reach a resolution. Resolution is part of the attachment-building process of repair. Repair happens after there has been a rupture and involves accountability, forgiveness, and taking action toward lasting change. We need to engage in conflict to be seen and known, and until we feel our partner understands our experience (which does not have to mean they agree or can relate) we cannot move on.

Think of conflict like a circuit. All the connections need to be in place for the light to be able to flick on. If we have a rupture still waiting on a repair, we have a broken loop, and we will keep coming back to it until it is resolved. In these moments we highly recommend saying, "I am not feeling understood right now, and it hurts," but that's not something many of us have been encouraged to express. What typically comes out is something more like: "You are making me feel bad, and you have to make sure I feel better," which doesn't make you or your partner feel good, isn't true, and does not invite resolution.

Conflict, like a good story, needs to have a beginning, a middle, and an end. Conflict can have an end (which does not mean it will not come back up ever; see chapter 15 about resentment and forgiveness) in which people feel heard and understood and that their experience matters. If there is action needed to be taken, we want to trust that this action will be taken by our partner. Repair is one of the most overlooked parts of a conflict. It requires accountability—being humble and sitting in someone else's experience, which may be unpleasant if you had a part to play in the negative experience. Repair requires forgiveness, which means being vulnerable, expressing how you have been hurt, and trusting your partner. It also means that you move through shame and forgive yourself when you've done something you're not proud of. Finally, repair means you take action to change.

Repair is not fun or glamorous, but it is essential to resolving a conflict. Repair cannot be rushed. If it is, it's not a real repair and you will find it's not actually over. Repair also cannot be faked, and if it is, the trust will not be there. This will be uncomfortable to do at first, but once it becomes more of a practice in your life, you will enjoy the powerful connection and sense of resolution repair brings to your relationship.

THE CONFLICT-TO-CONNECTION EQUATION

In over twenty years of working with couples, we've discovered the equation for making your fights less frequent and intense. This secret originated from both our professional experience and our personal lived experience as parenting partners to three kids.

At the point when we had our oldest, we both had advanced degrees in counseling psychology, had a few years of clinical work under our belts, and had been to individual and couples therapy for years. Stephen was also in the early stages of his PhD in a medical family therapy program. Theoretically, if there was any couple ready to have kids and weather the chaos of parenting and relationships, it was us. We had the knowledge and experience to make our transition from couple to parenting partners with minimal bumps along the way. Yet we struggled. We freely admit that we've had direct experience of every one of the thirteen conflicts we talk about in this book. All our education and lived experience wasn't enough to enable us to avoid the struggles so many couples seem to face in this life-altering transition. As we searched for help, we found it surprising how few research-informed, psychologically sound, educational resources there were available that specifically addressed couples in this stage of their life. There were plenty of parenting books, but not many addressed how a couple's relationship is impacted by parenting and how it can thrive during parenting.

So we went to work. We started developing resources based on our understanding of attachment theory, couples therapy, child development, narrative therapy, neuroscience, and countless other psychological principles. Then we began to apply them to this specific stage in a couple's developmental life cycle. During this process we discovered an equation that started to work for the couples that we were seeing. Did it work perfectly every time for every couple? No. But as we kept applying our equation and the specific tools within the equation we noticed couples began to change. Specifically, what changed is they went from hardened places of resentment and endless dead-end dialogue to connection and resolution. They began to heal. We also began to hear from tens of thousands of couples all over the world that this equation, our approach, and the resources we offered were helping partners feel seen and understood, improving how partners were communicating, and lessening the frequency and intensity of their fights. Couples were learning to move from conflict to connection.

So what is the conflict-to-connection equation and how does it work? It is:

$$A \text{ (Intentional Expressing)} + B \text{ (Intentional Listening)} = \text{Connection}$$

Part A of the equation refers to the partner who is initially expressing something important. Expressing is not venting and getting things off your chest. Healthy, intentional expressing is first and foremost describing your own experience, not blaming your partner or diverting attention away from yourself by focusing on your partner's experience. Remember Sasha and Alex from chapter 1? Sasha was angry with

Alex for coming home late from work and leaving her to handle dinner and bedtime. An unhealthy way of expressing this would be her saying to Alex: "You made me feel so mad because you were late. You are so selfish and completely absorbed in your own world. Do you even care about this family?" Healthy expression, according to our equation, keeps the focus on Sasha. It would go something like this: "I noticed that as I was making dinner, cleaning up, and trying to get Sofia to bed, I was feeling really angry with you. I feel so alone and like I am doing a lot of the parenting on my own." Sasha is keeping the focus on describing her own lived experience.

Second, the conflict-to-connection equation focuses on the *story* behind the feeling being expressed. So, what is being put into words is how the expressing partner understands they came to feel the way they do, based not on their partner's behavior, but on what part of their previous attachment experience is being brought to light in the present moment. Expressing partners are asked to understand themselves and describe themselves to their partner, which is no easy feat! It is a vulnerable, intentional offering of self.

Here are the four steps to move through when engaging in intentional expressing of the conflict-to-connection equation:

1. **Assess:** Evaluate if you feel triggered and your stress response system is activated. Slow down so you can notice and observe what is happening. Interrupt the stress response.

2. **Attune:** Tune into your body, mind, and emotions. What might these be telling you about the way you are feeling?

3. **Reflect:** Have you ever felt the way you feel before? What parts of your story are being repeated or are coming into your awareness? What are you trying to ignore? What is important about the story or stories you are remembering?

4. **Share:** Walk your partner through your process. Tell them the sensations, thoughts, and emotions you noticed. Relay to them the story or stories that emerged. Describe for them how the present moment relates to these things and why they feel important.

Now let's look at the second, and equally important, part of the conflict-to-connection equation. Part B of the equation refers to the other partner, the one who is listening. Listening is not just letting someone else talk. Listening is active and takes effort. Intentional listening requires two active postures that demonstrate to the expressing partner: "I am here and I am working to understand."

First, intentional listening requires a posture of humility. Humility shields the intentional listener from defensiveness. If one of the goals of intentional expressing is to avoid blame, then one of the primary goals of intentional listening is to avoid defensiveness. Humility involves a willingness to be open to your partner and to tolerate without protest their expression of their experience. It involves considering that you may have had a role to play in your partner's experience rather than dismissing their feelings or defending your actions.

Second, intentional listening requires a posture of curiosity. Curiosity is the opposite of being closed to and defensive about what your partner is expressing. It communicates to your partner: I am listening, I am taking you seriously, and I want to understand.

Take Sasha and Alex. Sasha can intentionally express that she is angry at Alex, but that really what she is feeling is alone in parenting. Intentional listening would not mean that Alex then launches into a long diatribe about all the things he does: "I help you all the time with parenting. I do the morning routine, most days I pick up Sofia, and tonight I was late because I had a huge client meeting. I am not usually late." Here Alex does not take a posture of humility and curiosity. In contrast to this, intentional listening would mean Alex says something like: "I can tell you are upset. I know feeling alone is terrible and scary. Can you walk me through what happened for you tonight?"

Notice in this response Alex showed humility by not dismissing Sasha's emotions and curiosity by asking her to describe more of her experience. Alex may be feeling the urge to be defensive, but he does not lead with this urge. He leads with intentional listening.

The four key steps in intentional listening are:

1. **Assess:** Evaluate if you feel triggered and your stress response system is activated. Slow down so you can notice and observe what is happening. Interrupt the stress response.

2. **Suspend defensiveness:** Don't lead with defensiveness. Defensiveness is often our default reaction when our partner begins to express emotions in a fight. It can come out as responding with anger, withdrawal, or a sarcastic remark. Suspend your defensiveness by responding with humility and curiosity.

3. **Believe the other person's experience:** This does not mean you have to agree with their interpretation of events, but you can acknowledge that this was their experience of it. You can be curious and say to yourself, "I might not agree, but this is after all my partner's experience. How can I engage them in a way that does not make them feel dismissed, like I don't care?"

4. **Repair:** Depending on the situation.

   If it is solvable: Apologize, take responsibility, decide together if a change needs to be made, and seek a solution. For example, you might repair the situation by saying, "I can see why my saying that in the moment was so hurtful. I did not think that through. I am sorry I said it. What about if next time I try _____?"

If it is a persistent problem: Move toward understanding and empathy. An example of an unsolvable situation could be that you got called in for work unexpectedly and had to leave your partner to care for the kids. You can repair this situation by saying, "I know this is hard and will cost you. I hate that. I am sorry this is happening."

A. Intentional Expressing	B. Intentional Listening
Assess	Assess
Attune	Suspend defensiveness
Reflect	Believe the other person's experience
Share	Repair

With practice, this equation can prevent fights a lot of the time, but even if your encounter turns into an unhealthy conflict—because that does happen!—knowing what's going on will help you get out of dead-end dialogue more quickly and move you toward connection and resolution.

TROUBLESHOOTING THE EQUATION

Couples won't be able to get it right every single time there is conflict. In a perfect world, both partners would come to a fight and instantly intentionally express and intentionally listen. As we all know, this is not how things always work. Sometimes a couple starts off on the wrong foot, and in the middle of the fight, they remember to try the equation. Other times one partner is trying to apply the equation and the other is not. Regardless of the situation, it's important to realize that you can shift into the equation at any point in your conflict. The key is understanding both your own and your partner's triggers. Before we delve into that, though, let's first define what triggers are and how they operate.

Triggers are the feelings or sensations that activate our stress response systems and are associated with past negative attachment experiences. For example, feeling lonely is a trigger for Sasha. It reminds Sasha of when she was a little kid. Because of her dad's work, the family had to move a lot. This meant that she had to go to multiple schools and start all over again in each one trying to make friends and find a place to belong. Sadly, this was not easy for Sasha, so she spent a lot of time sitting by herself at lunch or not having any playmates when her class went outside. For Sasha, loneliness is a trigger activating her stress response system.

Triggers can be set off by words, a tone of voice, facial expressions, smells, memories, stepping into a particular environment, being around certain people, and many other sensory experiences. Triggers are overwhelming because they initiate the feeling of a negative attachment experience, which is how an unhealthy conflict begins. Knowing your and your partner's triggers is key to the first step of the conflict-to-connection equation: Assess.

Know Your Triggers

The assess step in the conflict-to-connection equation is all about interrupting your stress response and trying to return to a more regulated place. So you've got to know the things that trigger your stress response system. Here are some questions that can help both you and your partner begin to identify your triggers:

- What things seem to trigger me?
- When I am triggered, what happens for me on a sensory and physical level? Do I get hot/cold? Does my heart start to beat faster? Do my hands sweat? Do I clench my jaw or tighten my muscles? Does my mind go blank? Do my ears buzz? Do I feel nauseated? And so forth.
- Think about my attachment needs for proximity (physical closeness) and responsiveness (attunement to, engagement with, and validation of our emotions, thoughts, and self). How is my trigger related to not receiving one or both of these needs?
- What are the past stories from even before my partner that made this such a sensitive spot? In other words, what earlier attachment experiences contributed to this being a trigger?
- How has my relationship perpetuated this being a sensitive spot?

Once you and your partner both become aware of these triggers, you'll be able to share these places through mutual vulnerability and curiosity with each other. Knowing each other's triggers will permit you to communicate with each other in a positive fashion. Yet, we are not perfect people, and many times we know what is triggering to our partner but it happens anyway. Oftentimes this is not an intentional act—it is just part of the everyday miscommunication that takes place in interpersonal interactions. Additionally, many times when we are triggered we do not instantly have the awareness that it is happening. Something is said or we experience a tone of voice in a particular way and our response is tense, terse, angry, withdrawn; you name it, and we are into a triggered place and fighting in the blink of an eye.

This is where the assess step is so important in the conflict-to-connection equation. It helps both partners take a breath and ask themselves: "Am I feeling triggered right now? Is my partner feeling triggered right now?" These questions can provide the escape hatch we need from a dead-end dialogue.

Recognize How You Get Untriggered

The second way to avoid falling back into your old stuck cycle is to understand how you and your partner get untriggered. Keep in mind that what works for one person may not work for the other. Very often one partner will try to de-stress the other in the way that de-stresses them. This is often a misstep and can make the hurt partner feel even more unseen and unknown.

So what are the ways you get untriggered? We know for us, fresh air and moving our bodies help us both. Whenever possible, we try to talk about important things while taking our dog on a walk or after exercising. For Erin, humor is almost always the surest way back to her untriggered soothed self. Because of this, Stephen has learned how to read the situation and offer some funny name for the fight we are having. For example, Stephen may say to Erin, "So from here on out, this will go down as the 'dinosaur-pants disaster.'" This humor gets Erin out of the stressed place she's in and reminds her that one day this will not feel as intense as it did just seconds ago. Stephen, on the other hand, appreciates a single sentence pointing out his stress response, then a few minutes to breathe and come out of his triggered place. For example, Erin may say, "Hey, you aren't sounding like yourself. You need a minute?" This comment helps bring Stephen into the awareness he is reacting in a stressed fashion and gently lets him know he can take a deep breath and reenter the situation with less reactivity.

IMPLEMENTING THE EQUATION

Let's look at Sasha and Alex's fight to see how the equation could have worked for them. What would conflict to connection look like in that situation?

A (Intentional Expressing) +
B (Intentional Listening) = Connection

Partner A (Sasha):

1. **Assess:** Whoa, I just lost it on him, didn't I? I guess I was angrier at him than I knew. I'm triggered.

2. **Attune:** Okay. I need to take a breath. What is going on? What about his being late feels so bad right now?

3. **Reflect:** I think I'm tired and overwhelmed. Today has been hard, and I felt really alone when he called me this afternoon to let me know he was going to be late. It took the wind out of my sails. I just kept thinking about how long the night was going to feel and that I wouldn't have any help. I hate feeling like no one can help me, that it's up to me to figure it out. Why can't I have help like other moms? I mean, my mom lives twenty minutes away and she can't even be bothered to give me a break on a day like today. I just feel angry about it.

4. **Share:** "Hey, Alex. I feel uncomfortable telling you this, but I think I just lost my patience with you because I am feeling sad and lonely about not having help. Like having a mom that could be helpful. I noticed I was getting pretty angry with you for not being home at the usual time. I mean, I know you called

to let me know about it, but it just made me so angry. And then I was sitting here looking at the clock counting down the minutes until you got home and my face was getting hot and it started to get ugly in my head, and then I just blurted out what was in my head. But I was trying to figure out why it felt so bad. I mean, you can't help being late sometimes. Then I realized when you called this afternoon, I just felt lonely. It was going to be a long night, and I found myself wanting to be able to call my mom and ask for help. A lot of my friends can do that, but I can't, and it just got me all out of sorts.

Partner B (Alex):

1. **Assess:** I couldn't handle what Sasha was saying. I just needed to get out of there. I couldn't even think straight. I think I am triggered.

2. **Suspend defensiveness:** Sasha is wanting to talk. She seems calmer, but I hear her saying that I am making her feel alone. I don't think that is true. I feel myself wanting to be defensive. Hold on. What is she trying to communicate about her experience? Don't get confused. Hold off on being defensive.

3. **Believe the other person's experience:** "I see how me being late could make you feel alone. I know not having help like some of your friends feels really hard. I know that when I am late, you are left to figure things out on your own."

4. **Repair:** "I really appreciate you telling me. I bet my just walking out of the room and not saying anything made it all feel worse. Granted I don't love being yelled at, but I got a bit overwhelmed and just took off. I can see that probably felt bad."

Through intentional expressing, Sasha is able to get to the deeper story of what was happening for her in the moment. She is able to talk about the attachment need that was being activated and she was able to see that her response to Alex was a stress response that contributed to an attachment-breaking interaction.

Alex is able to hold off being defensive and blaming Sasha. He hears the story, believes it, and responds to the attachment need that was present. This exchange does not involve blame and defensiveness. What comes to the fore is accountability, forgiveness, and action being taken to change.

ENGAGEMENT AND GROWTH

Through this scenario, we see that unresolved hurt and anger can drain our energy, but healthy engagement with conflict generates energy, sparks connection, and reminds us that we do like our partner and the life we are building together for our family. Of course you don't have to copy this dialogue; instead, use your own language and insert the specifics of your own story. But this will serve to show how people working to communicate clearly and effectively can sound.

We invite you and your partner to engage conflict for yourself, for your partner, for your relationship, and for the health of your family. In the next section, we will walk you through some versions of the most common conflicts parenting partners face. It's unlikely all of them will fit you perfectly—or perhaps they all will and you will realize how common and relatable so many of these conflicts are—but the idea isn't so you can have these conflicts in just the way we describe them here. The idea is that we are providing you with the framework to engage these conflicts in a way that creates connection and stops the stuck communication you and your partner have been having.

PART II

The 13 Essential Conflicts

CHAPTER 3

The "My Life Has Changed and Yours Hasn't" Conflict

JENN AND OLLIE have a nine-month-old, Astrid. They always knew they wanted kids and were very thankful for a relatively uneventful pregnancy and delivery. In fact, while pregnancy and the first few months postpartum were new and certainly involved learning and adapting, for the most part that period went off without a hitch. And now, after nine months, if you asked them directly how they are adapting to life as a family of three, they would happily tell you that they are grateful to be doing so well. And while that's the truth, it's not the whole truth. An important fight is brewing just below the surface.

Jenn is a director for a local nonprofit that focuses on helping provide legal services to underserved populations who cannot afford legal counsel. She has worked hard to make a difference in her community for the past ten years—first as an attorney for the nonprofit, and now as its director. When she thinks about the work she has done professionally, she feels proud and accomplished. She worried that after she had Astrid, her work would feel less important to her, but she has not found that to be the case. If anything, she feels even more inspired to show Astrid to work hard and follow her dreams and that she, too, can have real impact for good in this world.

Ollie works for a hospital managing a team of IT software engineers who troubleshoot issues with the hospital's electronic health record platform. Ollie has a hybrid work schedule where he is home three days out of the week and in the office two. Ollie has never been as passionate about his job as Jenn is about hers, but he is glad to have it and thankful the schedule seems to be conducive for their family at this stage.

When Jenn and Ollie got pregnant with Astrid, they were thrilled. One of the frequent conversations they had as a couple was how Jenn could balance her return to work and what life would be like for them both as they continued to pursue their careers and parent. They both expressed a desire to be a team when thinking of how to manage their lives together in their family unit. Ollie grew up with a single mom and wanted very much for Jenn to feel supported and know she was not alone. Jenn grew up with a stay-at-home mom, and while she liked and appreciated this experience, it was not the same path she wanted for herself. Jenn and Ollie did not expect balance to come easily, but they were both ready and willing to make it work for the good of their family.

Both Ollie and Jenn took parental leave and felt they made good use of their leave time as a family. Jenn has been back at work for six months now, and she is noticing the transition has been much harder than she imagined. She was not prepared for how her body would feel as she transitioned back into her routine post-Astrid. Between nursing at home, pumping at work, getting too little sleep, and her body still adjusting hormonally to having had a baby, she feels physically out of sorts. Sometimes she has energy, other times she's a little depressed, but most days her body just doesn't feel like it did before she had Astrid. She gets home from work, and before she knows it, the night is over and she's waking up to do it all over again. It's disorienting for her, and just the other day Ollie broached the subject with her.

OLLIE: Hey, you don't seem to be yourself. Are you feeling all right? I know you are tired, but you have seemed out of it for a couple of weeks now.

JENN: I don't know . . . I am just so tired all the time and I can't seem to get past feeling like I am playing catch-up or something.

Jenn has also noticed that she feels pulled in thirty different directions since coming back to work. When she goes to work, she feels like she is constantly thinking about Astrid. This is not a negative thing for her, but it takes up her brain space during a workday. Also, she must coordinate more with Ollie about the nanny's arrivals and departures, meals for Astrid, nap times, getting off work to get home, making sure she is pumping at work, and the list goes on and on. It's not infrequent that she has a somewhat regular text exchange with Ollie while pumping in a closet at work that goes something like this:

JENN: Hey, before you left this morning, did you tell the nanny that there is new breast milk in the downstairs freezer?

OLLIE: Why would I have told her that? I thought you told her . . . Do you want me to tell her?

JENN: Yes. It seems easier for you to go and tell her rather than me having to text back and forth with her.

OLLIE: Okay, sure. I need to wrap something up here, but I will talk with her.

Things between Jenn and Ollie have been good for the most part, and Jenn feels that they both are working hard to support each other. They have divided up the nighttime feedings for Astrid so they are both getting some sleep (or at least are equally not getting enough sleep). In so many ways things feel very positive between Ollie and Jenn.

Yet Jenn still has a nagging feeling that Ollie has it easier than she does, particularly when both of them are home from work. Astrid seems to want her more, especially in the evenings. It could be because Astrid wants to nurse, or maybe it's because she always seems to prefer Jenn when she's sleepy. On an emotional level, Jenn feels good about Astrid's wanting closeness with her after she has been gone all day, but Astrid's preference for Jenn puts a heavier burden on her. And because of all this, when they get home at night, Jenn feels like Ollie has it "easier." For example, when they both get home from work, Ollie can cook dinner by himself without any distractions. Jenn dreams of having that time to herself again.

Just the other night Jenn tried to understand her feelings on the matter by talking it out to Ollie, but she felt like Ollie got defensive quickly.

JENN: Sometimes I wish I could just be alone in the kitchen, like you get to be when you make dinner. It would be so nice to be doing something without Astrid on me.

OLLIE: I'll take Astrid if you want. I am only doing dinner because you said it was helpful for me to be fully in charge of dinner, beginning to end, when you got home.

JENN: No, it is helpful. I just . . . It would be nice to have some alone time in the kitchen, is all I'm saying.

OLLIE: I don't know if I would call it alone time. It's not like I'm on holiday in there.

JENN: That's not what I'm trying to say. I just don't think you know what it's like when Astrid always wants me and has to be attached to my body.

OLLIE: Okay. So let me take Astrid and you cook dinner. I'm not
trying to take the easy way out. I am happy to switch.

JENN: I didn't say you were taking the easy way out. I just . . . Forget it, you just can't understand.

OLLIE: Well, it's hard to understand because it sounds like you
want me to take Astrid but you also want me to cook dinner.
Which one do you want?

Jenn feels like her life has changed a lot since having Astrid, and
while many of these changes are welcome, Ollie doesn't seem to have
a clue about the cost to her body, hormones, work life, and daily routine. In fact, in comparison to hers, his life doesn't appear to have
changed at all. Jenn doesn't want to be judgmental and nitpick at
Ollie. She knows Ollie is exhausted. She keeps trying to tell herself
it could be worse, but over time she finds that the differences are
weighing on her. It's a feeling she can't shake, and one that is starting
to create some unresolved tension between her and Ollie.

WHY YOU NEED THIS CONFLICT

Having a baby changes your life in ways you couldn't imagine, and
before a couple can wrap their head around one major life transition,
a new one comes along that throws you off balance again. This experience doesn't always look and sound like Jenn's and Ollie's, but the
underlying need to address how this transition is experienced differently is universal. Of course couples are aware they have undergone a
massive transformation individually and as a couple, but creating the
time to reflect on and let their bodies, minds, souls, friendships, and
couple relationship catch up to these changes doesn't really occur to
them. And then like whiplash, the impact of so much change demands

to be acknowledged. Very often that demand comes in the form of feeling worn down, burned out, and overwhelmed.

Does having a kid change both parents' lives? Absolutely. Does having a kid change both parents' lives in the same way? Of course not. No two people experience anything in the same way. They don't have the same lived experience, they aren't triggered in the same ways, they respond to lack of sleep differently, and they have different hurts, hopes, and desires. Of course the experience of parenting is different for each partner, but sameness is not the solution to this conflict. In fact, it is the differences that can sometimes bring us together and provide perspective.

What Jenn is more than likely feeling here is some version of lonely and disoriented. Lonely in her experience. Not at all clear about who she is, what she is and isn't feeling, and no clue at all how to communicate the emotions she can't even begin to articulate. The way she feels in and about her own body has changed. Her brain has changed. Her sleep has changed. The way she does her job has changed. What she worries about has changed. Her friendships have changed. And every day, these keep changing and in different ways. For her, everything has changed, and what she needs is for Ollie to understand that. And not just to understand it, but to deeply feel the impact of these changes on her and how it affects every single area of herself and her life.

Until Jenn and Ollie really hash out this conflict, they are going to be stuck feeling lonely and misunderstood, pitted against each other. Yet, they are not against each other at all. That's just how that lonely feeling is coming out. What Jenn and Ollie really need—where connection comes for them in this conflict—is for Jenn to come to understand herself in this new world of parenting and for Ollie to move toward really grasping what's so different for her. Jenn needs Ollie to really see and empathize with how her life has changed, and how much being a parent has cost her. Which again, is not to say Ollie's life has not changed. She wants Ollie to acknowledge the sacrifices she makes second by second for her family, and she needs to feel that he understands the cost is not the same for both of them. That though he will never experientially understand exactly what it is like for her—he makes sacrifices, too, but it's different—he still sees her in it. This understanding, this moving toward each other, is what's needed.

HOW THIS CONFLICT GOES WRONG

Depending on their story, some people respond to stress by withdrawing and shutting their partner out, while others may become more hyperaware and critical. For many, it's a blend of both. They shut down and avoid the situation until it feels like too much, then boil over and lash out with criticism. In order to avoid the fight, Jenn backed away quickly and engaged in her flight stress response. At the time she didn't foresee that the conversation would go anywhere positive, but Ollie interpreted Jenn's backing off as a form of criticism, then her leaving the conversation as withdrawal. He takes this very personally because, having grown up with a single mom, he wants nothing more than for Jenn to feel like she isn't alone. In some ways he feels like he has been playing this role his whole life, and for Jenn to say he isn't good at it hits him in a very deep place.

Anyone can have this conflict go wrong—even us. Regrettably, this conflict took us six years and three kids to work out. Six years! Three kids! The earliest conversations we had about this were when we had our first child. Erin, like most of the parents in a similar situation, first tried to talk herself out of her complicated feelings about the impact of her postpartum life. Just like Jenn, Erin would begin to feel like things weren't even or fair between Stephen and her. Then she would quickly deny and try to reason her way out of her feelings. Truly, by any measure and all standards, Erin felt like Stephen was present and engaged with her and their kid, because he was.

But that feeling didn't go away, becoming more and more intrusive. She would feel the pang of irritation, often at dinnertime, bedtime, or early in the morning. Her annoyance would come out as a critical, snarky comment about how his life hadn't changed at all.

Initially, Stephen didn't say much about Erin's critical comments. He was confused by them, sure, but he had no idea where they were coming from and unknowingly decided it was best just not to engage with them. As these got more frequent, though, he grew angry, and he himself might respond with some defensive, snarky lob along the lines of "Sure, yeah, my life is the same as before we had kids, and I haven't sacrificed anything." This unhealthy conflict resurfaced over and over again. Then with our youngest we finally broke the stuck cycle.

For us it was a combination of factors. We had a series of raw, open conversations in which we were both able to finally understand and express what we really needed to. Through intentional expressing and listening, we finally experienced this conflict in a way that led to connection. Six years after we had started this fight, Stephen said, "I think what you are trying to tell me is that parenting is costing you, your body, and your freedom to tend to your own basic needs in a way it is not costing me. Is that right?" Yes! That is what Erin had been trying to say, and Stephen did not feel defensive about that in the least. The conflict wasn't about Stephen at all—it was simply an acknowledgment of what the real differences were and the freedom that came along with that validation. Because once the root of the conflict is exposed, the entire conversation can be about what action, if any, needs to be taken. Instead of you versus me, it's us, shoulder to shoulder, against the different costs to us both. We shifted out of an attachment-breaking interaction of blame and defensiveness into an attachment-making interaction.

CONFLICT TO CONNECTION: JENN AND OLLIE'S SESSION

Jenn and Ollie start their session with both effusively saying what a good parent the other one is, how much each of them is doing, and how hard each of them is trying to be there for the other. They know they want to talk about the growing tension they are feeling, but they fear this conflict will leave them stuck. As the session goes on, they begin to broach talking about their frustrations:

OLLIE: We both finish work tired and ready to see Astrid and each other. I have tried taking Astrid and letting Jenn make dinner, but that's never the solution, either. If that is what you're asking for, Jenn, I'm happy to do it. But I don't think that is what you are saying. If I take Astrid or if I make dinner, it doesn't really matter, because no doubt there was something else I did or didn't do that is going to upset you.

JENN: I'm not saying you don't help. I'm just saying you have no idea what it's like for me. I can't even come home and change out of my work clothes without holding Astrid, and I can't cook dinner alone because she gets upset when I put her down for even one second.

OLLIE: I'm happy to hold Astrid while you get changed if that'll help.

JENN: That's not the point!

OLLIE: How is that not the point? You literally just said it was!

It might not sound like it, but Jenn and Ollie are trying to connect. There is a need that they both are trying to express, but it is getting lost in translation.

> JENN: Ollie, you are missing the whole point. You won't even listen. You get so wounded and feel so easily criticized. I am trying to tell you I feel overwhelmed! I am trying to tell you something about my life, and all you can hear is how you are doing something wrong. Could you just get your head out of the sand and stop focusing on yourself and listen to me?!

The room is buzzing with energy. Right now, this is an attachment-breaking interaction. Jenn is feeling missed and does not sense Ollie's responsiveness to her, and Ollie is feeling attacked and blamed. If the conversation goes on like this, Jenn and Ollie will stay disconnected and hurt. They need some help to turn this conflict into connection.

> STEPHEN: Can we pause for a minute?

Jenn and Ollie nod a little and shrug.

> STEPHEN: Is this how it goes when you two try to talk about this? Does it look, sound, and feel like this?
> OLLIE: Yes, this feels like it to me. Jenn?
> JENN (nodding): Yes, some version of this.
> ERIN: What do you both notice about your energy levels right now?

Erin is trying to help Jenn and Ollie with the first step in the conflict-to-connection equation—assess. She is hoping that they can recognize that their stress response system has turned on because they are triggered.

> JENN: Well, I feel pretty keyed up right now. I feel hot. Like my cheeks are flushed.

OLLIE: I'm mad. I can tell because my brain feels a little stuck. All I can hear myself saying is "That is what she said. She wanted me to hold Astrid."

ERIN: So, Ollie, your brain feels stuck and you can't really hear anything else Jenn is saying?

OLLIE: Yeah.

STEPHEN: You are both feeling triggered, which is making it tough to express how you are feeling and listen to each other. Jenn, this might sound a bit strange, but when your cheeks are flushed, do you have any idea what this is signaling to you?

We are now moving into step 2 of intentional expressing—attune. Jenn has noticed that she is triggered. Now the focus is shifting to what emotions her triggered state might be illuminating.

JENN: Hmm . . . I get flushed when I feel like what I am saying is not reaching Ollie. It's almost like when a little kid is standing there with clenched fists and red cheeks because they are so angry they are not getting what they want. But it's not that I'm not getting something I want in terms of me pouting. I just feel so angry Ollie doesn't get it and I don't know what else to say.

STEPHEN: Is there anything else? Angry about what? Yes, Ollie doesn't get it, but because he doesn't get it, that leaves you feeling what?

JENN (quietly): Alone. It leaves me feeling absolutely alone.

OLLIE: How can you feel alone? I am bending over backwards to try and keep that very thing from happening.

Jenn gets ready to respond and the old pattern threatens to start all over again. Stephen jumps in.

STEPHEN: Ollie, obviously there is something that you feel is being missed about you. Maybe you even feel like that red-cheeked little kid that Jenn described. So let's try to do something different. Now, I know what I am about to propose might sound crazy, but just go along with me. Something about what Jenn has said feels like blame and you want to defend yourself. Right?

OLLIE: Yes.

STEPHEN: Okay. So here's the crazy part. Try and hold off on being defensive. Try not to engage in that emotion in the next five minutes and let's try and see if we can hear what Jenn is saying about feeling lonely. It might be tough, but block that defensive part off and maybe say, "Okay, Jenn says she feels lonely. I wonder what she means by that."

This is an attempt to move Ollie through steps 2 and 3 of intentional listening—suspending defensiveness and believing Jenn's experience.

ERIN: Jenn, you said you felt alone when Ollie does not understand. What are you wanting him to understand about your world as a mom?

JENN: I think I want him to hear that I just didn't know how hard it would feel. So many times in a day I feel pulled in a thousand directions.

ERIN: What are some of the directions you feel pulled in?

JENN: Being a parent and employee while navigating too little sleep, pumping at work, feeling anxious about how Astrid is doing, then coming home and wanting to be present to Astrid but going over in my mind if I responded to that last email and finished off all those loose ends at work. I want to hold Astrid, I want to cook dinner by myself, I want Astrid not to need me so much when I get home—but in all this I still love feeling important to her. I just didn't know there was going to be so much juggling of roles and that every aspect of my life would feel harder in some way.

ERIN: It all sounds like a lot, Jenn. Do you know how this leaves you feeling lonely?

JENN: Well, I think this is part of where Ollie and I get mixed up. I don't want to say something that is going to make him feel bad or get defensive.

OLLIE: Keep going, Jenn. I really do want to hear what you have to say.

JENN: Okay . . . I think I feel lonely because I don't feel like Ollie gets how constant this feeling of my whole world being turned upside down is. And that is not to say his world has not changed completely, too. It just doesn't seem like he has to deal with all the physical changes, pumping at work, Astrid being attached to him, and even some of the mental fog that comes with having birthed a baby. It doesn't feel as hard or different for him. So I feel lonely that it's not the same, and he doesn't seem to understand that it's not the same.

This is Jenn moving into steps 3 and 4 of intentional expressing—reflect and share. She is connecting her emotion to the story that is informing the emotion.

OLLIE: I can see that, Jenn. I get your life is way different than before Astrid. I get that you have had a hard time getting back in the flow of things and feeling normal. I do feel like you are having a harder go at it than me. The changes for you have been really intense. That's why I have been trying so hard to get dinner done and wake up at night to feed Astrid. I'm trying to be helpful, and I feel like you are saying I'm not aware and not doing anything to help. I feel like I am doing the exact opposite of trying to make you feel lonely.

STEPHEN: Jenn, what is it like for you to hear Ollie say that?

JENN: I believe him. I didn't know he even noticed things were different for me. I feel like when I try to say that, he just defends what he is doing. But I also hadn't put it together that he is trying to do more because he does see that things are different for me. I am not sure how to handle it or process it right now.

ERIN: Ollie, I'm curious about you saying you are trying to do the exact opposite of making Jenn lonely. Do you feel that Jenn has said you are making her feel lonely?

OLLIE: Yeah.

ERIN: It seems like it hurts for you to think Jenn is lonely. Does that feel true?

Now, Erin is trying to help Ollie shift into step 3 of intentional expressing— reflect.

OLLIE: Well, I don't think anyone wants their partner to be lonely.

ERIN: Of course not, but it feels like there is something extra meaningful to you about this.

OLLIE: I mean, my mom was a single mom, and stuff was really hard for her. She worked so hard and never had help. My siblings and I tried to make things easier for her. We cooked for ourselves, did our own laundry, and tried to clean the house. You know, basic stuff like that, but she just always seemed stressed and well . . . lonely. Wow, I don't know if I would have said that initially, but yeah, she seemed really lonely, and I just wanted her not to feel that way.

STEPHEN: So I imagine your hearing Jenn say she feels lonely is a hard thing to hear.

OLLIE: Really hard. I feel like I'm messing up or something.

STEPHEN: Jenn, what are you hearing?

JENN: I knew that about Ollie's upbringing, but I didn't realize that what I have been trying to express and how I am feeling were connected to it. Ollie, I'm not trying to say you are messing up or that you are making me lonely. I appreciate everything you do and feel so supported by you a lot of the time. I think I would feel lonely no matter what, and I just want to be able to share that with you and feel some understanding from you.

OLLIE: I can see how I may have been ignoring what you were saying because I didn't want to acknowledge it. Not on purpose, but just because a fear I have had is that you could feel lonely like my mom, and I never wanted that for you. I have been defensive, and I can see that hasn't been constructive. I am sorry.

JENN: I appreciate you saying that, and I understand why you have felt defensive. You are not messing up or making me lonely. I know that at times I can get upset and communicate in a way that is intense and makes it hard for you to want to listen. I'm sorry that happens.

OLLIE: I appreciate that.

Jenn and Ollie are now able to be accountable for their actions and forgive, which can lead to different action in the future. They are moving into the final steps of turning conflict into connection—repair and gaining resolution.

ERIN: Now that you have a better understanding of what has been happening, it may be helpful for you both to try and bring the other into the stories you told today. Jenn, you were telling a story of how your world has changed drastically. Ollie, you were telling a story about seeing your mom feel overwhelmed and lonely and how hard you tried then to keep that from happening. It may be helpful for you both to ask some questions of each other to understand how these stories are informing your present experience. This way you can understand other moments where these stories are triggered and have led to dead-end dialogues, and you can talk about them in a healing way like you did today.

BUT HOW CAN I ACTUALLY SAY ANY OF THIS TO MY PARTNER? SAMPLE SCRIPTS

Below are a few prompts for how both the birthing and non-birthing partners can express how they're feeling in this conflict so that it doesn't turn into a competition about whose world has been turned upside down more.

Intentional Expressing—Birth Partner

"I have been noticing lately I do not always feel like I know who I am anymore. I sometimes feel like, while I love so much about who I am as a parent, I do not always recognize myself anymore. And I miss some of who I was. Do you ever feel like this?"

"I wonder if sometimes I try to tell you about my experience by pointing out and criticizing yours. Do you feel like I do this?"

"Sometimes I feel like I have to prove to you how much I am doing or that my life is different now, too. I know you know it is, but it makes me wonder what might be going on for us. Maybe we are also missing something for each other. Is there something about your experience you wish I really knew or understood on a deeper level? I need to think, too, what about my experience I wish you knew and understood on a deeper level."

"I want us to pause and reflect on what all has happened for us since we had kids. Will you do this with me? I want us to take even just a few minutes (or longer!) to look at how much has changed, for the better and for the more challenging, since we had our kids. We have been through a lot. Here are a few things I am really proud of us for and things that have felt hard."

Intentional Listening—Non-Birthing Partner

"I have noticed that when we talk about who is doing what and who is tired and so forth that we seem to get into some kind of disagreement. I can get defensive, and I feel like you can get quiet or angry. I think I am missing something. Am I? I'd like to understand."

"Hey, I don't know if we have ever specifically talked about it, but what are some of the biggest changes you feel you are dealing with as a parent?"

"You know I get that we both are parents and having a baby has made our lives different, but one obvious difference is I did not give birth. How do you think that makes our experience different? Does anything feel harder or easier for you because you gave birth?"

QUESTIONS FOR REFLECTION

1. Do you ever feel like your partner's life hasn't changed?

2. Do you and your partner ever find that you try to prove to each other how your life has changed?

3. After kids, do you ever feel like you don't recognize yourself anymore? What about your relationship? Does it feel difficult

to recognize? What (if anything) do you miss about life for yourself and your relationship before kids?

4. Do you ever feel like you and your partner have a stuck conversation? If you were to step outside of the context (whatever the conflict happens to be about), is there a theme to what you and/or your partner may be trying to communicate?

5. Do you feel like you have been avoiding this conflict? Is there anything about this chapter that seemed to resonate with you? Did it stir any feelings or memories? Why might those feelings and memories be coming up now in the season of life and parenting you are currently in?

CHAPTER 4

The "I Can't Do Anything Right" Conflict

JADA AND LUCIA have been together for twelve years and have three kids. Parker is seven, Oliver is five, and Ella is three. Jada is an ob-gyn and works sixty-hour weeks, and Lucia works remotely part time as an accountant. Because Lucia works part time and her work is mostly seasonal, she is the one who is primarily with the kids.

From the very start Jada and Lucia had a great connection. Each felt like the other really got them in a way they hadn't known before. Before they had kids, they enjoyed camping and hiking. At one point Jada was into running races and Lucia would join her for some of her training runs. They have always loved movies and trying new restaurants, and that is something they find they still enjoy in their busy and kid-filled life. Even though Jada works long hours, she comes home and jumps right into the action: playing with the kids, cooking dinner, and straightening up the house, to name just a few of the nightly tasks.

Lucia knows that Jada works a demanding and stressful job. Yes, she gets to deliver babies and be a part of the happiest days of many people's lives, but she also has hard days where she is with patients at some of their darkest moments. Lucia is aware that Jada is doing a lot, but Lucia still feels that she is left to handle most of the parenting on top of working and maintaining a home. They have a good partnership, but if Lucia is honest, even before kids, she felt like Jada could be footloose and fancy-free in ways she is not able to. It's like Lucia does all the serious and "unpleasant" work and then Jada swoops in and has all the fun.

Jada is typically gone before she and the kids wake up and comes home right around dinnertime. This leaves Lucia to take care of all the planning, organizing, and implementing: getting their kids ready in the morning and off to school; signing them up for extracurriculars; planning the kids' social lives, as well as hers and Jada's; and managing the house. On top of all that, Lucia is always thinking about how the kids are doing emotionally and how their day is going. It's not that Jada doesn't care about these things, but she is not around to be involved. Lucia often feels this difference between them, which comes out in conversations like this:

JADA: This weekend I was thinking that we could have the Howells over for dinner. I sent them a text about coming over this Saturday, and they said that sounded good.

LUCIA: Jada, did you not look at the calendar for the week? Parker has gymnastics Saturday morning, Oliver has soccer in the afternoon, and Ella has a birthday party at the Vosses' house. We can't have the Howells over. It's already a really busy day.

JADA: Oh, I didn't know.

LUCIA: I put it in the calendar a week ago so that you would know. I didn't know it was my job to put something in the calendar and then remind you to look at it, too.

These kinds of interactions can leave Jada feeling blindsided by Lucia's critical and sharp tone, and Lucia feeling deeply missed by Jada's seeming lack of awareness of their life as a family and her role as a parent. In the past they might have tried to work this out, but lately it feels like more trouble comes from trying to have further conversation.

On one particularly difficult day, Jada, who was on call for the week, had to go back to the hospital twenty minutes after she got home. Lucia was devastated. She wanted Jada to be home and help so that she would not feel like she's responsible for everything happening in her family's life. When Jada did get home after the kids were in bed, she found Lucia sitting in the living room, seething.

LUCIA: For once, I wish your job came second to our family and me. Do you even know what goes on in our home? I get stuck most days doing everything around here. Do you know that we have parent-teacher conferences coming up this week? It seems like that doesn't even matter to you. I'm sure you'll be too busy to come and just leave it to me to deal with.

JADA: Oh, I'm so sorry you had such a tough day today, Lucia. While you were wringing your hands about parent-teacher conferences, I was dealing with a life-threatening labor. Lives were on the line, but yeah . . . I just left you alone.

LUCIA: Jada, I'm sorry that happened, that sounds awful, but here's the thing. Your work stress wins. What my day is like and how much I have to juggle and the stress I have are secondary because you have such a big important job. You get to hide behind what you do, and I'm just supposed to deal with it.

JADA: You always have some kind of critique about how I am working, parenting, or living. Maybe if I felt like you appreciated how hard I do work, how I try not to bring the stress of my job home, and that when I am here I do engage with the kids, I would be more open to hearing what you have to say. But you tend to be so negative, and I am getting tired of hearing it.

Both partners stared bleakly at each other. In moments like these, they begin to wonder if they will ever be able to get past this tired conflict.

WHY YOU NEED THIS CONFLICT

When you and your partner are both working hard and simultaneously feeling misunderstood, it may be impossible to believe your partner is on your side. Criticism will kill a relationship, and unfortunately, many parenting couple relationships are filled with it.

How does this happen? you might ask. Criticism puts whomever it's directed at on the defensive. If you or your partner feel as if they are constantly being told they are "wrong," "bad," or "failing," your relationship begins to feel untenable. This is not to say that partners cannot offer each other constructive feedback or hold each other accountable for actions or mistakes. That is actually healthy conflict! But if your partner feels that you are always accusing them of being a terrible parenting partner, the relationship will struggle to feel vibrant and hopeful.

Criticism often works its way into a relationship when a partner doesn't feel heard. Lucia is overwhelmed, and she does not believe Jada understands or sees how difficult life is for her. Her criticism is aimed at getting Jada's attention and convincing her to see that things are not okay. Very often, partners use criticism to make the point that not only is the situation not ideal, but they themselves are not okay. However, the partner who's on the defensive (Jada) is not really in a state of mind to hear from the one lobbing criticism. So, Lucia is pleading, "Listen to me," and Jada, who feels attacked, is unable to hear Lucia's true concerns and defensively responds, "Your life is hard? Well, my life is hard and all you do is complain."

This is an exhausting cycle, and when couples do this day in and day out for years, they get to the point of wanting to quit. This is how criticism can kill a relationship, and why this conflict is so important. You need this conflict because, for your relationship to survive, you have to shift out of a cycle of criticism and employ the conflict-to-connection equation so you and your partner can both be listened to and known.

HOW THIS CONFLICT GOES WRONG

People resort to criticism because they are desperate to be heard but don't know how to express that intense emotion. Being truly intentional in expression is vulnerable and, as we've discussed previously, scary. So often in such a conflict a partner dips just a pinkie toe into being vulnerable and tries desperately to express what they are feeling, but the second they feel misunderstood, they shut the attempt down.

Honestly, this cycle of criticism is somewhat inevitable when you are parenting. We personally hit our lowest point in criticism when our middle child was two and our oldest was four. Stephen was working full time and writing his dissertation and Erin was staying at home with two young kids. You know the story: neither of us was getting enough sleep, both of us were giving 100 percent, and we always felt like we were coming up short. We lived far from Erin's mom, who was our only support, and over time Erin was coming unglued. Stephen was overworked and exhausted but also felt like he could see the light at the end of the tunnel. For Erin, there was no light, just an endless tunnel.

Erin tried to tell Stephen how overwhelmed she was, but every time she broached the subject, it seemed to her that Stephen dismissed her concerns. His response would sound something like: "I know it is really hard right now, but it won't be like this forever. Just a few more years and we'll have more time." Stephen did not mean for his words to be hurtful, but they cut Erin like a knife. A few more years?! It had already been a few years! Erin was more than just fatigued—she was drowning, right now. Stephen wasn't exactly happy with the situation, but he realized that they really didn't have an option but to keep moving forward. The more Stephen tried to keep a positive spin on their situation, the more critical of him Erin got.

Erin didn't need Stephen to coax her out of her difficult place with idealism. She needed him to sit beside her and say, "You are not okay, and this is really hard. Honestly, I'm not okay, either, but I'm trying to cope by focusing on the goal." In his overwhelmed and exhausted state, Stephen needed Erin to say, "I am so sad and angry about how hard this is. I see it's hard for you, too, and I am trying my best to cope. I feel shut down by you, and I know I am being critical to try to make you see my experience. I know it's really hurtful to you."

Here's where this conflict so often goes wrong for many couples. Our different coping strategies can conflict, and when this happens, partners can turn to criticism to convey their frustrations and try to get their partner to understand their perspective. Stephen tried coping with our situation by focusing on the goal; Erin felt like Stephen was demanding she focus on the finish line and "be positive." But to Erin, that approach to managing his stress felt like a denial of her present overwhelm. Erin was trying to cope by sharing her experience and asking Stephen to come alongside her and "be" with her in it, but what she was saying felt threatening to Stephen. Her approach to managing her stress made Stephen feel like he had to "wallow" and get stuck in the mire. They turned to criticism in an attempt to get the other to understand their perspective and stop making the stress feel worse.

For Jada and Lucia, their criticisms are coming out over the "silly" and "smallest" things, which is extremely common for this conflict. Couples come to us almost embarrassed to tell us what the fight was about: forgetting to pick up something at the grocery store, parking the car in the driveway in a certain way, or even inserting the silverware "wrong" in the dishwasher basket. The truth is, it's never the action itself. It's about something so much deeper, but the specific event, no matter how seemingly insignificant, is what triggers the feeling at the time.

One partner criticizes, the other takes a defensive stance or maybe even ignores their partner, and the result of this is a feeling of distance. It's here where a lot of couples get stuck. They come to us feeling disconnected and miles apart. Thankfully this distance can be bridged with a little bit of tweaking as to how this conflict is engaged.

CONFLICT TO CONNECTION: LUCIA AND JADA'S SESSION

Lucia is open to the fact that in frustration she can turn critical, but Jada does not seem aware that how she responds is critical to Lucia. They know they don't want to be stuck in this cycle, but both are also painfully aware their partner may not be willing to budge, so they come in more tense than normal. The session feels intense from the start, with big emotions just at the surface.

LUCIA: I'm so sick of comparing whose life feels harder whenever we fight. Because Jada is a physician, she always wins. Meanwhile, I am at home working multiple jobs, putting in just as many hours as she is, and making just as important decisions for the lives of our kids. And a lot of the time I feel like I am doing this alone without any help and without any appreciation.

ERIN: I can feel your anger, Lucia. How do you think you express this to Jada? How does she feel your anger?

LUCIA: Jada is too caught up in her work to feel anything from me. I'd be surprised if she even knows that I'm upset.

JADA: I know you're upset, but nothing would make you feel better. You are constantly complaining about how hard it is for you to work and take care of the kids and that you have this impossible task as a parent. I could quit my job and just sit around the house waiting for you to tell me what you needed and you would still be upset.

STEPHEN: So you're saying it seems that Lucia has some imbalanced expectations and it feels like a losing battle to even engage her in the conversation?

JADA: Yes. I am aware that Lucia does a lot around the house and puts in a lot of hours at the same time she is doing all this work for our family. But she likes this type of work and chose this lifestyle. I deal with a ton of stress when I'm at work, and then I come home and jump into the chaos and work to be part of the family, too. I don't get a break. I'm up early, I go to bed late, I deal with life and death, and I make money so our family can have a good life. She seems to want a pat on the back when she has had a hard day making lunches for the kids.

LUCIA: Yeah, that's it, Jada. I need you to give me a hug because I'm struggling making lunches for the kids. That is such a condescending comment and shows you don't have a clue what I am talking about.

STEPHEN: It is condescending, for sure, but I think it shows you both don't have a clue what the other is talking about. When it comes down to it, you both think you are doing a lot. You feel like your partner takes what you do for granted, and you might even feel that what you are doing is the harder of the two. You are both doggedly determined to get the other one to understand your experience.

JADA: I don't know if I would have put it that way, but what I want is to be appreciated by Lucia and not told I am not doing enough or don't care. All I hear from her is criticism about every last thing I do or don't do.

STEPHEN: I see. And, Lucia, what do you want Jada to understand about you?

LUCIA: That I feel like Jada minimizes the importance of what I am doing and overemphasizes what she does. It's about her dealing with life and death and her being the fun one, but she is only able to do any of that because of me.

ERIN: You know what can happen in this conversation for couples? Each partner feels like they have to acknowledge the other partner's experience at the expense of their own experience being true. Jada, if you acknowledge that Lucia feels minimized, you would in essence be saying, "My experience doesn't matter or is not true." Does that feel like it fits?

JADA: Well, wouldn't that be what I am saying? Lucia feels like her experience is worse and she deals with more. For me to make her happy, I have to say she is right and how I feel about my experience is wrong.

ERIN: So that leaves you feeling like your only option is to dismiss and invalidate Lucia's experience?

JADA: Well, I don't want to dismiss her experience. I know she is having one, but I definitely feel like she is not seeing the whole picture.

ERIN: And to get her to see the whole picture, you tell her the intensity or energy she feels about what is happening for her is not that bad, which can be minimizing.

LUCIA: I feel constantly minimized and invalidated.

STEPHEN: I imagine you feel similar, Jada . . . or would it be more accurate to say you feel unappreciated? I believe you used that word earlier.

JADA: Yeah. I think I leave these conversations feeling more unappreciated than minimized. I guess if I felt like Lucia truly validated my experience, I would feel like she appreciated the intensity of my work, the effort I give to be a part of the family and care for her. But what she does is tell me all the things I'm not doing or how what I have done is wrong.

STEPHEN: She leads with criticism, which leaves you feeling broken down and like it is a waste of effort to try?

JADA: Exactly. Why would anyone want to try if they feel like they are just going to be told they were wrong?

ERIN: So in a way, you both want the other to understand your experience in such a profound way that you dismiss and invalidate each other's experience, which leaves Lucia feeling minimized and Jada feeling unappreciated?

LUCIA/JADA (with an exhausted sigh): That sounds relatively close.

ERIN: Well, that sounds like a solvable problem.

JADA: How so?

Erin: Well, this is where our conflict-to-connection equation can help. You both need some guidance to intentionally express and intentionally listen.

STEPHEN: There are three mindsets that have to shift so you can have the conversation. Shifting these mindsets will lead you through the process of intentional expressing and intentional listening. The first is to **stop thinking in terms of a competition (assess and suspending defensiveness)**—whose experience is harder or requires more—and accept that your experiences are different and both present challenges and struggles in unique ways. In short, you are both trying to explain to the other your different experience. The second mindset shift is that **acknowledging your partner's difficulty does not mean you have to deny your own (reflect/share and believe your partner's experience)**. It can be easy to get stuck in a cycle of hearing your partner say, "I'm tired" or "I'm busy" and then responding, "Well, I'm really tired and busy, too." This is how the competition mindset and the mindset of feeling like acknowledgment means denial get started. The third mindset shift is **criticism is not communication (repair).** Criticism is often used by partners to try and get the other to listen and pay attention. It's like turning up the volume so someone hears the urgency of their situation, but really all it does is make the other person feel threatened and cover their ears because things are too loud.

LUCIA: I can see how we get into a competition. Jada will say she had a hard day at work, and then I'll just jump right in with how hard my day has been because I don't want her to think she is the only one that had it tough. I see how I shortchanged her being able to say what is happening by jumping in with my story.

JADA: And generally there is some kind of dig about how I've done something wrong or just don't get it.

LUCIA: I can admit that. I have a good eye for what Jada is not doing.

JADA: I can see how I get caught up in a competition with Lucia. I feel like we often compare who had it worse or who was busier. I think sometimes I do that because I know you are working really hard and sometimes I even feel bad that you are having to do all the parenting by yourself. I just want you to know I'm not sitting on my hands doing nothing at work.

Jada and Lucia end up competing because they are triggered and feel threatened. This is what the assess step in intentional expressing and listening helps partners understand. The conflict is becoming contentious or getting off track because partners feel threatened and become defensive. This leads to dead-end dialogue and attachment-breaking interactions.

STEPHEN: Huh, that's interesting, Jada. Can you say a bit more about feeling bad that Lucia is at home doing all the parenting?

This question is an effort to lead Jada into reflecting and sharing. What is the story that is motivating her to feel bad and contributing to her defensiveness?

JADA: Well, I know my job is really hard and demanding. I also know that being with the three kids all day is constant. Unlike Lucia, I get a few minutes in a day to breathe and reset. In order to be more involved and engaged in our family, I get up early for work, come home as soon as possible, and try to do what I can in the few hours I have with the kids. But I can see how exhausted Lucia feels and I feel like I am not doing enough to help.

STEPHEN: That's an interesting phrase you used at the end there: "I feel like I am not doing enough to help." You said that when you feel Lucia is being critical of you that what she is saying is "No matter what you do, it's not enough or the right thing." It seems that maybe one of the reasons her criticism hurts so much is because you are already being pretty critical of yourself and feeling like you are not doing enough.

JADA: Yes, I do feel bad, and then I try as hard as I can to make up for it, and it just doesn't work. I just want Lucia to know I am working hard, too, for our family, and I get she is working hard for the family as well. I just want to feel more like a team and like we appreciate what the other does. I don't like feeling bad for the work I am doing when, honestly, I already feel guilty at times for not being around more.

LUCIA: I didn't know you felt bad for not being around as much. I don't mean this like it might sound, but it makes me feel good that you feel bad. I don't want you to feel bad, but I just didn't know you felt that way or even saw that I do take care of most of the parenting. I think my criticism is my frustration and anger coming out because I didn't know you even noticed me and I was feeling minimized.

Lucia is starting to move through the process now. She is noting what triggers her (assess), she is reflecting and sharing about what motivates her strong feelings in the conflict, and she is suspending her defensiveness and believing her partner's experience.

JADA: Well, I'm glad my feeling bad is helpful!

LUCIA: I know you work hard. I can't imagine what some of your days are like, and when you are home, you're a great parent and the house just feels better. Your working hard benefits us so much. I think I get lonely and overwhelmed at times, and your work as a physician is seen as so noble and important that I begin to feel my work as a parent goes unnoticed.

STEPHEN: Jada, did you know that Lucia felt this way about her work as a parent: that it is not as noble or respected as yours?

JADA: No. I think what she does is so important. Our kids are amazing, and (with a wry smile) at least 30 percent of that is because of Lucia.

LUCIA: Thanks for the recognition. I think another thing I am realizing is that I feel bad, too, for needing more help from Jada. I feel like she is busting her tail every day. I know she is working hard, and I can see she is exhausted. I think I feel embarrassed at times that I am overwhelmed and want more from her when she comes home. I mean, she is dealing with life and death every day and I don't want to be another burden to her.

JADA: Oh, Lucia, you don't need to feel bad! We are both treading water. I just think that is part of parenting. I want to help and I know you want to help me, too. We are just tired.

These comments reflect that Jada and Lucia are believing each other's experience and are moving into repair. They are becoming aware of how their reactions to each other are motivated by insecurities and fears about feeling bad or feeling embarrassed.

> ERIN: Lucia, I wonder if some of the criticism also comes from this feeling of embarrassment. You feel like Jada has the respected job and you have the thankless job. Sometimes we can criticize to try and get the attention we want even if it actually pushes people away.
>
> LUCIA: Yeah, I feel like I'm not supposed to be having a hard time or that I shouldn't need help. "Parent culture" is pretty full of partners complaining about how their other partner is never around. I think I feel overlooked, and then I feel embarrassed for feeling this way because it seems petty and needy. Then I get angry that parents are overlooked and made to feel bad, and it just builds up.
>
> JADA: I can understand that, Lucia. At the same time, I think what makes me frustrated is that I don't feel like I am one of those partners that doesn't help. I am gone a lot, but I feel like I'm not clueless about the burden you carry.
>
> LUCIA: You aren't an uninvolved partner. I just think I get overwhelmed and start looking around for some help, and sometimes you aren't there. It can feel like it is all too much.

Notice how Lucia and Jada are not backing off of the way they have felt or holding each other accountable. They are acknowledging each other's feelings, and that their defensiveness elicited during their stress response has hurt the other. Yet the tone is connective, not critical. This is an attachment-making interaction because both partners are having the experience of feeling validated and understood.

STEPHEN: We suggested that you needed three mindset changes in order to turn this stuck conflict into connection, and whether you have been aware of it or not, for the last few minutes, neither one of you has been competing, avoiding acknowledging the other's experience for fear that your own would be dismissed, or criticizing. Did you notice how that happened?

LUCIA: Not consciously. I think what shifted for me was hearing that Jada sees that I am doing a lot of the parenting and it's hard. I don't feel minimized.

STEPHEN: Yes, she acknowledged your experience without following it up with how her experience is hard, too. This is how you shift out of this negative attachment-breaking interaction. You have to **cut the competition, acknowledge your partner's experience, and stop the criticism.** These mindset changes can initiate intentional expressing and intentional listening. When you acknowledge your partner's experience, it becomes an invitation for them to do the same. There won't be a need to compete if your partner hears you saying, "I can see how you are working hard" or "I get that." Also, there won't be a need to criticize if you feel like you are a team rather than opponents on competing teams.

LUCIA: I can see that. When Jada said she sees that I do a lot and she felt bad about it, I didn't feel like I had to protect my experience. She got it, and this helped me feel invited to share and to acknowledge her and see that what she wants is to be appreciated.

JADA: Yeah, I see that, too. It just feels hard to remember to do this in the heat of the moment.

ERIN: Sure it is, but this is something you learn to do. Something that, as you continue to navigate this conversation, you get better and better at doing.

BUT HOW CAN I ACTUALLY SAY ANY OF THIS TO MY PARTNER? SAMPLE SCRIPTS

You are both working hard as parents. What this means for you and how you feel the burden of what hard means are different. Competing about whose life is harder and criticizing each other in an effort to convince the other you are winning the "harder" game is a recipe for relationship ruin. If you are steeped in this pattern of competition and criticism, there is a way out, but you will need to change your communication to move from conflict to connection. Here are some potential scripts you can use to keep the ethos of acknowledgment at the center of this conflict.

Intentional Expressing

"I have been noticing that whenever we start to talk about who is tired or who is doing what around the house or for the kids, things don't go so well. It feels like we are competing with each other to make a point or to be understood. I don't want to make you feel like you need to compete with me, and I don't like feeling like I have to compete with you. Can we try and talk about our experiences without competing? I'll really work to listen and not jump to being defensive."

"One of the things I think I have heard you say is that I don't listen to you or try to understand your perspective. I don't disagree. I think I do feel criticized by you, and this shuts me down. I imagine that is frustrating for you. It's frustrating for me to feel criticized. I would like to have this conversation in a different way. When you are feeling critical of me, can you tell me what is going on for you? Can I tell you how it feels to me to be criticized?"

Intentional Listening

"I realize that when I feel overwhelmed or alone in parenting, I can get really critical. I can't imagine that you enjoy my talking to you in such a negative way. I want to be less critical and not approach you in a way that shuts you down. Can we try and have this conversation again and I will work to be less critical?"

"I think that lately we might be feeling the same way. I am feeling like I am working really hard and doing a lot and that you are not understanding how I am feeling overwhelmed. I think you would say the same thing. What am I missing for you? Can I try and explain what I feel you are missing for me? I just want the conversation to feel different because I think we are both really frustrated with how it is going so far."

QUESTIONS FOR REFLECTION

1. Did you see your own parents become critical of each other?

2. What is your favorite thing about yourself and your partner as parents right now? Do you feel like you spend more, less, or equal time encouraging your own and your partner's parenting or offering feedback and ways to improve?

3. Do you ever feel minimized in your parenting? Do you ever feel unappreciated as a parent?

4. What is the most stuck place for you in this conflict? What feels like the most important thing to you in this conflict? How did it come to be that important to you? What's at stake for you?

5. Do you feel like you have been avoiding this conflict? Is there anything about this chapter that seemed to resonate with you? Did it stir any feelings or memories? Why might those feelings and memories be coming up now in the season of life and parenting you are currently in?

CHAPTER 5

....

The "I'm All Touched Out" Conflict

MATEO AND CARRIE have three kids. They met and began dating in law school, and both felt it was seamless becoming a couple. They look back fondly at that time in their life. It was challenging, to be sure, but also a sweet time for them.

> CARRIE: We got each other. We were in the same graduating year, so we were doing classes and projects together regularly. When we were not doing schoolwork, we just enjoyed each other's company. We could have fun doing absolutely nothing together.
>
> MATEO: It's true. We spent many long nights studying and stressing, but I felt like I had my best friend with me and we were going through this really intense part of life as a couple. We thought if we could do that and come out closer, we'd be able to do anything.

Following graduation, they both got jobs in separate firms and started their careers. After they had their second kid, and after much discussion and deliberation, Carrie decided she wanted to stay at home to care for their kids for a period of time. They arranged their schedules, finances, and life to make that happen. This again felt like a time when they were aligned and shared the same values and vision for the next stage for their family.

> CARRIE: Mateo was really supportive during this time, and it was a tough decision. A lot of work had been put into my becoming a lawyer and I knew that stepping away would put me behind in my career. I knew it was what I wanted, but I debated with myself if I should want it. If I really wanted it. If my old self would be disappointed in me and if I was creating a difficult situation for myself in the future.
>
> MATEO: I know Carrie is a hard worker, and I also know she loves time with the kids and really wanted to explore staying at home. My thought was she could always come back to the profession if this arrangement didn't feel like it was working. At the end of the day, I think it worked pretty well.

Four years later, Carrie is still a stay-at-home parent, and they have welcomed their third child into the family. They feel like their current work/life situation is working, even though Carrie occasionally thinks about if she eventually will want to go back to work. She doesn't know when or how or even if that will ever happen, but she finds herself musing on it from time to time. Carrie and Mateo have always felt close—like they can really understand and relate to each other, having gone through so much as a team. However, there is one thing they don't feel like they can talk about, at least not with any hope of having it lead somewhere productive: physical touch.

To be clear, we aren't talking about touch as a cute pseudonym for sex. We mean touch as in physical closeness: a touch on the arm in passing, a long hug of reconnection after a day apart, or sitting near each other on the couch for a show. It's been years, and Carrie and Mateo both still aren't sure how to talk about touch without one or both of them leaving the conversation feeling misunderstood and misrepresented. This conflict leaves them both in pain, each not sure what is really happening for the other one. Physical touch used to be a go-to reconnection strategy for them, and since that isn't working now, they are feeling more and more disconnected. They oscillate between confused, frustrated, and angry, and they would both agree they are growing more distant over time.

Carrie used to initiate physical touch often and found that this closeness helped her feel connected to herself and to Mateo, but now, though she hates to admit it, she feels more repulsed by than drawn to Mateo's physical proximity. She wishes she didn't and even tries to tell herself that it isn't so, but she keeps thinking these thoughts no matter how hard she tries to push them away. Over time she has tried to bring up these feelings to Mateo, and her attempt often comes out as something like "I think I just feel overstimulated, and one touch more feels like too much." That statement on its own is fine, but it never quite moves the conversation to a place where she feels more understood. She's really not sure exactly what she's trying to say or how she hopes Mateo will respond. Mostly she just finds herself recoiling when she anticipates that Mateo may be coming in for a hug, a kiss, or a touch on her arm.

While Carrie hasn't said anything to Mateo, he definitely feels it. He sees Carrie tense when he steps nearer to her. He isn't blind to the fact that she used to like to snuggle up during movies or have an occasional out-of-the-blue hug or kiss. Now that seems like a distant memory. He tells himself he says nothing about this because he doesn't want to pressure her or come off as a jerk. He wants to say, "I'd love a hug when I get home from work," but rationalizes: "She has a lot going on with the kids all day." "Maybe it's me." "Maybe I'm just not attractive to her anymore." "Maybe I'm wanting too much."

"I don't want to pressure her, so I'll just keep my distance and wait for her to approach."

He would never try to be mean or want to make Carrie feel responsible for making him feel better, but sometimes he blurts things out after he gets that cold feeling from Carrie. Just last week he tried to say something directly instead of being passive while Carrie was sitting on the couch, and it didn't go well.

MATEO: You know, I came into the room and thought for a second about coming and sitting next to you, but I just figured you'd tell me to scoot over and give you some room. It feels weird that I don't feel welcome to even sit by you on the couch.

CARRIE: Mateo, I don't mind you sitting by me on the couch. We've sat by each other on the couch plenty of times. Sometimes I just need some space. There are a million little hands touching me all day. I feel like you're being overdramatic.

MATEO: Well, sometimes it seems that you need space from me *all* the time.

CARRIE: I don't want space from you.

MATEO: So if I came over and sat by you right now, how would you feel?

CARRIE: Well . . . I am feeling a little overwhelmed at the moment, so I might scoot over just a little to get a bit of separation, but I wouldn't get up and move.

MATEO: So you need some space from me.

CARRIE: Mateo, I don't know how to explain what I'm trying to say. I am not trying to hurt your feelings.

Carrie would like to feel close and physically connected to Mateo again, but she doesn't know where to even start. Mateo wants to understand, but he doesn't and it hurts. Mateo wants to find that ease and connection that brought them together all those years ago, but he's worried that maybe that's not possible. He knows Carrie's life has changed drastically since they met, but he thought this was what she wanted and he fears that she doesn't want him anymore. Carrie keeps trying to remind herself she likes Mateo, but the tension just won't melt. They both hate the growing chasm between them but have no idea how to get to the root of the problem without blaming the other and making it even worse than it is already.

WHY YOU NEED THIS CONFLICT

Couples need to talk about their experience of the physical changes that took place (and may still be taking place) before, during, and after pregnancy. Throughout the months from the first confirmation of pregnancy to the birth experience itself, partners experience a physical disconnection. One partner is having something otherworldly take place in their physical body and the other is not. It's impossible for the non-pregnant partner to know how the other partner feels. This happens not because the non-pregnant partner is willfully trying to disconnect from their partner's physical experience. It simply is a result of the differences between the physical experiences of each partner.

Here are just a few of the physical, psychological, and emotional realities a pregnant and birthing partner might experience:

- the pressure and thrill of trying to conceive
- sore breasts during pregnancy
- the joy of experiencing those first kicks in pregnancy, or the fear that a sharp pain means something more
- the constant anxiety about losing the baby
- throwing up and nausea
- weight gain and weight loss

- the unknowns concerning what this labor and delivery will be like—how long it will be and what toll it will take on your body
- fretting about whether the baby will arrive safely and be healthy
- a traumatic birthing experience
- a beautiful birthing experience
- the fear of going to the bathroom after birth
- the sting of stitches
- the fear of walking up or down steps for the first time after birth
- feeling completely helpless to what is happening to and within your own body

Carrie has been pregnant and given birth to three young children. Her body has done incredible things, but a lot of the time her body does not feel like her own. What she maybe senses but hasn't yet put into words is that physical touch has come to mean someone taking from her. She accepts that her children will use her body as a jungle gym, but when Mateo approaches, that feeling that he also needs her body is tiresome. She doesn't want him to need or take from her.

This has an impact on the other partner as well. Think about the current conflict between Carrie and Mateo. Carrie's feeling of being "touched out" influences Mateo's experience of himself. He is wondering if Carrie still wants him. He doesn't want to be a jerk and pressure Carrie or to be perceived as needy, and he definitely doesn't want to take anything from Carrie. Both partners are having an experience of pregnancy and birth that is shaping their whole world and the emotions they feel about each other and themselves. Right now, both feel misunderstood and take each other's responses as personal.

Each partner must come to understand the holistic impact (good, bad, uncomfortable, scary, beautiful, panicked, ugly) of the journey to parenthood through the lens of the body. One partner has to grapple with the impact of pregnancy and childbirth on the body, and the other partner has to learn not to take these life-altering changes to their partner personally. This takes work, because while it is about you, it really is not about you. It is about understanding the journey you and your partner have been on and working through the impact of those changes on you and your relationship as a whole.

HOW THIS CONFLICT GOES WRONG

This conflict gets right to the heart of what is personal for almost everyone. The dreaded fear: Do you want me? On paper, this conflict can seem to be about Mateo's feeling he is not wanted anymore. He is thinking to himself, *Maybe she just doesn't want me anymore.* But the opposite is likely true as well. Carrie's internal dialogue might run like this: *I do not just want to be needed to make him feel better about himself. I also want to be wanted. I want my experience and my body and my needs and wants to matter.* This feeling is unquestionably valid.

In our relationship, Erin falls more into the "touch leads to connection with partner and self" camp, and Stephen lands more into the "having had personal space leads to wanting touch and connection" category. Touch is often regulating for Erin, while touch is often dysregulating for Stephen, a difference that can hinder communication.

Here's a small example of how this difference played out between us. Erin often wanted Stephen to move toward her and the baby she was growing in a very physical way. Erin might say something like "The baby is moving! Come feel!" And Stephen more than likely would have come to feel the baby move, but clearly not because he wanted to. Depending on the day, that lack of enthusiasm could hurt Erin's feelings. What she could have said that might actually have moved the needle would have been something like "I would really like for you to try to enjoy me and this baby in a way that is meaningful to me." Instead, what usually came out was something like "Stephen, you can't even try to connect for the sake of our baby?!"

Understandably, comments like these hurt and confused Stephen, who really did want to connect with Erin and the baby. Feeling Erin's stomach move actually felt strange to him. Stephen wanted to connect with the baby and with Erin in his own way, so he might have said something like "I saw someone sent a new book for the baby. Is it okay if I read the book aloud to the baby?" Erin loved times like this, but it almost certainly would not have registered to her as Stephen's making the effort to connect, because it was not how Erin would have handled it.

What we had to learn about each other was how touch was related to our styles of regulation, and how pregnancy and birth informed how we both experienced touch—just like it did with Carrie and Mateo. What helps parents find the connection they are longing for with their partner is not arguing about whether they need space or need touch. What helps parents is figuring out how they regulate their bodies and feel a sense of connection, and what impact pregnancy and birth have had on these.

CONFLICT TO CONNECTION:
CARRIE AND MATEO'S SESSION

Mateo and Carrie are clients we have seen for a while, and when the topic of touch arises with them, it's almost always in a passive-aggressive fashion. They know it is something they want to talk about, which is why it keeps coming up, but they are also afraid of hurting each other and of feeling misunderstood and hurt themselves.

STEPHEN: Mateo, you told us the story about coming into the room and seeing Carrie on the couch and thinking about sitting next to her but deciding not to because you felt she would need space. What were you hoping that Carrie would understand about you by telling her this?

MATEO: I don't really know if I was trying to say something about myself. I think I was just trying to note I felt sad that this was my thought process. That I thought about being close to her but then second-guessed myself.

ERIN: How would you prefer your thought process to have gone, Mateo?

MATEO: Well, I would have liked to come into the room and thought, *I'd like to sit next to Carrie to be close,* and then been able to have done so and for her to reciprocate.

CARRIE: The way you are describing me doesn't feel fair. I am not averse to being close to you.

STEPHEN: How would you describe things, then?

CARRIE: I really don't know how to explain it. Mateo is not wrong in that I am not as affectionate and physical as we have been in the past. I don't always love for him to come sit by me on the couch or just randomly come up and hug me. Sometimes he just wants to hold my hand while we are driving in the car, and that feels like too much. I get that it can be confusing for him and that he might even feel like it's his touch that I don't like.

STEPHEN: Mateo, is this how you feel sometimes, that Carrie just doesn't want to touch you in particular?

MATEO: I mean, yeah. She seems fine when the kids are jumping all over her and she has endless hugs and kisses for them, but when it comes to me, she just seems hesitant and standoffish. I even notice it when we are saying goodbye in the mornings. She gives the kids a big hug, and then gives me a side hug and maybe a kiss on the cheek. It's hard not to feel like she doesn't want to be near me.

STEPHEN: Carrie, you said you don't know how to explain it. There's something about how you feel regarding touch that is mysterious or like you just have to be in your body to get it. Does that seem true?

CARRIE: What feels true is that part about having to be in my body to get it. I don't know why, but when I think about that, I feel really overwhelmed and I want to cry.

ERIN: What do you think your body is trying to tell you?

CARRIE: I don't know. I just feel like the whole getting pregnant, having a baby, and parenting has taken way more from me physically than I thought it would.

MATEO: What do you mean? I thought you loved being pregnant, nursing, and playing with the kids. You seem to love all the physical aspects of being a mom.

CARRIE: I do love it, but that doesn't mean it hasn't taken a huge toll on my body. I mean, I have been pregnant and having babies and nursing for the last seven years, not to mention working in a really demanding job for part of that time before baby number three. I am just exhausted.

ERIN: I can hear the overwhelm in your voice. It feels like even trying to think about how to describe what your body has been through, both beautiful and hard, is like climbing Mount Everest. It's just indescribable.

CARRIE: Exactly. To be fair, it has been wonderful as well, and I am proud of my body and how I have been able to care for our kids. I think that is some of the confusion, too. There are days that I just feel like I can't nurse or pump one more time or pick up one of the kids and hold them while they are crying, but I also cherish these moments. It's so confusing!

STEPHEN: And then when Mateo wants to be close physically, it can feel like just one more thing on your list to take care of and push through?

CARRIE: I mean, I feel terrible saying it, but yes, that is how it feels sometimes.

STEPHEN: And this is what you feel from Carrie, Mateo?

MATEO: Yeah, I mean no husband wants to feel like just another task on their partner's to-do list.

ERIN: Mateo, can you hear, though, that this is not what Carrie is actually saying?

Mateo: What do you mean? It is what she said, and it is how it feels with her. I mean, how can sitting by her on the couch be such a huge ask?

Mateo is having a hard time listening to Carrie. He is getting stuck in feeling defensive. At the same time, Carrie is not able to hear what Mateo is trying to communicate, either. They both need some help with intentional listening.

STEPHEN: This is the stuck pattern, Mateo. Carrie is trying to tell you something about her experience, and you are getting caught up in your experience and missing hers.

MATEO: So I just have to forget about what is happening for me and suck it up?

STEPHEN: I see how that is what it sounds like I am saying. Hang with me a minute. What I am saying is that oftentimes partners get caught in a standoff when they are trying to communicate. It goes something like this: "I am not going to hear from you until you hear from me." There is no solution here if this is the approach. You both lose. But when we engage in intentional listening, the standoff can end. Mateo, in order to do this, you first need to suspend your defensiveness.

Note the first step in intentional listening (assess) has been done. Clearly Mateo sees the conversation as triggering and responds defensively. So onto the next step: suspend defensiveness.

> MATEO: I feel a little defensive hearing you say that, but go on. What does that look like?
>
> STEPHEN: I think what you just did is the key. You have to realize that you are defensive and suspend it for a moment so that you can hear what Carrie is saying. I like to imagine it this way. Let's say your defensiveness is any kind of object: a book, a coffee mug, anything. What object do you want it to be?
>
> MATEO: I don't know. A book.
>
> STEPHEN: Okay. A book. Suspending your defensiveness simply means that you are taking your defensiveness, the book, and putting it on a shelf for a few moments. You can come back to it. You can pull it off the shelf and talk about it later. You don't have to stop being defensive. Honestly, your feeling defensive most likely means you have something important that you feel is being missed and you want it acknowledged. So don't quit being defensive. Just suspend it for a moment. Put the book on the shelf.
>
> MATEO: All right, I can do that. I can put it on the shelf.

Note this visual image of how to suspend defensiveness is used to help stop Mateo from feeling triggered and to encourage him to intentionally listen.

> ERIN: Carrie, now that Mateo is making the effort to suspend his defensiveness, what do you wish he was getting about your experience of touch right now?
>
> CARRIE: I think I am dying for Mateo to understand what it has been like for me these last seven years to lose every inch of independence and physical space that I used to have. Sometimes

it feels like he cares more about whether I hold his hand than he cares about understanding why it might feel so hard for me to touch. It feels like he is being selfish.

ERIN: I imagine that is hard to hear, Mateo, but can you see how Carrie ends up at this place?

MATEO: I understand what she is saying. I really don't know what it feels like to lose your space. Honestly, I feel a little embarrassed to say it, but I haven't ever considered how Carrie has been nursing, pregnant, or holding a baby in a carrier for the last seven years straight.

This is Mateo having the capacity to shift into step 3 of intentional listening—believing Carrie's experience—because he is not holding on to his defensiveness. He is open and intentionally trying to be receptive to what she is saying.

STEPHEN: Carrie, what is it like for you to hear Mateo say he realizes he doesn't get what it has been like for you?

CARRIE: I can't believe it. Just hearing that simple recognition feels so good—to recognize that I have been through something that has changed how I feel about my physical space. I get that he can't understand that experience firsthand. I don't even know how to explain it, but it feels like he is focusing on me and not himself when he says he knows the last seven years have been tough.

ERIN: Mateo, what do you think about what Carrie expressed?

MATEO: Well, I am glad she feels like I am hearing her. I want to do so. I think there probably is a lot more to understand about what she is saying. Clearly I've been missing something.

CARRIE: Mateo, I really appreciate how you are working to hear me. It feels so good. I think you might feel the same way—that I am missing something. What would you say I am missing?

Carrie is now moving to suspend her defensiveness so she can intentionally listen to Mateo.

MATEO: I feel a little hesitant because I don't want to dismiss what Carrie is saying about her experience.

CARRIE: I can put my book on the shelf, too, Mateo.

ERIN: Yes, Mateo. Intentional listening is not one-sided. What are you hoping Carrie gets about your experience?

MATEO: I want Carrie to understand how lonely and disconnected I feel because touch has changed in our relationship. It's not as simple as just wanting to hold Carrie's hand. Touch helps me feel connected as a couple in a way that Carrie doesn't get, and I believe she is not trying to understand. I don't know what the balance is between trying to respect her and also connecting in a way that feels meaningful to me.

ERIN: I think that feeling of being stuck and not knowing how to explain how touch means something different to you than it does to Carrie is an important part of your experience. Carrie, what do you hear Mateo saying?

CARRIE: I don't quite understand it, because touch doesn't mean something so deep to me. I like touch, but it seems like something really connective for Mateo that I haven't paid attention to. It sounds like I'm touched out and Mateo maybe feels touch deprived.

ERIN: Mateo, what you are talking about is a very fundamental part of human attachment and feeling connected. Proximity or physical closeness is a primal need we have to feel safe and connected. Granted, we all feel this need with different levels of intensity—you and Carrie obviously feel it differently at this stage in your relationship—but it's an important part of how you feel attached to your partner.

CARRIE: It sounds like part of why Mateo feels so much intensity about touch is because it really does help him feel connected and close in a way that it doesn't for me. In this way, holding hands is not as benign as I think it is. When Mateo wants to be close, he really wants to connect.

STEPHEN: Mateo, does that sound about right?

MATEO: Yes!

Suspending defensiveness has helped the intentional listening process happen. Both Mateo and Carrie are hearing each other differently. Now what can the couple do practically to repair?

ERIN: Now that you both get what this is about, I hope it can lead to some different actions.

STEPHEN: I hear two primary needs in this conversation. Carrie, you need Mateo to know you need some space, and, Mateo, you need Carrie to know you want some closeness. Are there any ways, although not perfect, that you feel you are able to get these needs met?

CARRIE: Mateo has been taking over the morning routine so that I can wake up and take a shower in the morning. That has been so nice. We've been doing this for the last three weeks, and you would be surprised at how it changes my whole day.

MATEO: Huh . . . I didn't know it was such a big deal.

STEPHEN: But now you do. Now you both do. So this can be something that registers for you, Carrie, as "Mateo gets it. He is waking up and doing the morning routine so that I can have space because he gets what my body has been through." And, Mateo, you can be aware of why the shower is so important and keep protecting that time for Carrie.

ERIN: What about you, Mateo? What is a way you are able to be close to Carrie?

MATEO: Well, one thing I like is when we walk our dog with the kids and we hold hands. It is pretty simple, but there is something about it that makes me feel like we have a good, connected life together.

STEPHEN: Carrie, does holding Mateo's hand while walking the dog feel like a hard thing to do in this place of being touched out?

CARRIE: No. I love our walks, too.

STEPHEN: Great! Then let this be a big deal. Carrie, you can hold Mateo's hand on the walk and this can be a message to him that you get how important touch is to him. Mateo, this can be a message to you that Carrie is making movement toward you. Sometimes you might have to take new action, but many times there are things that you are already doing that you can see in a new light and allow them to be significant.

MATEO: I get that. It actually helps that it doesn't feel so impossible.

CARRIE: I agree. I bet if we think about it, there are other ways you give me space and I am close that we don't even notice.

ERIN: Maybe so. This week let the shower and holding hands on the walk be special and maybe keep an eye out for other things that you are already doing for each other.

BUT HOW CAN I ACTUALLY SAY ANY OF THIS TO MY PARTNER? SAMPLE SCRIPTS

Mateo and Carrie were struggling to figure out how to have the "touched out" conflict, which can feel like such a sensitive subject. Many times couples don't say anything so they don't "make things worse" or "make each other feel bad." But by engaging in this conflict in a healthy way, both partners can feel seen, heard, and ultimately closer to each other in their lives as a parenting couple. Here are a few scripts that might help the conversation get started for you and your partner.

For the Touched-Out Partner

"My body does not feel like my own. I don't know if I like it or hate it or feel completely neutral about it, but I feel like a stranger in my own body. I want to be able to talk about this more with you. I don't need you to understand, I just want you to listen."

"I know it's been a while, but I realize we never discussed all my body went through during pregnancy and birthing up to this point. Honestly, it makes me really sad not to have acknowledged this about myself for all this time. I have gone through a lot for our family. I'm not seeking praise or compliments, but I do need you to see it is important to me to feel like you understand this."

For the Touch-Deprived Partner

"Lately I've been feeling disconnected from you. One thing that helps me feel close is physical touch. I don't want to pressure you or make you feel like you have to do another thing, but can we talk about this tension and see if there are any changes that can be made?"

QUESTIONS FOR REFLECTION

1. What has your relationship to your body been throughout your life?

2. Have you and your partner taken the time to map out the experiences your bodies have been on throughout your parenting journey?

3. After kids, have you been able to take the time to get to know your body in this new way? What about your partner? Have the two of you spent time getting to know each other's bodies and how they have reacted to having kids? What, if anything, do you miss about your body and your physical relationship with your partner since having kids?

4. Do you ever feel like your partner hurt you in the "touched out" conflict? What do you feel you are missing about their experience? What do you want them to understand about yours?

5. Do you feel like you have been avoiding this conflict? Is there anything about this chapter that seemed to resonate with you? Why might certain feelings and memories be coming up now in the season of life and parenting you are currently in?

CHAPTER 6

The "Stop Micromanaging My Parenting" Conflict

HARVEY AND WENDY have been together five years and have two kids: Quentin, four, and Lilah, two. Harvey works full time and Wendy has chosen to stay at home with the kids.

A large part of Wendy's passion for being a mom is a desire to give her kids an experience similar to what she had growing up. Wendy loved her childhood and felt that her parents did a great job, giving her a warm and loving environment to thrive in. Harvey also valued the environment he grew up in and is glad his dad showed him the value of hard work as a way to take care of your family. He is proud of his role in his family unit and glad that Wendy has the option to stay home, but he also feels that he is missing out on Quentin's and Lilah's childhoods because he is gone a lot for work.

Wendy spends a lot of her free time researching the latest studies on parenting and studying up on what kind of parenting style is "best" for the kids. She reads all the blogs, follows all the social media parenting influencers, and is highly focused on how she and Harvey can be the best parents for their kids. She is the primary decision-maker in the house on all things parenting. She has made up the plan for how the kids and family should eat. She sets the tone for how she and Harvey discipline the kids. She has established the nighttime routine. The list goes on and on.

Harvey sees Wendy's passion for parenting and appreciates all that Wendy does. He is gone a lot, so it makes sense to him that Wendy would have a lot more to say about parenting. After all, she has more time to research and set a plan for their family. He believes in the vision Wendy has for the family and trusts Wendy with their kids entirely.

Yet Harvey sometimes goes off the books when he is alone with the kids. There are moments when he pushes the limits of the bedtime routine or allows foods Wendy might not in the name of having some fun and not being so regimented. When Wendy is around, he feels like she runs the show and he is just there to support her and her decisions. He says he is fine with that, but sometimes it irritates him. Wendy knows Harvey "cheats" on some of the rules and she tells him it's okay, but sometimes it irritates her.

One Saturday, Harvey was watching the kids while Wendy was spending time with her mom and sister, who live in town. Harvey was looking forward to this one-on-one time with Quentin and Lilah, but throughout the day he got multiple text messages from Wendy checking to make sure he was sticking to the nap schedule for Lilah, feeding the kids the prescribed foods, and checking to make sure the kids were not getting too much screen time. At first Harvey didn't take offense to the text messages, but as the day went on, the comments in the text thread got more tense:

HARVEY: Wendy, I know the nap schedule, and yes, the kids have eaten. I fed them what you had prepared in the fridge.

WENDY: Well, just checking, because you like to follow your own interpretation of the routine.

HARVEY: Have you enjoyed your time with your mom and sister? With the amount you have been texting me, I bet they are getting jealous of how much time we are spending together today.

WENDY: Forgive me for not trusting you can handle the situation. It is only the third time in a year that you have been alone with the kids.

HARVEY: My third time? Come on! I am with the kids plenty when you are not around.

WENDY: Yeah, but I'm usually around a little more to supervise. Watching the kids while I'm occupied at home doesn't really feel like the same thing as being left alone for the whole day.

HARVEY: I don't need your supervision, Wendy.

Then, when Wendy got home twenty minutes after bedtime and the kids were not in bed, things got even more heated.

WENDY: So you don't need supervision, Harvey? Why is it that I always feel like you are parenting by the seat of your pants and not sticking to the plan?

HARVEY: Would you just let me be a parent, too, and stop telling me how to do things? We were heading to bed. It just took a little longer than expected. It's not the end of the world.

WENDY: Not the end of the world for you, but I'm the one that is going to have to deal with overtired kids tomorrow because you can't be trusted as a parent.

HARVEY: Wendy, that is a little extreme. Twenty minutes is not that big of a deal, and calling me untrustworthy is a low blow. You act like I'm some helpless guy that can't tie his own shoes. I am their parent, too, you know.

WENDY: Well, it sure doesn't feel like you are a parent when I have to follow behind you and fix what you have done.

Despite this interaction, Wendy does think Harvey is a good father. She mostly feels supported by him, but part of her feels he's not really engaged or invested. Harvey is highly competent at work, but at home it just works best for everyone when he follows Wendy's lead. On a day in, day out basis, each is not aware of any growing resentment for the other, but when parenting does come up, or when Harvey is in charge of a parenting task for any reason, they both prepare for the worst. Harvey isn't trying to be disengaged, but the truth is, that's what he feels is being asked of him by Wendy herself. It's not that he needs things to change drastically around the house or with parenting, but he gets the distinct feeling Wendy thinks he is incompetent and his engagement only seems to perpetuate that narrative.

This is one of those chicken-and-egg situations we talk with couples about a lot—where both partners can see, at least to some extent, where the other partner is coming from. For example, Harvey may be able to say, "I can see why Wendy thinks I am more disengaged at home and more dialed into work. But at work people trust my intentions, and at home I feel like Wendy is on my back and questioning everything—not only if I know how to take care of my own kids, but also it feels like she doesn't trust my decisions. If she could back off and trust me, I would feel excited to step up and be more engaged around the house. But she won't, so I can't." And Wendy may be able to say, "I would love for Harvey to be more engaged! But he can't dial back from work for long enough to drop the kids off at school without taking a work call on the way. So no, I don't trust him to be engaged and step in without having to double back and check how things went."

This is one of those times when Harvey and Wendy are holding those big thoughts and feelings in—albeit not intentionally. They fear what they might discover if they analyze these big feelings and deeply hurtful things they sometimes think and feel about each other. On the surface they think they are working together well and make a good team, but in actuality they are chronically disconnected in a way that feels too big to fix.

WHY YOU NEED THIS CONFLICT

For Harvey and Wendy, and possibly yourselves, this conflict involves words like *trustworthy, disengaged, disinterested,* and *controlling.* Other couples facing this conflict throw around phrases like:

- "You're always nagging me."
- "It's like I have three kids and not just the two we actually have."
- "Get off my back about it."
- "You are so selfish."
- "You are so condescending."
- "If you want a say, then you have to do the research, too."
- "You act like I'm the only one who ever gets frustrated here—you do, too!"

This conflict is about couples wanting to continue or correct attachment experiences in their own family. As discussed in chapter 1, one of the reasons for conflicts feeling so different when couples become parents was because parenting touches on each partner's own attachment experiences as kids. Depending on the quality of these experiences, partners want to replicate or change their own caregiving experience when they become parents. This conflict in which one partner micromanages the other is a common way this fundamental dynamic emerges.

Wendy cherished her experience growing up. She had a warm and loving home and a mom who was present and involved, and made her feel special. This is how she wants her kids to feel with her and in their home. Her dad was gone a lot, and although she understood he was working his hardest to provide for her family, she missed him and wished he was around more. Harvey had a good experience growing up as well, and one of his core values is that he works hard to give his family a good life just like his dad did. At the same time, Harvey missed having his dad around more. So one of the things he tries to correct in his family is that when he is around, the experience is memorable and fun.

This is why couples need this conflict: the desire to give your kids the best is so strong that any perceived deviation from your plan or your expectations as a parent can feel threatening. You can easily begin to distrust that you and your partner are on the same team, which can lead to communication breakdowns. Rather than communicating from a place of openness and collaboration, you try to control each other, and your communication is closed, directive, and critical rather than collaborative. You need this conflict so that you can approach parenting as a couple who trust each other and communicate expectations and fears openly. For Harvey, this conflict is about feeling micromanaged and constantly criticized by Wendy, which leads him to feel Wendy doesn't trust him. For Wendy, this conflict is about feeling she has to micromanage Harvey because his not sticking to the plan is not what is best for their kids. The deeper fear for Wendy is that Harvey doesn't care enough about her and the kids to bother trying.

When engaged in a healthy way, this conflict allows couples to stop reading their partner's actions through a worst-case scenario and hurtful lens, and instead to understand their partner's hopes for their family during this stage of parenting. In this conflict we are motivated by our desire to give our kids the best, but we are misguided in our fear that our partner will not help us get there. The conflict-to-connection equation can help couples respond to each other without fear, mistrust, and micromanagement.

HOW THIS CONFLICT GOES WRONG

We are not strangers to this conflict. Each time we welcomed a new kid into our family, we had some version of this unhealthy conflict. One of the simple daily ways this happened for us was when Stephen came home from work each day. He was employed at a hospital in town and would work a nine- or ten-hour day. Thus when Stephen walked in the door from work, he was tired, distracted, potentially on his phone, and stressed about what other work he needed to get done that evening while finishing up his dissertation. Erin and the kids were excited about his coming home. At the time we had only one car, so Erin and the kids had been cooped up all day in the neighborhood and were ready for some fun with Dad and the whole family. Erin was also excited to have another adult in the room to help give attention to the kids and to get some support after parenting alone all day.

The conflict typically looked like Stephen walking in the door and being met with excitement and questions and hugs and calls for his attention. Stephen's response was typically something like "Hey, whoa, hang on. Just give me a minute to put this stuff down." He did not exhibit much interest or excitement when reuniting with the family. Erin saw this response, sensed the disappointment in the kids (not to mention her own disappointment), and would begin to make comments like "Could you try to show a little excitement? We have been waiting all day for you." After a while, she even began to monitor Stephen's every move when he walked in the door. "When you came in the house today, you had your phone out; you need to put that away right when you get home." Or "You didn't even look at the kids when you walked in the door. You said hi, but you didn't look their way."

Stephen started feeling like Erin was constantly watching his every move, mood, and interaction when he came home and was judging him. He felt like Erin was treating him like he didn't know how to parent and interact with his kids. This conflict would continue to fester over time, and when it was at its worst, Stephen felt that he was being told he did not know how to parent and could not be trusted, and Erin thought Stephen didn't want to engage with the family. We were stuck having the same unhelpful conflict, and neither one of us was able to intentionally express why we felt such strong emotion around such a mundane and routine event like reuniting after work. After working through the conflict-to-connection equation, we eventually reached a point where we both were able to intentionally express.

Erin realized that one of the things she loved the most about her attachment experience with her mom was how engaging, fun, and present she was when she was with Erin. Erin had her mom's full attention even though she was a single mom that worked full time. One of the things Erin wanted to replicate with our kids was this same feeling of presence, an important value she had based on her attachment experience. Stephen did not disagree with this attachment value in principle. He understood the importance of being engaged and present with children, but during Stephen's childhood, his dad was rarely engaged and present. His dad was either away working in the evenings or home sitting on the couch watching TV rather than spending time with Stephen and his siblings. Stephen hoped to be more available to his kids than his dad had ever been to him, and in many ways this did happen. However, Stephen didn't feel those experiences were ever noticed or acknowledged by Erin. However, he also knew that at times he fell short, and when Erin highlighted these moments, he found himself being defensive.

A lack of trust often leads to the feeling that someone or something needs to be controlled. Erin realized that she had become fearful that Stephen would not be present and engaged as a dad and therefore was hyperattuned for any moment that proved her fear legitimate. Stephen began to understand that one of the things he cared about the most was not giving his kids an attachment experience similar to his. He worked hard to be different and be engaged. So when Erin pointed out his disengaged demeanor when he came home from work, it felt hurtful to him. She seemed to be looking for ways to highlight his worst moments and completely overlooking and minimizing all the interactions where he was present and engaged. This left him feeling defensive.

We needed this conflict so that we could understand how our attachment experiences were contributing to our communicating out of fear and defensiveness. As parents we all want a positive, healthy experience for our kids—but there's always room for our own growth and healing, and by openly and honestly engaging in conflict, couples can find the way forward together.

CONFLICT TO CONNECTION: HARVEY AND WENDY'S SESSION

We have seen Harvey and Wendy for a few sessions before this conflict comes up, and when it does, neither is initially comfortable diving into the deeper emotions they're feeling. They tend to skirt around the topic until they reach a boiling point and it becomes clear we need to address the elephant in the room.

HARVEY: Wendy is a great mom, she really is. I appreciate all she does, but she acts like I have no idea how to parent the kids, and I don't think that is fair.

WENDY: Of course you can parent the kids, but I am the one that is in charge of parenting the majority of the time. You are gone at work, and I am running the show at home.

ERIN: Wendy, is this division of labor—Harvey working and you running the show at home—the way you want things to be?

WENDY: Yes, I wanted to be able to stay at home with the kids. My mom stayed at home, and it was wonderful for me and my siblings. I always imagined that I would be able to do the same thing, and thankfully Harvey has a great job and works really hard and I can have the choice to stay home. Harvey is a great dad, too. When he is home, he is available to the kids and we divide things up relatively well in terms of household stuff.

STEPHEN: So that all sounds positive to me. How do you get from feeling like you have a pretty good thing going to the point where, Harvey, you feel like Wendy doesn't think you know how to parent?

HARVEY: I don't know. Wendy does have more responsibility for our home life and the kids. She has done a lot of research into different parenting styles. I a hundred percent take her lead and read the research she suggests and feel we are on the same page in terms of how we want to parent the kids. I feel like she thinks I am not on the same page with her or work against her in some way when it comes to parenting.

STEPHEN: Wendy, how does what Harvey just said land for you?

WENDY: I agree we are on the same page when it comes to parenting, but I do feel like Harvey works against me sometimes. I have always wanted to be at home with the kids, and I work so hard to make our home an amazing environment. I remember with my mom she made everything feel so good when we were home. It was clean, it was organized, and it was fun. We made messes and laughed, and things made sense. It was a safe, loving place. Part of how I try to achieve this same feeling in our home is to have a daily schedule and rhythm. The kids like it, I like it, and it helps each day feel smooth. Harvey is constantly messing this up.

ERIN: How does Harvey mess things up?

WENDY: He changes the routine. He changes the plan. Like when I left to spend time with my mom and sister. I had food set aside. I didn't prepare it, but it was food for lunch and dinner that I wanted the kids to eat. Harvey will end up just ordering food out. Or with bedtime—it helps the kids to have a consistent bedtime and not stay up too late so that they are not disasters in the morning. Harvey is always pushing the limits on bedtime and not getting the kids to sleep on time. It's little stuff, but when Harvey changes the plan or doesn't follow through with what I expected, it ends up making things harder on me. If the kids are tired in the morning, then I have to deal with that, and I don't want to have cranky kids and get into it with them because they are tired.

ERIN: Because cranky kids and messed-up routines negatively impact what you have been working so hard to create: a calm, fun, positive feeling home environment.

WENDY: That's right. Harvey's changing the plan is fun for him but not for me or ultimately the kids, so I feel like I have to check on him to make sure he isn't messing things up.

HARVEY: I think that is an overstatement. I don't change the plan all the time, and the kids and I have a lot of fun together. Maybe you are just being a little uptight, Wendy. I still don't see how going to bed late matters that much.

STEPHEN: It feels like we are getting into the dead-end dialogue you typically have around this issue. Wendy, you feel like Harvey is dismissing you and not listening, and, Harvey, you feel like Wendy doesn't trust you and is trying to control you.

HARVEY AND WENDY: Yes.

Neither partner seems too upset or triggered at the moment. They know they are frustrated, but neither understands the story potentially informing

*why this is a stuck place. We can start shifting the conversation to focus on
steps 2 and 3 in the intentional expressing process—attune and reflect.*

STEPHEN: Harvey, do you ever push the limits a little? I mean, you
did keep the kids up a little later when Wendy was out with her
mom and sister. Are you saying things like this have never happened before?

HARVEY: I do deviate from the plan. I will admit.

STEPHEN: Why do you think you do that?

HARVEY: What do you mean?

STEPHEN: Well, I mean how come you think that is a good idea? I
can't imagine you go through your day thinking to yourself,
"How can I upset Wendy?" It's important to you to deviate
from the plan when you do in the ways you do for a reason.
How so?

HARVEY: Well, like the other night when we stayed up past the
normal bedtime, Quentin said that he wanted to help with
making dinner. Normally, I would have said no and just tried to
rush through dinner to keep from having some big mess. But
then I remembered how Wendy loves to play in the kitchen
with the kids and she lets them bake and make all kinds of
messes because this is something she got to do as a kid and
loved. So I thought I'd give it a try and just not stress about the
mess and the schedule and have some fun with Quentin.

ERIN: What about having fun with Quentin felt so important?

HARVEY: I miss Quentin and Lilah. I don't always get to be home,
and when I am there, I want it to be something memorable
and fun.

STEPHEN: Harvey, do you ever feel bad for not being at home
more?

HARVEY: Totally. My dad was gone a lot, and I remember missing
him and wishing he wouldn't work so much. I feel torn because

as Wendy said, she can stay home because I do work a lot, and this is really special to her and the kids. I want to give them this and work hard. That is something I appreciate about my dad. At the same time, I missed him a lot, so I think when I am home, I want to make it memorable.

STEPHEN: Wendy, did you know that this is how Harvey felt or what he thinks about when he is home?

WENDY: Maybe . . . I know he wants to work hard because that is something his dad did and it provided a good life for his family, but I don't know if I knew Harvey felt bad about being gone so much. I guess I didn't really consider what it meant to Harvey to not be around.

ERIN: Wendy, what do you hear in what Harvey is saying?

WENDY: Well, that he cares about not being around as much and worries how the kids are impacted by it and wants them to have a good experience of him.

ERIN: Harvey, does that sound right to you?

HARVEY: Yes, it is true. I just want the kids to know I care about them, and even though I am gone, I want to be important to them and not have them feeling like I did, that I missed out on my dad a little.

STEPHEN: Wendy, in some ways I hear a lot of what you have said about what you want for the kids in what Harvey just said. Did you hear it?

WENDY: I am not sure. What do you mean?

STEPHEN: Well, if I understand what you have said, you want to create a warm, loving environment similar to what your mom created in your home growing up. You want your kids to know you care and you want to be important to them just like your mom was, not in a selfish way, but because when kids and parents have strong relationships, it makes for healthy kids.

WENDY: Yes, that's right.

STEPHEN: I feel like I am hearing you and Harvey say the same thing about what you want for your kids. A warm, loving home environment where they know that both their parents care about them and they have positive memories of their parents. You want to create an attachment environment that is positive and safe for your kids.

WENDY: I guess we are saying the same thing. I think it doesn't feel like we are saying the same thing, but I get what you are saying.

ERIN: Harvey, do you see how you and Wendy might actually be on the same page in terms of what kind of environment you are trying to create for your kids?

HARVEY: Yeah, I see it.

ERIN: But, Wendy, you said it doesn't always feel like you are on the same page, and Harvey, I think you would agree. It seems that on some level your good desire to create a strong attachment environment for your kids ends up putting you at odds with each other.

Here Erin is focusing the couple on how their reflection on what they want for their kids, based off of their own attachment experiences, is confusing their communication. Intentional expressing is leading the couple into intentional listening by suspending defensiveness, believing each other's experience, and moving toward repair.

WENDY: I do feel at odds with Harvey at times. I get fearful that the kind of home I want for our kids won't happen. Honestly, most of the time, things are fine, but it's these instances where Harvey changes the plan or deviates from the plan that activate my fear. Then I try and plan what he does so things go the way I hope.

HARVEY: I don't think I really understood how my changing the plan isn't just a small thing. I can see how it makes Wendy afraid that I won't be with her, helping her create a positive environment for the kids. I think I just get focused on my fear that they will miss me and end up feeling like I felt about my dad.

WENDY: I for sure was not aware that you were feeling worried about the kids missing you and that part of your changing things was an effort to have a memorable moment with them. I get it. I don't love the changing of plans or when you go off script, but I understand how it happens.

HARVEY: I don't want to make you feel like I am not with you, Wendy. I am. I love the home we have and all you do to make it feel the way it does. Our kids are really fortunate to have you as their mom. I'm sorry that my deviating from the plan has caused you to feel like you can't trust me. I understand how it has felt that way.

WENDY: Well, I get how you have felt micromanaged, too. I don't want to make you feel like you are not a good dad or husband. We are so grateful for you, and I know my fear of what might happen has caused me to be controlling toward you. I don't want to do that anymore.

Part of repair is then game planning for taking different action. This is what comes next.

STEPHEN: So you both realize that you want the same kind of attachment experience, but how can you get on the same page so that you don't feel like the other is a barrier to your creating the type of environment and relationship you want with your kids?

WENDY: What feels true is we both want the kids to have a memorable attachment experience and we can go about trying to achieve this in different ways. Then we both feel our way is the right one in the moment, and I try and micromanage Harvey and he tries to create a special moment at the expense of the routine or agreed-upon plan.

STEPHEN: Excellent! I am hearing that you both need some affirmation about different things. Harvey, you need to know that Wendy trusts you as a parent and will allow you to create memorable moments, and, Wendy, you need to know that Harvey values the routine and plan, because it is part of creating memorable moments and a positive attachment experience for the kids.

HARVEY: I think that sounds right.

WENDY: Yes, that feels true.

ERIN: So when you are feeling like you are wanting to micromanage Harvey, and, Harvey, when you are feeling micromanaged, what really might be happening is you are both wanting these things to be affirmed?

WENDY/HARVEY: That sounds accurate.

STEPHEN: So how can we skip the miscommunication and start with communicating these needs? I like to think about this little formula in these situations:

> *Name the situation, ask for clarification, affirm each other,*
> *and come up with a game plan for next time.*

This is what I mean: Wendy, let's go back to the situation where you come home after a day away and find the kids not in bed yet. You are already feeling a bit of energy because you have that worry that maybe you and Harvey are not on the same page. Part of it is recognizing you are already a little elevated. Harvey, you know Wendy is going to come home and not be pumped about the kids not being in bed, so you are probably a little elevated too. Naming the situation and asking for clarification looks like this.

Wendy saying something like:

"Hey, Harvey, I see the kids aren't in bed yet and can feel myself wanting to assume a lot about this situation. I don't want to bring that negative energy to this conversation. Can you help me understand?"

and, Harvey, you saying something like:

"I thought you might wonder why the kids aren't in bed yet. I know this can make you feel like I am not on your team. I do have a reason. Can I get the kids in bed and then talk about it with you?"

Then tell each other the stories you just told us today. Wendy, tell Harvey the part about wanting to feel on the same page and how you can get fearful at times that Harvey doesn't want the same thing as you when he deviates from the plan. Harvey, tell Wendy the part about wanting exactly what Wendy wants and the tension you feel to create memorable moments with the kids because you are gone a lot. Remind each other what your motivations are and how they do align. After that, you can **affirm each other,** which looks like this.

Wendy saying something like:

"Okay, that is a helpful reminder, Harvey. I get how you were trying to create a special moment with Quentin and not trying to work against me."

and Harvey saying something like:

*"I know being a great mom and having a magical home
environment is really important to you. That is one of the
things I love about you, and I am really grateful that you are
our kids' mom. I want the same thing. I get how coming
home to the kids being up past bedtime can feel like I am not
with you."*

Then you can **make a game plan for next time like this.**
Harvey saying something like:

*"So, I get tonight was not ideal. Would it be helpful next time
if I give you a heads-up that the kids are not going to be in
bed because we were* (with a smile) *creating some memorable
moments?"*

and Wendy saying something like:

*"I don't know. I think it could help or it could make me
frustrated, and then I won't enjoy what I am doing.
However, I think it would be better to let me know and I can
work through any frustration on my own. I think it will
help, too, that knowing part of the reason you are letting me
know ahead of time is so that we can be on the same page. It
feels caring rather than like a surprise."*

Harvey saying something like:

*"I still realize that the kids being in bed is really important.
So maybe I can be more thoughtful about asking something
like, 'Hey, would it be okay if we stayed up a little later
tonight?' Or maybe I don't bust up the routine at all and I
just plan something like taking them to breakfast in the*

*morning. I just want you to know I am not trying to
frustrate you or disrespect you."*

and Wendy saying something like:

*"Well, having the conversation like we are and then knowing
that we are on the same page helps me think about how you
sometimes operate outside of the routine. But I probably
would have preferred that you do something memorable
that doesn't interrupt the routine (like going to
breakfast). I like your suggestion about trying to have a bit
more foresight."*

Harvey saying something like:

*"I can work toward doing that and I appreciate your
flexibility around if that does not happen there is a way for us
to communicate about it more clearly and with more of a
heads-up."*

Does this sound like it would be a helpful approach?

WENDY: Yes, it would feel so much better.
HARVEY: Absolutely.

BUT HOW CAN I ACTUALLY SAY ANY OF THIS TO MY PARTNER? SAMPLE SCRIPTS

One of the challenges when your communication has broken down
due to a lack of trust is getting the conversation started. Things
can easily devolve into the old pattern of feeling like one partner is

micromanaging while the other is on the defensive and not listening. So here are some possible ways to get the conversation going.

Intentional Expressing—Partner Feeling Micromanaged

"Hey, I wanted to talk with you about something that feels important to me. I feel like there are times you don't seem to trust that I know what to do with our kids if I am with them and you aren't. I might not be reading it right, but I was wondering: Do you notice feeling like you have to monitor how I parent? If so, can you help me understand what is happening for you?"

"I get the feeling sometimes that you think we are not on the same page as parents. I love how we are parenting and appreciate your ideas. Is there something that I am doing or not doing that makes you feel like we are not on the same team?"

Intentional Expressing—Partner Feeling Like They Can't Trust Their Partner's Parenting

"You know, I am noticing that I am feeling some anxiety about our parenting. I am not trying to say you are doing anything wrong, but I find myself wondering if we are on the same page as parents and it makes me uneasy. I want to be on the same page. Can we talk about what we are doing and how we are thinking about parenting?"

"There are times when I feel like we have discussed a plan of action when it comes to parenting and then I feel that you deviate from that plan. I think you and I are on the same page, so I don't think you are saying you agree and then trying to do something different. I am curious, though. Could I give you an example of what I mean and then you can help me understand what you were thinking? I don't want to make assumptions."

QUESTIONS FOR REFLECTION

1. Do you ever feel like you aren't allowed to get something wrong in parenting without it upsetting your partner?

2. What are the areas specifically where micromanaging seems to happen in your couple relationship? Do you and your partner both know and understand what about these topics are so significant?

3. What were some of your favorite things about your own childhood? Do you know if you have intentionally or unintentionally tried to carry those through now with your family? Does your partner know about those things and how significant they were for you?

4. Is there anything in parenting your partner does that feels ongoing and you feel like you have to manage?

5. Do you feel like you have been avoiding this conflict? Is there anything about this chapter that seemed to resonate with you? Did it stir any feelings or memories? Why might those feelings and memories be coming up now in the season of life and parenting you are currently in?

CHAPTER 7

The "I Am Carrying the Mental Load" Conflict

G ABRIEL AND ANYA have been together for nearly ten years and have two kids, ages six and four. They both work full time, but Anya feels she works full time plus the third shift that begins when she gets home, whereas when Gabriel comes home from work, Anya feels like he sees it as "Work is over, now I can relax." It's not uncommon for them to have an exchange like:

> ANYA: It must be nice to have a housekeeper to pick up after you and do your laundry.
> GABRIEL: What are you talking about, Anya? I just finished cleaning the kitchen.
> ANYA: Yeah, but you did that only because I told you to.
> GABRIEL: Wait a second. Are you mad at me for doing what you asked me to do? That makes no sense.

Gabriel wants to help. He believes he has tried, but it all feels futile to him, so they are both exasperated, and he focuses his energy on being with their kids as much as possible. Anya recognizes what a great dad Gabriel is, but even that makes her resent him because she is taking care of everything behind the scenes, doing all the invisible work that allows for Gabriel to relax and enjoy their kids in the way he does. Their dynamic has Anya feeling stuck in productivity mode. For example, while she is preparing dinner, she makes sure to get the laundry started and go through the kids, backpacks to see if anything has been sent home from school for her and Gabriel to see. When Gabriel does dinner so she can play, she feels like Gabriel just does dinner and misses all the other things there are to do so Anya can actually just play like Gabriel is able to.

ANYA: Gabriel, did you not notice that there is a load of laundry sitting here waiting to be put in?

GABRIEL: No, I didn't see it. I was focused on dinner.

ANYA: This is why my playing with the kids doesn't work. When I cook dinner, I look around the house to see if there is anything else that needs to be done.

GABRIEL: If you wanted the laundry done, why didn't you just ask me to do it?

ANYA: That's just it, Gabriel. I don't want to have to *ask* you to do the laundry. I want you to notice the pile of laundry waiting to be done while you are cooking dinner and do both at the same time, like I do. When I check back in from playing with the kids, I want you to have taken care of the things that need taken care of. Now it just feels like I went and played with the kids and now still have a ton of work to do before the night is over.

GABRIEL: Anya, I could have cleaned this whole house while you were gone and you still would have found something to be upset about.

Gabriel feels like no matter how hard he tries, no matter how many tasks he can accomplish, he's a disappointment to Anya. Each feels like the other makes them out to be some awful person trying to make the other miserable, but that is the last thing either wants. They want to feel connected with each other, but most days they are just trying not to provoke each other into having a fight they are sure will get them nowhere.

Frequently, Gabriel and Anya get in arguments over household tasks. Gabriel is generally exasperated at how the list of chores seems unending and what he manages to accomplish is never enough, but he tries to quietly do what she asks and avoid a fight. Lately, though, he frequently has thoughts like *I could do everything she tells me to do and she would still find fault in what I did* or *She really does hate me. My worst enemy wouldn't talk to me this way.*

Anya is feeling more and more frustrated as well. She has noticed that she is increasingly finding it acceptable to utter unkind, pointed statements at Gabriel when she is feeling angry and overwhelmed. In fact, Anya and Gabriel bring out the very worst in each other these days. She hates that her kids see this unhealthy dynamic from them. She certainly doesn't want to be seen as a nag, and she especially wants their kids to see two parents putting in the work so that both get to enjoy the kids. At this point, she worries that all their kids sense is two people trying not to let their loathing boil over. Their fight sounds like this:

ANYA: Doing laundry, cleaning the dishes, and keeping the house straight doesn't feel like things adults should have to be reminded of, Gabriel.

GABRIEL: So you're saying I don't know how to act like an adult?

ANYA: Adults don't need someone to remind them of all the tasks that need to get done to have a home that functions.

GABRIEL: Anya, I want to help you, but you don't want my help. You want me to magically predict what you want done, when you want it done, and how you want it carried out. So yes, I do find it best to ask for you to direct me to save time and so that I am doing what you want.

ANYA: I don't want help, Gabriel. I want a partner! I want you to understand what it takes to live life, have kids, and work together.

Gabriel and Anya both want to do what needs to be done to find more connection and less hurt and anger. At this point their conversations toward this end go immediately sideways. They can have a gigantic argument about a glass in the sink before nine A.M. or about a sock by the tub right before bed, but this issue is much bigger than that. Until they can learn to engage in this conflict in a positive, connective manner, the hurt and anger will grow deeper, and the gap between them will continue to widen.

WHY YOU NEED THIS CONFLICT

This conflict is a very common area of really, *really* big hurt. Big like "If we can't resolve this, if you can't see me in how I am crying out for you to be with me in this, then I don't know if I can be in this partnership" kind of big. We frequently hear some version of Gabriel's and Anya's story, and it's never less than heartbreaking.

What this chapter is ultimately about is acknowledging that there is inequity between parents. This inequity is referred to as the mental load, a term meaning that one partner is inordinately responsible (the default choice) for the physical, emotional, psychological, and practical needs of the family. What makes this reality so divisive and contentious is that it is also intimately tied to societal expectations about the roles assigned to women in a family system—societal expectations that say women are responsible for the home and men are not.

Granted, the dynamics of one partner carrying more of the mental load (the default parent) than the other are found in same-sex households, too. Yet there is a particular challenge that presents itself in mixed-gender couples, one centered around gender roles and patriarchal societal systems. Gabriel and Anya are encountering this challenge.

Gabriel must come to understand that there is a reality to Anya's world that is not the same for him. Anya is drowning because she is expected to serve as a full-time employee, partner, parent, social coordinator, household manager, cook, school email recipient and responder, researcher, emotional needs monitor—this list goes on and on. Her combined work is beyond 24-7. When she says, "I am drowning," it's because she doesn't have the space to feel like there is ever a moment to pause and come up for air without something else falling apart that she will also have to clean up. Does Gabriel mean to perpetuate this? Almost certainly he does not. But his intention does not mitigate the fact that he does perpetuate this dynamic when he relies on Anya to tell him how to "help" her. Part of why Gabriel does not understand this is because he has never had to. Men in mixed-gender relationships or non-default parents in same-sex relationships face a huge learning curve. There are not equal expectations of men or non-default parents in parenting partner relationships. Society expects women and default parents to do far more than men and non-default parents, and these expectations are generally invisible to everyone except the people they fall on.

This conflict is essential because Gabriel and Anya need to get down to the nitty-gritty of a couple's division of labor, and how the inequity inherent in this dynamic perpetuates destructive societal expectations about women and default parents. This conflict is not about Gabriel's not doing the laundry or Anya's having impossible standards. This conflict is about the hurt Anya feels because Gabriel does not get the impossible expectations put upon her. One of the ways she tries to make him aware of these impossible expectations is by loading him up with all the stuff he is not doing just like she herself is loaded upon. What Anya needs to communicate is how impossible and unfair things are for her and how bad it hurts that her partner isn't working to understand her experience and make radical changes to help make her experience different. Gabriel also needs this conflict because he first needs to acknowledge the reality of the mental load and its harmful message to women and to see how inequity in the division of labor perpetuates this harmful message. Second, he needs this conflict so he and Anya can practically move toward an equitable division of labor in the home. Third, he needs the conflict so that he can express he has been hurt by how Anya has communicated her hurt and anger, without being told, "how you feel doesn't matter."

HOW THIS CONFLICT GOES WRONG

This is a really exhausting one to have go wrong, and unfortunately, the longer this conflict goes wrong, the harder it is to recognize the roots. It zaps all the energy from a relationship and even kills the motivation to find that energy again. *Work to repair? With them? Why bother? They have turned into a monster I don't much like, and I turn into a monster I despise when I'm around them.* These feelings can seem insurmountable, but finally feeling seen in it, finally having your partner truly understand the hurt and anger, can be the lifeline for a relationship.

Anya needs Gabriel to acknowledge the inequity in her carrying the mental load and to employ a system for equally separating out the tasks of family life—together. They waste a lot of time arguing about the fact that Gabriel is not doing enough or just "helping"; this misses the core of why Anya is angry and hurt.

Our own version of this got progressively worse over the first six years of our being parents and then came to a boiling point. Erin would often try to express that she was completely overwhelmed with navigating how to balance care of the kids and the house, her grief over a pregnancy loss, school planning, meals and snacks, our social calendar, and on and on. Erin felt overwhelmed and not okay. Stephen did as much as he possibly could when he was around, but it never felt like enough to either of them.

Honestly, Stephen was legitimately perplexed about how Erin could feel he was not being helpful enough. Erin oscillated between feeling defeated and saying nothing and feeling angry about how chronically overstimulated and overwhelmed she was. In some ways she felt she didn't have the right to feel the way she did because it wasn't like Stephen was just sitting around all day—he was working hard—but also, she felt like no matter how she tried, he had no idea the depth of how bad she was feeling.

What Erin was trying to tell Stephen was that things did not feel equitable. He left in the morning at 7:30 A.M. and didn't come back until 7:00 P.M. All during that time, she was working, too, and her work felt constant. We didn't have any family nearby for help and didn't have any money to hire someone. What she did have was two little kids at home that she was thankful to be with. But she didn't get to leave for a few minutes to go to the bathroom or go take a lunch break and have a little quiet time. Even when Stephen was home, the kids would bypass Stephen and seek out Erin for help or to let her know they needed a snack or a hug. She was always needed and on call, always thinking about someone else, and when she wasn't, something was falling through the cracks that she was going to have to work to fix later.

When Stephen came home, this feeling of "always" didn't stop. It just seemed to get added to because he would ask, "What can I do?"

or "Are we having the Sloans over for dinner this weekend?" or "Did you not call the dentist today and schedule appointments?" or "Of course you can't find your wallet, you're so scattered." There was a level of work that Erin had to do to get Stephen up to speed and involved in the family, and he didn't see it. It was invisible labor, but we could see the disconnection between us. Stephen didn't mean to be oblivious, but his intentions were not enough to mitigate the harmful impact. He got defensive when Erin tried to express her experience. This response from Stephen left Erin increasingly disoriented, sad, and angry. Stephen grew increasingly defeated, exasperated, and defensive. Stephen began to think there was no way he could make Erin happy. Erin began to feel that Stephen would never get what she was trying to say.

Just like Gabriel and Anya, Stephen and Erin were stuck, but there is a way to reshape this conflict by using the conflict-to-connection equation to first recognize the inequity, validate the burden caused by the inequity and the hurt caused by the couple's unhealthy communication, and initiate specific practical action to address the inequity.

CONFLICT TO CONNECTION: GABRIEL AND ANYA'S SESSION

Gabriel and Anya had briefly described this stuck fight in our initial consultation, so in their first session we helped them address the fact that they needed to divide up their household tasks. They needed to understand what the household tasks were and to come to an agreement about what all was entailed in completing each of those tasks from beginning to end. They came in for their next session cautiously optimistic that things could feel different for them. Each wanted to acknowledge to the other that they knew they weren't perfect, but also that they failed to grasp what the other one was trying to say to them.

ANYA: Gabriel doesn't help me unless I tell him to help or nag him until he is worn down.

GABRIEL: That's not true. I am happy to help. I do ask you what you want me to do because typically you have a very specific way you like things done. For example, I clean the kitchen, but then you'll come back behind me and reload the dishwasher because you don't like how I did it. So I find it better to just wait for you to say what you want or ask you what you want.

ANYA: That's just another way of saying my expectations are too high when the problem is you're sloppy and do things halfway. I'll ask you to help in the kitchen and you'll load the dishwasher but then leave all the pots and pans in the sink and not wash them. How is that helping? How do you not understand what a clean kitchen means? I feel like you are another child that I have to teach how to do basic things around the house. So no, your help is not helpful, and yes, I do come behind you because you don't seem to know how to do daily tasks on your own.

The hostility in the room feels intense, the kind of energy generated when partners are triggered and stuck in their stress response. Neither one is able to suspend their defensiveness and intentionally express or listen.

GABRIEL: Look, it's not my fault you are so particular and high-strung. You want things done to a level that I don't think is necessary.

ANYA: So my expectation of wanting the pots and pans to be included in the meaning of a clean kitchen is too much for you?

STEPHEN: Okay, I think I get it. This is what it sounds like when you two are in conflict. It seems like it can get pretty sharp and mocking.

GABRIEL: Yeah, Anya is not afraid to let me know that she thinks I'm dumb or inept.

ANYA: And you're not afraid to let me know that you think I'm being reactive and nagging?

STEPHEN: So what are you wanting to change, Anya?

We are looking to shift the conversation out of the triggered attachment-breaking interaction into the conflict-to-connection process. This question can help Anya move to step 2 (attune) of intentional expressing.

ANYA: I don't want to feel like I am the only one doing "adult" things in the house.

ERIN: Can you explain a little bit more about what you mean by "adult" things?

ANYA: Well, Gabriel plays with the kids and has a lot of fun with them, but I am left to take care of everything else. There is laundry to do, dishes to be cleaned, school lunches to be made, groceries to buy. The list is endless. If I want something done, I either have to do it myself or create a very detailed checklist of what Gabriel needs to do and then stay on his case for it to get done.

GABRIEL: Look, I can help with that kind of stuff. Just ask me to do it!

ANYA: Why do I have to ask you to do things that should be self-explanatory for the household we both live in? It is just more work for me to have to sit there and think about trying to help you get involved.

STEPHEN: Anya, what would you prefer? If Gabriel was also doing the "adult" things, what would that look like?

ANYA: It would be his knowing what goes into making our house and family function. It would look like his anticipating the needs of the kids and household because he knows us and knows the needs. It would look like his not letting everything fall on me, knowing I'll pick up all the slack.

ERIN: Gabriel, what do you hear from Anya in what she has just described?

This is an effort to shift Gabriel into intentional expressing and keeping him moving through the steps of attuning to what he is feeling as he hears Anya talk.

GABRIEL: I mean, it's not anything I haven't heard. She acts like I don't want to help. I am happy to help. At the same time, the way she asks for help isn't really welcoming. Honestly, she gets angry and then just starts calling me names, saying I'm useless, and it pretty much makes me want to leave.

STEPHEN: Your disconnect is in how Anya treats you when she is feeling like you are not helping or being an "adult."

GABRIEL: Yeah, I mean even the use of the word *adult* is belittling. I *am* an adult. I go to work, I have a lot of responsibility, I do all of our finances, I take care of our kids and Anya. I am an adult, and she sits there and mocks me. I don't like it, and I don't want to help her. I don't think it's kind or fair.

Both Anya and Gabriel have been able to drill down below the content of the conflict (dishes, laundry, etc.) and get at the core feeling of the conflict, the things that hurt. They are moving through the steps of attune and reflect in intentional expressing.

STEPHEN: So how would you like it to go, Gabriel? How would you like these conversations to happen or what would you like them to feel like?

GABRIEL: I want to feel like we are a team. That we both have things we do, we both have responsibilities, and we interact with each other like we are on the same team. We can disagree or have different roles, but we don't have to attack each other. We can solve a problem together and treat each other with some kindness.

ANYA: Being kind doesn't get you to listen to me, Gabriel. I can ask you to do something with a smile on my face and while batting my eyelashes, but unless you think it's important or want to do it, it won't get done. And honestly, you don't want to do any of the things that need to be done in our house.

ERIN: And this is the old stalemate again. Anya, you are past being nice because you feel angry. And, Gabriel, I think you feel hurt that Anya has turned against you, maybe switched teams, and you don't want to listen to her or help, which is how you express your anger. Anya uses words to express her hurt and anger and you hear it in her words. Then you stop listening and doing things, and your hurt and anger is exhibited in your actions or, better said, inaction.

ANYA: I'm definitely over it and feel angry. I'd rather just do this on my own rather than expect anything from Gabriel.

GABRIEL: I don't know if I would say I'm angry, but it does hurt and I find myself starting to become indifferent.

STEPHEN: Yeah, and the indifference contributes to the inaction.

GABRIEL: Yeah, I see that.

Here we are modeling how intentional listening looks. We are guessing at what Gabriel and Anya's experience might be like to try and help them get to the step of believing their partner's experience and then engaging that experience with repair rather than defensiveness, blame, and dismissal.

ERIN: We hear this and see this a lot with other couples. First of all, how you all are experiencing this conflict is unique to your relationship, and at the same time this dynamic is actually very common. What we have found is that there are two things that can help. Gabriel . . .

GABRIEL: Yes?

Erin: It seems to me that Anya is not asking for your help; she is asking for a partner. Do you know what that distinction is?

GABRIEL: Not really.

ERIN: Think about it in business terms. You are equal partners in the firm that is your household. Partners don't help. Partners set the vision for a firm. They strategize for the firm's future. In short, they are the drivers of the firm's direction. Partners know the numbers, know the potential problems, know the way to move toward solutions, and actively set the tone. I think Anya is saying she feels like she is the only partner in the firm that is your household. Anya, does that fit for you?

ANYA: Yes, a hundred percent. I don't want someone to help me. I want someone to be my partner.

ERIN: Gabriel, do you see the distinction between helping and being a partner?

GABRIEL: Maybe.

STEPHEN: Gabriel, to put it plainly, I don't think you get it because you have never been challenged to get it. Let's stick with the work analogy. How many hours does a typical workweek entail?

GABRIEL: Forty hours.

STEPHEN: And it is my understanding that both you and Anya work full time, so you both work forty hours a week?

GABRIEL: Yes.

STEPHEN: Yet what Anya has described is that she gets off work and then comes home to work. She clocks in for her third shift and starts coordinating meals, homework, housecleaning, social calendars, and much more. She does all of this in addition to her full-time job, and it takes a massive amount of mental energy, emotional energy, physical energy, and cognitive energy. Would you agree?

GABRIEL: Yes.

STEPHEN: This additional energy she has to expend is then something you add to by not being a part of doing this extra work, too. You come home, and it's not that you lie around and don't do anything, but you rely on Anya to tell you what to do. Even though you are more than willing to carry out any given task, Anya has to expend mental, emotional, physical, and cognitive energy to bring you into the work of being a part of running the household. What Anya is saying is that she wants you to come home and clock in for the third shift just like she does. She wants you to share in the mental, emotional, physical, and cognitive energy to be a partner with her in the work, not someone she has to tell how to help her do the work. This is the mental load. This is what she does not want to keep carrying all by herself.

GABRIEL: Okay, I'm seeing it. By my coming in and saying, "Hey, just let me know how I can help," I end up adding to the work. I can see how that isn't fair. But practically I don't really see how this works differently. Honestly, it feels like Anya says she wants a partner, but I don't think she does. She wants to run the firm and she wants me to do what she says.

STEPHEN: I imagine that is how it feels and maybe even what Anya communicates sometimes. We'll get to that. First, let's go back to the partner analogy Erin was mentioning to answer your question about how this looks different practically. I think we have a strategy that can help. I like to say it like this:

1. Do the research
2. Make a plan
3. Carry out the plan

This is what I mean. *Do the research* is your shifting from being a helper to a partner. As partners, you both need to know the kids' schedules, you need to know and be aware what laundry needs to be done, you both need to know or have mutually decided the meal plan for the week, you both need to know the pickup and drop-off schedule, you both need to know what tasks are involved in running the house. This is not something Anya needs to tell you. As partners you also do the research, you pay attention, you observe the processes, and you make them a priority.

Make a plan is where you look at your life and the tasks that need to be done and you coordinate your work schedule, your workout schedule, your hobbies, and whatever else with the tasks that need to be done. In other words, you create a business plan for your firm and show how you are part of making the plan happen.

Carry out the plan is where you and Anya sit down and divide responsibilities, exchange ideas, problem-solve, and set the plan in motion.

Anya, how does that sound to you?

ANYA: If that actually happened, I would be so blown away.

ERIN: Anya, if you pause for just a few moments and imagine that Gabriel does the research, makes a plan, and carries out the plan, what are you aware of in terms of how your body feels or what emotions come up for you?

ANYA: I could tear up at how much that would feel like a relief! I can just feel my shoulders get a little lighter and my chest doesn't feel so tight. It would feel so good, and it would feel like Gabriel and I are a team. It would feel like we are together rather than miles apart.

ERIN: Gabriel, what is it like for you to hear Anya say that? To hear her say she wants to be a team, too?

GABRIEL: I mean, it's nice. It doesn't always feel like she wants to be a team, but I would love it.

STEPHEN: So, Gabriel, what Anya has just said is this is what would make things feel like you are on the same team. This is how you get to be teammates, partners.

GABRIEL: Sure, but like I said earlier, I don't think Anya wants me to be a partner. She wants to run the show and she wants me to do what she says.

STEPHEN: Right. So like I said, we would come back to this. Anya, do you understand what Gabriel is saying? Do you want to be in charge?

ANYA: Well, I know what he means. I do and I don't want to be in charge, and sometimes I wonder if that impulse has gotten stronger just because I have been angry and don't feel like Gabriel is a partner.

STEPHEN: So perhaps in your hurt and anger, that has been coming out as controlling and shutting him down.

ANYA: Yeah, that has happened. I don't want that to be true and I really don't want to make Gabriel feel controlled. I think sometimes I don't trust that he can be a partner.

STEPHEN: Gabriel, do you see how you not acknowledging the mental load can contribute to Anya's not feeling like she can trust you? She needs you to get it.

GABRIEL: Anya, I am seeing it. I have not been aware of the mental load and have been so defensive that I have not listened to you and how overwhelmed you have felt and how imbalanced things have been. Of course you wouldn't trust me. I missed it and I am sorry.

ANYA: Thank you, Gabriel. That means a lot to me.

STEPHEN: Anya, I appreciate your being honest there. I bet it is tough to trust that Gabriel can be a partner. Yet part of being in a partnership is accepting his partnership. One of the things that makes a firm strong is having a diversity of partners. You can't all be the same, and you can't all go about solving problems the same way. I think where accepting Gabriel's partnership will come into play is in your partner meetings after he has done the research and made a plan.

ERIN: Yeah. And you both have the accountability to trust each other's partnership. Gabriel, you can build trust by doing the research, making a plan, and carrying out the plan. Anya, you build trust by accepting Gabriel's partnership. These are the areas that have caused the disconnection in the past and drive the conflict.

STEPHEN: What does this sound like to both of you?

GABRIEL: It sounds hard. I can see why Anya feels like she needs to take control. I don't do the research. I just see parenting as her world, one in which she is in charge. But I get how this puts a lot of pressure on her and perpetuates her having to carry the mental load.

ANYA: I want his partnership, but I definitely send out the vibe that it is a partnership my way. I can see how this is not very welcoming. And, Gabriel, I can see how I have been really harsh and unkind in how I have communicated my anger. I do say you are not an adult or that you are selfish, and this makes you feel like I despise you. I get why it would feel hard to believe that I want a partner. I'm sorry that is how I expressed myself.

GABRIEL: I really appreciate that, Anya. It has hurt, but I can see how I wasn't acknowledging the inequity and this was making it hard for you not to be angry and for that to come out like it did. I'm sorry I didn't listen when you have tried to tell me you are overwhelmed.

Gabriel and Anya have repaired. They have both taken accountability for how their actions have impacted each other, they have forgiven each other, and they have moved toward implementing different action.

BUT HOW CAN I ACTUALLY SAY ANY OF THIS TO MY PARTNER? SAMPLE SCRIPTS

This conflict is highly charged for many couples, but we are certain this conflict, when done in a healing way, can be navigated and become an attachment-making interaction. Here are some scripts that may help you and your partner begin to have the conversation in a new way.

Intentional Expressing—Partner Feeling the Inequity

"I feel like we fight a lot about how the tasks in our home are divided up and about who feels they are doing more. This is an awful fight, and I don't love having it and I know you don't, either. I feel at a loss to know how to talk with you about this. Could we try and get some outside help? I feel like I need some guidance on how to express myself to you and to listen to your perspective."

"There is this term that parenting partners talk about a lot nowadays. It's called the mental load. Have you ever heard of it? I would really like to talk with you about how I feel like our relationship is being impacted by the mental load. I want us to be close and to understand each other, and I think this would help me be able to describe to you something I am feeling."

Intentional Expressing—Non-Default Partner

"You know, I am realizing that I have not acknowledged that there is an inequity between what is expected of me and what is expected of you as a parent. I think you have been trying to tell me that you are held to a different standard and that this standard is overwhelming you and unfair. I have missed it and I have even perpetuated it. I am sorry."

"I know that I can't just say I get there is a mental load. I have to do things differently to actively work against the inequity. I have not been doing this. I have thought through some ways I can practically make changes. Can I share these with you?"

QUESTIONS FOR REFLECTION

1. Growing up, what roles did you and your partner see your parents play? How, if at all, was the division of labor divided between them?

2. Do you and your partner ever find that you try to prove to each other what all you are doing in a day? Do you feel like you have to be able to make a list detailing all the times you were specifically contributing to the daily tasks of a household?

3. Can you imagine what would feel good for you in terms of household division of labor? Are you far from that currently? What is one thing that could change this week to move you closer to what would feel good for you? When that one thing starts working, what is one more thing that could change to move you closer to feeling more balanced?

4. In this conflict for partnership, are there hurt places you need your partner to know about and really move toward you in? What about for your partner? Are there places of anger you need to receive apologies for? Are there places you need to ask for your partner's forgiveness? What are the unresolved places in this conflict for you?

5. What, if anything, about this chapter resonated with you? Did it stir any feelings or memories? Even if they predate your current relationship, what emotions arose in you? Why might those feelings and memories be coming up now in the season of life and parenting you are currently in?

CHAPTER 8

··

The "You're Too Stressed" Conflict

PAUL AND DOUG are a couple with a one-year-old, Ty. Paul is a stay-at-home dad and Doug works in commercial real estate. They both have wanted to be parents for a long time and through surrogacy were finally able to have a baby together. Paul is a self-described chill guy and loves to approach life with spontaneity and a "let's see what happens" attitude. Doug is more organized and structured. Routine and order help Doug feel balanced and less anxious. When things get out of order or his routine is altered, Doug finds it tough to recover and not become irritable and thrown off by the change. Outsiders wouldn't know Paul ever feels anxious, but some of how Paul deals with stress is procrastinating and sometimes shoving stress down.

In Paul and Doug's case, opposites did attract, and they appreciate how each of them helps the other access a more challenging part of themselves. Paul helps Doug take risks and enjoy the moment, and Doug helps Paul stay focused and set goals for the future (not to mention live in a clean house).

Before kids, Paul and Doug would sometimes get frustrated by their differences, but they were able to accept these and felt like the differences made their relationship stronger. Since Ty arrived on the scene, they are beginning to see that the differences that had been merely irritating before are feeling more and more like barriers to their parenting but also to their overall happiness with each other.

Paul loves to play with their son, and at times it can look like a whirlwind has spun through the house. Doug can practically follow the path of Paul and Ty through the house. Toys are strewn about the living room, the gooey breakfast concoction is on the floor by the table, the high chair is now crusted with food, a diaper is lying on the steps, and Ty's pj's are on the floor on the way into his nursery. When asked, Doug would say this is a daily occurrence, while Paul would maintain that this has definitely happened but is not at all common.

Doug resents being left to clean up after "good time" Paul, and when this happens, he badgers Paul, pulling him into a fight, like this:

DOUG: Hey, no worries, I'll just come behind you like a house-keeper and clean up your mess.

PAUL: Oh, I'm sorry I didn't realize that making sure the house was ready for a magazine photo shoot was more important than paying attention to Ty and being engaged.

DOUG: Well, someone has to pick up. You know, if you would help with the house every once in a while, I could hang out with Ty, too.

PAUL: Doug, you wouldn't even know how to have fun with Ty. You care more about having a clean house than about being a good parent. Your idea of playing with Ty is taking him on an errand you need to run and calling that quality time.

DOUG: What are you talking about, Paul? That is a really cruel thing to say.

PAUL: Doug, you choose to make yourself stressed. You don't have to tear through the house cleaning up and huffing and puffing all around. You are making the situation worse than it needs to be.

Paul and Doug feel blamed and criticized about the way the other copes with stress. Doug wants Paul to keep the house in order and organized so he can keep his calm and feel more able to engage. Paul wants Doug to set aside his desire for order and organization and play and engage and put things right later. Paul feels Doug has an endless list of things to get done; he believes that engagement and relaxation will never happen because in Doug's view of the world, there is always one more thing to do. It didn't bother Paul as much before Ty, but Doug is constantly wound up and Paul doesn't want that kind of negativity for himself or for Ty. On the other hand, Doug feels Paul makes his stress worse. He feels like Doug disregards his need for external cleanliness and order and creates stress and chaos for Doug to have to clean up. Paul and Doug have both taken to making passive comments about how silly the other's needs and coping strategies are, and these comments are becoming the norm rather than the exception.

WHY YOU NEED THIS CONFLICT

Stress impacts us all. It impacts us differently, but no one escapes it. Stress cannot be avoided in life, and it definitely cannot be avoided in parenting. Being parents changes your life so completely and in so many unexpected ways, it is only natural for you and your partner to experience stress. Stress gets in between couples because it pits our different techniques for coping and dealing with stress against each other. This is a typical statement from a partner in this type of conflict: "I am stressed, but my stress would be cut in half if you weren't

making it worse by continuously adding more and more to my plate!"
Parenting partners need to engage in this conflict so we can learn our
own stressors and approach stress with a "It's you and me against the
stress" mentality instead of this refrain: "Our different coping strategies make it you and me against each other."

For Doug and Paul, the stress seems to center around the messi-
ness of the house. So many of the couples we work with identify with
this conflict, and for good reason. Our internal and external worlds
are connected, and oftentimes when we feel chaos in one area, we
seek to gain control in the other. For example, if a partner is worried
about work, this internal tension may become externalized by that
partner's trying to have a spotless house. In this way, this partner is
trying to bring order and control to at least one part of their world.
Or if a partner feels their external world is chaotic, they may retreat
inward and zone out on their phone or just be less engaged in general
in an effort to quiet the external chaos.

Every partner is triggered by different things and is soothed by
different actions. Many times, partners feel as if their triggers are
obvious, but they are not. What sends one partner into an activated
stressful place may not send the other one there. One partner may
actually need for the laundry to be put away before they can go to
sleep at night while the other partner seems not to even realize there
is a gigantic laundry basket full of unfolded clothes sitting right on
the bed. But that same partner who seems oblivious to the laundry
stress may get into the car and feel instantly overwhelmed by the
state of the car and the car seat.

What causes stress varies. For some the overwhelm is:

▪ The noise. You walk into a room and your kids are yelling at
   the top of their lungs (either in distress or just having a great
   time), and your first impulse is to try and return the room to
   a normal decibel level. You feel you do this so you can hear

your kids and yourself think, but your partner feels you do this because you feel entitled to walk into a room and "change the environment to suit you and your delicate needs."

▪ The mess. You step into the kitchen and are faced with open boxes of cereal and cups of half-consumed juice precariously balanced on the countertop edge. You move to clean up the mess, but your partner says, "I was going to get that! We aren't finished yet."

▪ Lack of structure. Maybe it's how your partner models disorganized behavior and you see your kid picking up on that.

▪ Work stress. Maybe it's a partner who has a hard time shaking the stress of work or can never quite leave work behind.

▪ Being rigid. Maybe it's the constant refrain of "Don't leave that there," "Pick up your shoes," or "Let's stick to the schedule" that sets you off. You want to be able to have a more flexible approach to raising kids.

Just as partners do not stress about the same things or even experience the same stress in the same way, they also don't cope or deal with their stress in the same way. Many people find these to be stress-reducing activities:

▪ Exercise
▪ Time with friends
▪ Sports leagues
▪ Eating out
▪ Long showers or baths
▪ Intimacy (sexual and nonsexual)
▪ Watching TV/movies
▪ Sleeping
▪ Focusing on a healthy diet

This is why you and your partner need this conflict—because your different triggers, your different ways of coping, and the lack of available outlets for coping will intensify your stress and cause numerous conflicts. You need this conflict so that you can be stressed, cope with your stress differently, collaborate on realistic coping strategies, and feel like a team rather than opponents.

WHERE THIS CONFLICT GOES WRONG

Coping with stress is one of life's most persistent tasks, and finding a solution that works for you can prove difficult. Just as you thought you had a handle on it, add the element of parenting to stress and people can be pushed to their physical, emotional, and mental limits. Ask many parenting couples how they are doing, and they will say something like "We are just surviving" or "We are so busy that we are just trying to make it right now."

Now imagine factoring your partner into the stress equation. While you're trying to cope with your stress, you might not even be aware of how your partner is attempting to cope with theirs. It tends to catch most partners off guard that they and their partner have very different ways to handle their stress, and that disconnect can lead to more tension in the home. The tension is often brought on because the way one partner copes might be in direct opposition to how their partner manages, which activates their stress even more. One partner might want to just sit and relax with their partner on the couch and "do nothing for five minutes," while the other wants to be physically active and exercise. There is limited time already, so it's not possible to meet everyone's coping needs. Whose coping strategy wins?

One of the primary ways we see this conflict go wrong for couples is when one partner believes that their way of coping with stress is the "right way" and their partner's way is "wrong." Stephen can very easily feel that Erin is wasting time or trying to distract herself from getting things done when she wants to go for a walk or have a hug because she is stressed. Inversely, stopping stresses Stephen out, so he sees Erin's way of coping as inefficient and a time suck. Erin can look at Stephen and criticize him for being a robot and not caring about anyone else or even needing others. His task-oriented "I'll take care of it myself" mentality can be seen as mechanical, not relational. In moments when Stephen and Erin are trying to cope with their stress, they can feel like the other is actively and purposefully trying to increase their stress.

Another very common way this conflict turns couples sideways is when one partner makes sure to get their need for stress relief met while the other feels there is no time or way for them to get their need met at the same time. You can probably see how this dynamic leads to anger, and fast. "I see you got your run in today. How entitled of you." "It's not my fault you didn't get a run in. You could have made time just as easily as me." And while both partners need to prioritize inserting stress-relieving activities into their routine, it is not as easy for a default parent to do this as it is for the non-default parent. The non-default parent can more easily find and take the time to relieve stress, and the default parent likely has an uphill battle to do the same. The non-default parent has to recognize that the opportunity to just get out the door is not the same, and both partners will have to work to make sure the default parent has the same opportunities for stress-relieving activities as the non-default parent has.

As this happens to a couple, they move from being frustrated with each other to feeling hopeless about the relationship. But neither partner is really trying to sabotage the other or drive the other to hopelessness. We're all just working toward coping with stress so that we can connect with each other. Yet how can this happen when our needs are so different in these stressful moments? It is possible to have these differences and be a team when it comes to parenting, and it starts with a shift away from the wrong versus right mindset to a mindset of "you and me against the stress, not against each other."

CONFLICT TO CONNECTION: PAUL AND DOUG'S SESSION

Doug and Paul came to their session quiet and tense. You could feel how frustrated they were.

> DOUG: When Paul said that I wouldn't want to hang out with Ty even if I helped around the house and that I wasn't a good parent, that was it for me. It hurt and was unkind. I don't want to keep having this conversation, and honestly, if that is what Paul thinks about me, then what are we doing together?
>
> PAUL: But it is true, Doug. You walk around spewing your anxiety about all the tasks that need to be done, like keeping the house organized, and maintain that you miss being engaged with Ty because of me. So in a lot of ways I feel the same. If this is how you are going to be, and soothing your anxiety is more important than being with me and Ty, what are we doing together?
>
> STEPHEN: And this is how this conversation begins to feel really serious for you both. You all are asking questions like "Why are we together?" "Should we be together?" "Is this how I want things to be for the rest of our relationship?"
>
> PAUL: Yeah, it feels really scary. I love Doug, but we just aren't connected anymore. I don't know if we can get back what we used to have.

ERIN: What did you used to have together?

This is a question that gets Paul into intentional expressing. Erin asks him to reflect (step 3) on the story that is part of why this all feels so bad. Things weren't always this way, and the loss of how it used to be is part of what triggers both partners.

PAUL: We enjoyed each other more. If we did get in an argument or see things differently, it didn't feel like such a big deal. Doug has always been a little anxious, but it was cute and I could handle it. I've always been a bit of a free spirit, and it annoyed Doug, but now I think it just makes him rage.

ERIN: What would you say, Doug?

Erin invites Doug to reflect as well. This reflection also allows Doug and Paul, to attune (step 2) to the emotions that drive the intensity of the conflict.

DOUG: I think Paul pretty much described it. We just seemed to have more space for each other to be different and it didn't feel so abrasive or hurtful when our differences came up. Now it feels so personal. Ty is wonderful and makes our lives fuller, but there are so many things that need to get done, and adding parenting to full-time work and trying to maintain a house just feels like too much. I need Paul's help and he doesn't seem to care, which hurts.

PAUL: I do help you. It's not like I'm a slob or Ty is wreaking havoc on the house. So much of your anxiety is self-generated. You have to have things perfectly in order to feel all right, and that's not realistic when we have a kid. I don't like being told I'm the problem when the problem seems to be your anxiety. Ty and I can't be responsible for making you feel better. That's what feels personal to me. You are anxious, and then we have to pay for it.

Doug: You know what, Paul, I am anxious. Order and systems help me not feel out of sorts. I like the house to be clean. I don't need it to be immaculate, but when it looks like every toy in the house has been taken out and thrown on the floor and breakfast is still sitting on the high chair at dinnertime and the kitchen is a mess, I do get overwhelmed. I don't get why you can't take a few moments to clean that stuff up. You are home. I'm at work. How can this not be part of the work you do?

The tone has shifted to blame and defensiveness, which is blocking intentional listening.

Paul: Because I consider the work of engaging with Ty and playing and giving him my full attention the ultimate priority. If you would stop working yourself up about the mess when you get home, we could tackle it together after Ty is in bed. I don't need you to tell me how to work while you are gone. I don't tell you what to do at your job.

Stephen: Doug, would it be fair to say that when the house is a mess and the high chair is crusty from breakfast, you feel that this, in a way, is Paul saying he does not care about you or consider your needs?

This question is meant to refocus the conversation on intentional expressing. The suggestion is offered to shift Doug's focus from defensiveness to attuning to his emotion and seeing how this relates to his triggered state.

Doug: Absolutely. I'm not asking Paul to be perfect, I just want to know he cares. So yeah, I am anxious, and I feel like he does not think to acknowledge that or even act like it's important to him. Rather, he says it's my problem and I'm the reason everything is not working at home! How is that being a partner?

ERIN: Doug, I wonder if sometimes it even feels like Paul cares
more about Ty than you? Like giving Ty his undivided attention
each day is more important than giving you any attention?

PAUL: He most certainly does. He says that, and I can't believe it.
He feels threatened by a little kid, our own kid. It just seems so
insecure and another way his anxiety gets in the way.

*Paul is having a tough time suspending his defensiveness and believing his
partner's experience (steps 2 and 3). This has to shift if the couple is going to
be able to practice intentional listening.*

DOUG: Well, thanks for being so understanding about my anxiety
and trying to make me look foolish, Paul. That feels so welcoming and understanding. It most certainly couldn't be that you
are so hyperfocused on parenting and anxious about being a
terrible parent like yours were that you hover over Ty like a helicopter every second. I might be anxious about keeping a house
clean, but your anxiety makes you an overbearing parent and a
disengaged partner.

STEPHEN: Hmmm . . . Paul, what do you hear in Doug's words?
This sounds like a part of the story we have not heard yet.

PAUL: I don't like hearing him say I'm a helicopter parent, but he
has said it before. I think I'm different from my parents, but I do
know I feel a lot of stress about being a parent. I didn't have the
best experience with my parents. They were disinterested in me
and my siblings and treated us like we were in the way a lot.
They both had involved jobs and were focused on their careers
more than us.

STEPHEN: So how do you see that contributing to your anxiety
about parenting?

PAUL: I don't want my kid to feel like I don't want him or that he
is a burden to me.

ERIN: I wonder, Paul, if sometimes when Doug is feeling anxious about the mess and disorder at home, you feel like he is saying Ty is a burden. I'm not saying he is actually trying to say this, but it might tap into that place for you that kids are a problem and get in the way, like in the way of having a clean house and so forth?

This question is meant to help Paul assess (step 1) his own triggers. If he can connect to how he is triggered when Doug is anxious, we can begin to move toward intentional expressing and listening.

PAUL: Yeah. I don't think I have made that connection directly, but it feels right.

STEPHEN: And so you see Doug's anxiety as selfish and "wrong," similar to your parents', and you dismiss it as his problem, not yours?

PAUL: Yes. That's exactly how it feels, and honestly, I don't think it's my problem to figure out.

STEPHEN: Okay. Doug, I imagine when you feel like Paul's anxiety is causing him to be hyperfocused on Ty and to dismiss you, it feels like his anxiety is winning and you are paying for it. In a lot of ways, this sounds very similar to how Paul says he feels your anxiety wins and he pays for it.

DOUG: Exactly, and he doesn't see it that way. He sees what he is doing as "right" and what I am doing as "wrong." When the truth of the matter is, we are both anxious about certain things and we make each other pay for it.

STEPHEN: Paul, did you know that Doug felt very similar to you regarding how anxiety is mucking up your communication and connection?

PAUL: No, I don't think I realized that he felt like my anxiety made him pay. I guess I still think being anxious about being a good parent is better than being anxious about the house being clean, but I get that it is a bit hypocritical to say it's all Doug's fault.

ERIN: So it seems like the deeper story is you both have some areas of life that you are anxious about and these anxieties influence how you communicate with each other.

DOUG: I can see that. That feels a bit more balanced, in contrast to it's just my issue.

PAUL: I can go with what you are saying.

ERIN: So, Doug, Paul had begun to reflect on his parents and how his experience with them may be contributing to his anxiety about being a good parent and his frustration with your anxiety.

This is encouraging intentional listening and is important because as someone shares (step 4 of intentional expressing), their partner has to suspend their defensiveness and believe their experience so that they can understand their partner's perspective. In the end, what this will help Doug and Paul do is work with each other's anxiety rather than feeling like one of them is right and the other is wrong.

DOUG: Yeah. I have met his parents. I get what he is talking about. In fact, they even treat Ty like he is an inconvenience to their schedule. Whenever we ask if they have time to watch him or want to come over to see him and play, they just seem put out. It makes me upset.

STEPHEN: So, Doug, can you see how Paul might have some extra energy around making sure Ty has all of his attention and that toys all over the place or crusty food on a high chair is not going to distract him from his mission?

DOUG: Yeah, I get that.

These questions are part of helping Doug suspend his defensiveness and believe Paul's experience and how it influences him and contributes to his anxiety and his feeling triggered when Paul becomes anxious.

ERIN: Paul, what do you think is part of the story for Doug and the things that make him feel anxious about the organization in the house and so forth?

PAUL: Well, I know Doug's mom was intense about keeping things straight in his house, and he has said that he sometimes felt like he couldn't touch anything. I don't think he is that way, but I do see how having things out of order could feel pretty threatening to his sensibilities if he was always told that was wrong.

ERIN: So, a room full of toys on the floor could feel threatening? Isn't that strange how something like toys on the floor can become such a big deal because it would have been a big deal with Doug's mom? This likely would have made Doug feel pressure to "do the right thing" or "fix" it so that she wouldn't be upset . . . What does that sound like to you, Doug?

DOUG: I don't know if I was totally aware of that, but my mom would get so upset if something was out of place and I would get really scared that I needed to fix it. So in a weird way when Paul leaves a mess, I feel like he doesn't want to be close to me because he's not trying to keep things clean.

Both Doug and Paul have started intentional expressing and intentional listening. As they engage in this process, the conversation starts to move away from who is coping correctly or incorrectly, and there is a sense of understanding about how the anxiety emerges.

ERIN: Yeah, so crusty high chairs can feel like a big deal.

DOUG: Whoa! Paul, I don't think I ever noticed that, but I do feel like that sometimes. I get that it's not true, but I still feel it.

PAUL: Yeah. That makes sense. Especially why it feels like such a big deal.

Doug: And I can see how me being more focused on a clean house and not Ty can feel bad to you and like I don't care about you and Ty.

Doug and Paul are moving into step 4 of intentional listening: repair. They are moving toward being accountable, forgiving each other, and taking new action toward change.

Stephen: So rather than telling the other "You are too much" or "You are anxious and just need to get it together," you say, "I can see how what is happening right now might not feel good to you and makes you anxious."

Anxiety is always located in a story or stories that we feel are getting played out again in our life and we don't want them to be played out again. So, we get defensive, closed, and push against our partner by saying, "Stop being anxious" or "Stop making me feel anxious." I don't know if you are aware of this, but telling someone to not be anxious is a great way to make them more anxious.

Instead, through intentional listening you can say, "What's going on here? Help me understand, I can see that you are having a hard time." But that is not all. We can respect the anxiety, but that does not mean that it's okay to dump the anxiety on our partner.

Doug: Which is where Paul and I keep getting stuck. So what next?

Erin: You both will have to give a little when it comes to your anxiety. This means you will have to help each other regulate and you will have to bear a little bit of discomfort. For example, Paul you mentioned something earlier in our session that could be an example of this. You said that when Doug gets home you wish he would check in with you and Ty, engage, and then you both can tackle straightening up the house.

For you, Paul, it helps soothe your anxiety for Doug to come home and jump in with you and Ty. Doug, for you your anxiety is soothed if the house is straightened up. So the goal is not to tell the other not to be anxious in these situations. You are going to be anxious. Respect it. You have stories that say it's a good idea to be anxious in these situations.

Now working with each other to address the anxiety is figuring out a system that works for you. Doug, can you wait until after bedtime to clean the house? Paul, maybe Doug would like to take twenty minutes to just straighten up before he jumps in. Could you work with him and let this happen?

In whatever scenario, you are trying to help your partner regulate and need to accept that you will have to bear a little discomfort to meet your partner where they are at.

PAUL: Okay, I see it. So we don't need to fight the anxiety and tell the other to stop it. We just need to figure out how we can help each other, and it will take a little give-and-take.

DOUG: Easier said than done, it seems. I mean I get it, but I don't know if we can do it.

STEPHEN: So we know the story behind what generates your anxiety when it comes to this transition in the day. And let's say that even though you might not understand the other's anxiety, you are willing to respect it. Meaning, Paul wants you to engage with him and Ty when you get home, Doug, and, Doug, you want the environment to feel a bit calmer so that you can engage. How do you want to do it? This transition can feel better for you both, but it might not be perfect.

PAUL: Well, I guess I could try and pick up the house a little bit before you come home, Doug.

STEPHEN: I like how you are wanting to meet Doug where he is at, Paul, but I think this might still be working with the old system, where you feel the pressure to do what Doug wants and Doug feels the pressure to jump right in when he gets home.

I wonder how you could allow each other to deal with your anxiety and then come together. This is what I'm thinking. Maybe, Doug, you let Paul know when you are heading home and this sets in motion the transition routine. Paul, you take Ty upstairs or on a walk right before Doug gets home. Maybe, Doug, you can come home, set a timer for ten minutes, and pick up the house a little. Then, Paul, you and Ty can come home and, Doug, you can greet Ty and Paul fully engaged and ready to be present.

DOUG: I don't know. That sounds nice because I can soothe my anxiety by getting the house back to order and then I won't be distracted. Paul, I know when I come home you like for me to greet you and Ty and check in and be present. Would it be hard to let me have that ten minutes?

PAUL: I mean, if I know it's coming, I think that makes sense. If Ty and I just act like you are not home for that ten minutes, then it would feel like we are greeting each other as if you just came home and I wouldn't be waiting for you to do a flyby, saying hello and then getting busy cleaning. It could work.

ERIN: And that's the thing. It could work, it could not. But the idea is that you try and find something that does work for you. The goal is for you to figure out what works, which honestly is very different from how you have been having this conversation up until this point. Figure out what works for you both, but keep in mind that you are trying to work with each other and your anxiety, rather than dismissing each other and telling the other that they are the problem.

DOUG: I like that, working with each other. I want to figure this out with you, Paul. I know I can be anxious and that can put a burden on you. I don't want to do that. I would love to figure out a way for us both to feel good about these kinds of conflicts.

PAUL: I want the same thing, Doug. You know, I think I just assumed you were the one who was anxious, but I can see how there are some things I am anxious about, too, and need some help with. Let's give this idea a try and see how it goes. We can tweak it if we need, but let's give it a shot.

BUT HOW CAN I ACTUALLY SAY ANY OF THIS TO MY PARTNER? SAMPLE SCRIPTS

It is easy for couples to feel at odds with each other when trying to cope with their individual stress. The conflict can center around whose way of coping is "right" or "wrong." Through the conflict-to-connection equation, couples move from this dead-end dialogue toward feeling like they are working together against the stress rather than each other. Here are some scripts that can help you and your partner have an attachment-making interaction as you cope with stress.

Intentional Expressing That Invites Intentional Listening—The "Stressed" Partner

"I get the sense that how I am trying to handle my stress is actually adding to yours and vice versa. Can we talk about this and try to figure out a way to support each other even though we are coming at this differently?"

"It feels obvious to me that we handle our stress differently. I am sure I don't understand how you handle your stress, and I don't think you really understand how I handle mine. I feel like we should talk about it and try and see if we can feel more connected with each other about all this."

Intentional Expressing That Invites Intentional Listening—The "Non-Stressed" Partner

"I am noticing that I am feeling frustrated with you for being stressed. I'm not saying this is okay. I don't want to feel this way. I think we are handling our stress differently, and I want to try and understand what is happening for you and what is helpful to you when you feel stressed. Can we talk about it?"

"I can tell that I am not being helpful to you in your stress. In fact, I think how I approach stress annoys you. I don't want that to be the case. Can you help me understand what is happening for you and what helps you not feel stressed?"

QUESTIONS FOR REFLECTION

1. Before kids, what was your go-to activity to reduce your stress?

2. Do you ever get the feeling that your partner feels entitled to reduce their stress without also making sure you have the same opportunities to reduce yours? Do you ever feel like your partner is upset with you for taking time for yourself? Could that be because they do not feel they get that time for themself?

3. Do you feel like you and your partner have a good handle on knowing what the most common stressors are for each of you? Do you feel like you validate each other in those stressful moments?

4. In this conflict about how our stress can cost our partner, are there hurt places you need your partner to know about and really move toward you in? What about for your partner? What are the unresolved places in this conflict for you?

5. What, if anything, about this chapter resonated with you? Did it stir any feelings or memories? Even if they predate your current relationship, what emotions are stirred in you? Why might those feelings and memories be coming up now in the season of life and parenting you are currently in?

CHAPTER 9

The "I'm More Tired Than You" Conflict

A DAM AND GWEN found out that Gwen was pregnant with Ana just a few weeks after their honeymoon. They both wanted kids, but a pregnancy in their first year of marriage was not how they had imagined it. After their initial shock, they started getting excited and making plans for their quickly growing family.

Gwen had expected to be tired in pregnancy, but she had no idea she could be as tired as she was. Gwen was not herself, especially in the first trimester. She napped frequently, even during her lunch break at work, and would come home and fall asleep early. As the pregnancy progressed, she found she didn't need a nap every day, but she was sore and achy all the time. She felt like her feet, calves, back, and shoulders couldn't be rubbed hard or long enough. She woke several times at night to pee. But thankfully that was coupled with the fact that baby Ana was very active, and Gwen loved getting to feel the baby move. Gwen felt very attuned to her body and to Ana, and the discomfort and exhaustion was worth it because she was going to get to meet this little one soon! She was excited and anxious, and it felt like she could be all of the emotions in the span of five minutes just thinking about getting to see and hear Ana.

Adam had also been preparing as he awaited the arrival of Ana. He had a list of things he wanted to make sure he had finished before Ana arrived—like making sure the house was babyproofed and dealing with insurance issues concerning the birth of the baby. Then he worried whether Gwen would have a safe labor and delivery. He was full of questions: "Are we really ready for a baby?" "How are we going to be able to afford child care?" "Will I be a good parent?" "Will Gwen and I lose touch with each other, like so many couples we know do?"

Luckily Baby Ana's arrival went pretty much according to the birth plan, and before they knew it, they were leaving the birthing center and putting the car seat into the car. They exchanged a look that meant: "I can't believe we are leaving here with her. We are really doing this!" In that moment they knew there was no one else they would rather be doing this thing called parenting with. Gwen wanted to breastfeed, and again she was surprised by how many demands this placed on her. She loved Ana and nursing, but she felt that no one had told her the whole story about how exhausted and overwhelmed she would feel.

Adam could see how demanding having a newborn was, especially on Gwen, and wanted to be as great a support as possible. He kept finger foods on hand so Gwen could have food ready to eat even if her hands were full or if she couldn't prepare something herself. He would wake up with Gwen while she was nursing because sometimes she said it helped her not to feel so lonely having him there. He would change Ana's diaper after she had finished nursing and put her back to sleep, or would bottle-feed Ana when Gwen wanted and needed to get some sleep. At the same time, Adam was working full time as a medical sales rep. He adjusted his travel schedule, tried not to be gone on trips overnight, and still was straining to make his monthly quotas. He also had no idea how exhausted he would feel. They still frequently exchanged that look between them of, *"I can't believe how hard this is AND I am so glad to be doing this with you."*

Adam and Gwen got into a routine of sporadic, inconsistent sleep and attempts to work hard during the day so they could be available for Ana and each other. Gwen had to figure out how to bond with Ana, breastfeed her, and navigate the emotional roller coaster of postpartum healing and weighing the next steps for after her parental leave. Emotionally and physically, she felt like during the day she was making it, albeit some days just barely, but as the sun set each night, she often hit a wall, convinced that she might not ever feel rested or like herself again. Adam felt pulled in every direction. He was trying to keep advancing at work so that he could support his growing family. He missed Ana and Gwen when he was gone, but felt overwhelmed at home trying to be engaged, and he was trying to understand his own relationship with Ana. He was just barely holding on.

One week a big client asked Adam to come to some meetings that could result in a significant commission for him. He would need to be out of town for two days and nights. Both he and Gwen felt like he needed to go, and they discussed what Gwen might need for support while he was gone. They didn't have help nearby, so they asked Gwen's mom to come out for the two days and felt like they had a good plan in place.

Adam flew out early in the morning the day Gwen's mom was scheduled to come in. Unfortunately, Gwen's mom got sick with the flu, and it seemed best for her not to come and risk getting Gwen and/or Ana sick. Gwen understood and let Adam know that she was going to be okay and to stay focused on the work he had to do. Gwen handled the weekend great, but she was exhausted from the constant attention to Ana and ready for Adam to come home. Adam's trip also went great; he worked long hours while he was gone, needing to perform at his highest level for two days straight. He was also anxious to get back home. When he arrived home, he was depleted physically and mentally, as was Gwen. Right as he walked in the door, he greeted Ana and Gwen and then said:

ADAM: Hey, I am wiped out. Is there any way I can take thirty minutes and get a quick nap? I feel so tired.

GWEN: Oh, *you* feel wiped out? Was that quiet hotel room loud at night? I bet it was difficult to have to sit through a hot meal someone prepared and cleaned up for you. Was that round of golf you played yesterday really taxing? You have a lot of nerve. I have been here with no help, getting no sleep, doing everything! You don't know what tired is!

ADAM: Gwen, it wasn't an easy trip. I was stressed out the whole time trying to make sure it was the perfect weekend for the client and not to mess up this massive deal. A deal that is going to make us a lot of money, by the way, because of how hard I worked all weekend!

They both were surprised by how intense their reactions were and how quickly it got heated. This moment might have been the flash point, but they both realized that something about this conflict struck a nerve. Gwen was remembering the nights she sat awake nursing a child while Adam slept beside her or the days when Adam would head off to work and have time for himself there but she was constantly on call for Ana. Adam was also aware of that feeling he has had where Gwen looks at him like he's not allowed to be tired or sick or in a bad mood or even momentarily break eye contact with Ana for one second. He started to feel angry and found himself thinking, *I know she's working hard and that she does have a lot going on during the day, but my days aren't carefree. I am always thinking about work and about needing to get back home so Gwen doesn't feel like she is doing everything. I can't win.*

Neither of them has been consciously maintaining this list of emotions; in fact they weren't even aware they had these feelings. For the most part, they know they are working hard and feel like the other is pretty good at acknowledging how much they are doing for the good of the whole family. Granted, the weekend was mutually exhausting, but Gwen can't shake the feeling that Adam is selfish, putting himself first. Adam is sure he was not trying to behave in an entitled fashion but rather was simply attempting to get a little fuel so he could give Gwen as long a break as she needed. He feels like he has reworked his life to put Ana and Gwen first.

Neither of them wants to feel so worked up about this or keep a record of their partner's "wrongs," but they are also immersed in big emotions that lead to resentment on both their parts. They keep trying to talk about this, but the conversation keeps going off the rails. Gwen points out how when she wakes at night and sees Adam sleeping, it can make her angry, and then Adam brings up all the times he woke up with Ana or when he changed her diaper and Gwen went back to sleep. Adam says he would love to be able to stay at home and connect with Ana all day and Gwen responds: "Yeah, because we just take strolls to the park and laugh and coo all day."

Gwen and Adam are stuck trying to figure out what is going on by pointing out tension-filled moments that hurt them. Then each of them takes the moment (and completely misses the feeling) and deconstructs it and provides counter evidence as to why the other person shouldn't feel how they're feeling. If they weren't tired already, this conflict would be enough to completely exhaust them.

WHY YOU NEED THIS CONFLICT

Parent tired is different. You are tired deep in your bones. It is a "I have worked with every fiber of my being and loved with my entire soul for every last second of this day" kind of tired. *Tired* is often the word used, but it can mean so many different things. Very often until this conflict is engaged, neither person really knows what kind of tired they are talking about or even how to differentiate between the options. One thing is certain, though: physical exhaustion exacerbates emotional experiences every single time.

Let's go back to the interaction between Adam and Gwen when he got home from his work trip. Adam led the conversation with the fact he was tired, likely physically and emotionally. Gwen was definitely physically tired in that moment, but just as equally emotionally drained, because she was feeling some version of threatened from Adam's comment. She just spent the whole weekend alone holding out for the moment her husband would arrive home and take over, and instead of taking over, Adam asks for help from her. This ask directly threatened and thwarted Gwen's need for sleep, and because they hadn't had this conflict yet, her reaction was swift and scathing.

Gwen is reacting before she has even registered that she is having a big reaction. For Adam to put his need for a break above her need for one sparks her anger, and then that anger comes out as her invalidating that Adam could even be tired. Note that we are not saying Gwen should not be angry. Our emotions are important and tell us where the conversation needs to go to get resolved, but when Gwen counters with minimizing Adam's experience because she feels like that is what he has done to her, we have lost her experience. In other words, the reaction in this moment is causing Adam to look away from her sadness, hurt, and anger, by pointing the finger at him and saying he should feel nothing but rested and happy. Her experience and her emotions surrounding it matter a lot, which is why how we communicate about them matters.

Shifting to Adam's perspective, he comes in without having read the room and is therefore insensitive to the meaning underlying his "simple" request. His question has a loaded and hurtful impact, though this wasn't his intention, so he is blindsided by Gwen's outburst. The emotions stirred up by the situation signal something big is happening and something important is being felt. The couple needs help thinking through impact along with intention—an important lesson that will help them have this conflict the right way in the future.

This conflict about who is more tired is a must-have. Gwen doesn't really think Adam isn't tired, and Adam in no way is trying to say he is more tired than Gwen. Of course Gwen knows that Adam has just been through an exhausting weekend, but when he expressed the fact in that moment and in that context, it felt like the single most selfish thing he could possibly have said. It hurt, and it made Gwen worry he would never see the disparity in their parenting relationship. Although this example concerns a weekend work trip, it could just as easily have been about a normal Tuesday night in which Adam slept terribly, but every single time Gwen was up with Ana, Adam seemed to be sleeping just fine. This conflict is about weekends away and regular old Tuesdays. It can come up when your partner says they are starting to feel sick or may need some time with friends. It can come out different ways, but the underlying conflict is essentially the same.

We need this conflict because we and our partners need to feel free and safe to express how we are feeling, and more than anyone else, we need our partner to be there with us in it. Everyone needs to be able to be tired from time to time, but we have to take our partner's context and story into account in how (and when) we express that.

HOW THIS CONFLICT GOES WRONG

This conflict is weighty for so many couples. The words *I'm tired* coming from your partner's mouth can feel like a full-on assault to your nervous system. *I'm tired* is just an expression, but it feels self-centered and can easily lead many of us to point out how ridiculous our partner is to say this when their difficulties can't hold a candle to ours. These competitive thoughts can come out as: "You mean to tell me that after you snored peacefully beside me while I got our kid water, took a different kid to pee, and nursed a baby three times last night, *you* woke up sleepy? Oh, you poor thing." Or "You're sick? You mean, you finally have the same cold I have been pushing through for three straight weeks? You have a little tickle in your throat, so you need a day in bed. Sure, sounds fair to me."

These thoughts always look awful written out like that. No one wants to say those things, and the truth is, we probably don't really even believe them. In the heat of the moment, feeling invisible in all that we have pushed through, we point out what an incompetent and selfish partner we seemed to have bogged ourselves down with.

We hear this pain point in relationships all the time. The "You've got a lot of nerve" narrative is one that starts when your child is born and then grows with time. Again and again we have heard some version of how the day after the baby arrives, the non-birthing partner wakes up and makes some comment about how uncomfortable it was sleeping on the couch or how they were cold because they didn't have a blanket or how they woke up a lot because of all the sounds in the hospital. Of course the non-birthing partner says these things because they are true. Sleeping on a cold couch in an unfamiliar place that does have a lot of lights and sounds is truly an uncomfortable way to spend a night. However, the non-birthing partner is saying these things to or at least in earshot of their partner, who just spent a lot of hours in labor pushing a human through their body, or having undergone a major surgery to get that baby out and experiencing hormonal and physical changes many partners could never even fathom.

The issue is not that the non-birthing partner had a great night's sleep. It's just that in the context of having stitches in places no one wants stitches, wearing a diaper, feeling sore everywhere, and having breasts that essentially triple in size overnight (or the anxiety about why this hasn't happened), that one comment can feel more than a little out of touch. Feeling suddenly like their partner is the single most self-absorbed person on the planet, the birthing partner begins to filter everything through that lens. A phone pickup? Chronically disengaged. A late night at work? Absorbed only in their own world.

When the birthing partner begins to communicate shock at how their partner is so oblivious to their experience, it comes out as invalidation and criticism. Again, their anger at their partner's lack of attunement to their experience is legitimate, but it gets lost in the often biting way they communicate their frustration and hurt. Non-birthing partners end up feeling attacked, and rather than lending a listening ear to their partner's frustrations, they defend themselves, which only perpetuates the cycle. This conflict must be had to provide each partner with a new take on what is actually going on. A new view that takes both partners out of the place of feeling misunderstood and invalidated and into the place of being curious and empathetic, and taking action to demonstrate they get what their partner is saying.

CONFLICT TO CONNECTION: ADAM AND GWEN'S SESSION

When Adam and Gwen show up to sessions with us, they are tired. Their emotions are right on the surface, even though each partner has a different take on the experience. Adam says they are tired of the dynamic, so much so that they will speak about it in front of some strangers (us). Gwen maintains she is tired of the dynamic, too, but she despairs that we can be of any help. "What's wrong with us? We used to really like each other, but now we have somehow turned into a couple that minimizes the other's experiences."

Neither one really wants to go first. They don't want to talk about it because they don't want to resume the old conflict and they are tired of going back and forth about it. Adam eventually speaks up, using the out-of-town example to demonstrate what the argument looks like.

ADAM: I understand that my asking Gwen for a break when I got home was probably not the best idea. She had a tough weekend. I think it frustrates me that she feels like she is more tired than I am. Implicit in that is the thought that she is working harder than me.

GWEN: This is so frustrating. I *am* actually more tired than you are. Have you ever tried to breastfeed? Do you know how much energy it takes to do that all day long? I'm not saying you are not tired or working hard, but there is just no comparison. What I am doing is harder, and it drives me crazy to hear you wanting some kind of concession from me to help you get some rest.

ADAM: That's ridiculous! How do you know how tired I am? I have turned my life upside down to try and support you and be with you as you breastfeed and figure out how to be a mom. I wake up early. I work long hours late at night. I wake up with you when you feed Ana and offer to bottle-feed her during the night. I say no to travel when my boss tries to pressure me into it, and I am constantly trying to make sure I am doing my part because I get that you are tired. All I am saying is that I am tired, too, and I don't think you even notice or acknowledge what I am doing. In fact, you don't! You just said what you are doing does not even compare to what I am doing.

GWEN: Ugh . . . You want some kind of gold medal for the "work" you are doing, and you need some kind of recognition for being a parent? I *am* doing everything! I feed Ana, I change Ana, I am awake with Ana, I worry about Ana's development, I research what she needs, and you assist. I am exhausted physically, emotionally, and psychologically. You are just tired because you don't get enough sleep. It is different.

Both Adam and Gwen are triggered. They need to slow down and assess (step 1 of intentional expressing and listening). We interrupt to try and stop the stress response they are both having.

STEPHEN: Whoa, do you hear it, too, Erin?

ERIN: I hear it.

ADAM: What are you talking about?

STEPHEN: Well, you and Gwen are caught up in an exhausting couple's game show we like to call *Whose Life Is Harder?*

ERIN: Yep, it's a game where everybody loses and nobody wins.

STEPHEN: It is probably the most commonly played game in couple relationships, and it is one of the biggest conflict generators. Over time, the losses each partner feels, because everybody loses in this game, really stack up to some heavy resentment.

GWEN: Well, it sure does happen a lot in our relationship. I feel like we are typically pretty good as a couple until one of us says they are tired and then everything breaks down.

ERIN: Gwen, what are you wanting Adam to understand about your experience that you feel is being missed?

Erin is moving the conversation into intentional expressing by asking Gwen to attune to her experience and describe the emotions she is feeling (steps 2 and 3).

GWEN: I think Adam believes I have some level of "free time" in the day where I am just sitting around holding Ana and taking it easy on the couch while he goes off and works. I am working hard every day, and I don't know how to explain the exhaustion

I experience. This is one of the hardest things I have ever done. And I have done really hard things before! This requires every ounce of my strength. I don't think Adam gets what is happening for me right now and what tired actually means when I say I am tired.

ERIN: So there is something about your current experience as a parent that is being missed by Adam?

GWEN: Yes.

ERIN: Adam, what are you wanting Gwen to understand that you feel is being missed?

Now it is Adam's turn to attune to the emotions he is experiencing.

ADAM: I don't know. I just don't want to feel like I am less than her or unappreciated. She is not the only one having a hard time and feeling like her life and world are turned upside down. I am trying to make my life fit with Gwen and Ana. I'm invested. I'm here. I'm trying. I'm tired and overwhelmed, and I don't want to feel like Gwen wants me to pay for how she feels. I just want to feel like we can respect each other's efforts.

STEPHEN: This is a tough conversation, and it makes a lot of sense that it feels so charged with energy. Here's an idea of how you both can hear and be heard by each other. A lot of times this is considered validation, but there is a key component to validation that is more than just hearing what your partner is saying. It is having the feeling they get it, like they may not relate, but they really do get what you are expressing. For validation to happen, both of you have to feel felt. This is a fancy way that neuroscientists [specifically Dan Siegel] talk about what validation feels like.

But validation is not just feeling felt. Validation also needs to lead to action. So, here's how we help couples work through the

Whose Life Is Harder? game. First, you need to feel the validation. Second, you need to demonstrate the validation.

So this is how it goes: We have five questions you need to ask
each other to feel the validation and five questions you need to
ask to demonstrate validation.

Here are the five questions to help you feel the validation:

1. What are three words you would use to describe how tired
   you feel?
2. Are there any physical components to your feeling tired that
   you want your partner to know about?
3. What has changed about your life since having your child
   that feels hard/sad/like a loss?
4. When you feel like you are trying to describe your experience
   to your partner and they don't get it, how does that leave you
   feeling? What two words would you use to describe what you
   feel?
5. Name a time when your partner *did* get it, or at least you felt
   like they were trying. You may want to react and say, "It's
   never happened." But really think about it. Even if it was not
   a perfect moment, when has this conversation had a different
   feeling or tone that has been toward the positive?

Here are the five questions to help you demonstrate validation:

1. Is there anything practically that needs to change for your
   experience to feel different?
2. When you say you are tired, is there a way that I can respond
   that will feel better than what I have been doing?
3. How can I tell you I am feeling tired in a way that does not

feel like I am competing with you? Is there a way we can both talk about what is happening without starting the *Whose Life Is Harder?* game?

4. If we start getting caught up in this old dialogue, what cue can we use to stop, regroup, and connect rather than disconnect?

5. What is one thing we can do right now to help each other feel a brief moment of pause or relief from feeling tired?

This is a very structured way to guide the couple through the conflict-to-connection equation. We do this because this conflict is one of the most sensitive ones for couples and in our view needs a more directive approach. The first part, which is focused on feeling validation, walks the couple through intentional expressing and listening. The second part, focused on demonstrating validation, is an in-depth look at how to repair (step 4 of intentional listening).

ERIN: Let's try and walk through these conversations. Who wants to go first?

ADAM: Gwen, how about you go first? I really do want to get what you are saying.

GWEN: Okay . . .

1. What are three words you would use to describe how tired you feel?

Drowning, trapped, and *withering away.* I know that's four words, but I think those are pretty accurate.

ERIN: Those are powerful words. It seemed like those were difficult to say. Was it difficult to say this is how you are feeling?

GWEN: Yes, I don't want to sound like I don't like being a mom. I love it. It is so hard sometimes. I think I do feel embarrassed because I don't know if other moms feel this way. I don't know how to do everything sometimes.

2. Are there any physical components to your feeling tired that you want your partner to know about?

Oh, I don't even know how to describe my body right now. I love it. I hate it. I feel proud of it and I feel betrayed by it. I worry that my body has changed so much, it will never be the same. My nipples hurt all the time. I get clogged ducts periodically that feel awful. I feel like I am always being touched by Ana. There is pressure that she needs my body to survive, which makes me feel like I don't have control over my body. I used to feel in shape and strong, but now I often feel exhausted and tired. I am also proud of giving birth and what my body can do and how it has changed so we have Ana. My body just feels confusing and like one more thing to figure out.

ERIN: Your body feels confusing. That sounds really hard. I imagine much of this happens outside of your awareness most of the time. We get so used to our bodies that we forget to pay attention to them. It's like if I twisted my ankle, I would know I did it, but if I didn't treat it or pay attention to it, I would start to adjust to the injury and live with the discomfort. So much is going on after having kids that unfortunately, unless we know not to, we forget about all we have been through and keep pushing through. The changes to our body are monumental, but we also have to focus elsewhere and keep going. Maybe the way you feel about your body gets rolled into how tired you are and it's so much more than feeling just sleepy tired.

GWEN: So much more. It's almost like having a body I don't recognize anymore. I don't know how to describe it.

3. What has changed about your life since having your child that feels hard/sad/like a profound loss?

Well, definitely what I just said about my body, but also I feel like I lost myself. I used to have a job that felt important to me, but that matters a lot less to me now. I also don't know if I am thinking about this all in the right ways. I don't have the bandwidth or the brain space to think about my career. Also, I miss time with Adam. We had more time and space together to connect and have fun. Now we are sitting here with you struggling and feeling disconnected.

4. When you feel like you are trying to describe your experience to your partner and they don't get it, how does that leave you feeling? What two words would you use to describe what you feel?

Alone, and it's *maddening.* I can't get him to see that this is more than a transition or a big change. There are no words to describe what my body, mind, and spirit have gone through. I feel like he treats what I am saying like it's some new "challenge" in life, an opportunity to hunker down, game-plan about, and tackle with confidence. I am not some business challenge, though.

ERIN: So there is something otherworldly that is happening. Something that neither you nor Adam have experienced before, and you want him to get this.

GWEN: Yes. Saying all this right here is helping me realize it for myself. I don't think I have known how massive a change this has been for me.

5. Name a time when your partner did get it, or at least you felt like they were trying. You may want to react and say, "It's never happened." But really think about it. Even if it was not a perfect moment, when has this conversation had a different feeling or tone that has been toward the positive?

Well, I think I feel like Adam gets it when he wakes up with me at night to nurse. It's a small thing. He reaches over and rubs my back, but I feel like he is with me. Like he sees it is so hard. I remember we talked about how waking up at night felt lonely, and after that talk, he started waking up with me. It has really meant a lot to me.

ERIN: So Adam can understand and has understood, and there are moments that he doesn't.

GWEN: Yes.

ERIN: Adam, what about you?

1. What are three words you would use to describe how tired you feel?

ADAM: *Exhausted, crowded,* and *not enough.* I used four words, too, Gwen.

ERIN: What do these words capture for you in your experience, Adam?

ADAM: I guess the feeling of persistence or the constant nature of parenting. There is no downtime. I spend every minute of every day either working or parenting, and if there is any other time, it is used to get ready for work or parenting or trying to do something that will make work or parenting feel easier. It never stops.

2. Are there any physical components to your feeling tired that you want your partner to know about?

Maybe. I mean, hearing Gwen talk, I was blown away. My body definitely is not as impacted by kids. I'm tired and can hardly feel my face most days. I wish I had time to work out like I used to, but my physical body does not seem to suffer, at least not in any way that feels like how Gwen described.

ERIN: Not being able to feel your face is a great descriptor. And even in what you just said, you can see that there are some differences in how your bodies have been impacted. It's not to say that there is no impact to you or that the impact on you is not important, but you seemed to hear some difference between your experience and Gwen's.

ADAM: Yes, I had no idea that Gwen was feeling some of these things and that her body felt so different. I mean, of course I knew some of it. I can see how it would be such a big change with everything she has gone through, but no, I haven't thought about it like she described.

3. What has changed about your life since having your child that feels hard/sad/like a profound loss?

I would echo what Gwen said. It's hard not to have as much time to be together and connect. I miss the freedom we had before Ana. Granted, I love Ana and wouldn't trade her for our free time, but it really has been a shock and hard to navigate.

4. When you feel like you are trying to describe your experience to your partner and they don't get it, how does that leave you feeling? What two words would you use to describe what you feel?

Hmm. I think it makes me feel like I am *failing* and I'm *misunderstood*. I think I can feel like Gwen is telling me what I am doing and how I am contributing is not that important. It's like I'm secondary to what she is doing, and because of that, my feelings are not important. I wake up every day wanting to be a part of this family and wanting to love Gwen and Ana with all that I have. So when I'm told I'm not tired or I'm not having a hard time, I feel like I'm being told I'm not a part of what is happening in our family.

ERIN: That seems like it would be crushing to feel like you are being told you're not that important.

ADAM: Yeah. Crushing is a good way to put it. It makes me feel defeated, like I am wasting my time trying.

5. Name a time when your partner did get it, or at least you felt like they were trying. You may want to react and say, "It's never happened." But really think about it. Even if it was not a perfect moment, when has this conversation had a different feeling or tone that has been toward the positive?

You know, there are times that Gwen has said to me she knows I am working hard and trying to be present and balance work and being home. I was glad to hear her say she appreciates my waking up with her at night. I think moments when she sees I am trying feel good to me.

STEPHEN: Gwen, have you heard Adam share some of these things before?

GWEN: Maybe. Probably yes. He has said this, but typically we are in the heat of an argument or something and it doesn't really register with me. I realize that sounds insensitive, because I do care.

STEPHEN: So slowing down like this and hearing from each other feels helpful?

GWEN: Yeah. I think it was even nice for me to hear myself say what was happening for me, and of course I was glad to hear from Adam. I feel like I can get where he is coming from a little better.

ADAM: I feel the same way. I think that word *otherworldly* really connected with me. Gwen is experiencing something that is completely new, and it's really different from how I feel about it. I am experiencing something new, too, but there is something uniquely different about our experiences that I have not been paying attention to.

STEPHEN: I really like that, Adam. You both can be tired, of course you are. You both can be experiencing something, and it can be different. There does not have to be effort made to compete about whose experience is worse. There just has to be an effort made to connect to how the experience feels different and what that means for you as a couple.

GWEN: I for sure have been making it a competition. I imagine that hasn't been the easiest thing to deal with, Adam.

ADAM: I do the same thing, Gwen.

ERIN: So now is the opportunity for you both to move from "feeling validation" to "demonstrating validation." Let's have you two go home and go through the next five questions just as we did the first five today. Then when we see you next week, we can talk about how the conversation went.

Adam and Gwen want so much for the other one to understand their experience, but in talking about it, they realized that even they themselves did not know what exactly they were feeling and what they were wanting their partner to get.

This is a conflict you and your partner need to have. Do sessions always happen just like this? Nope, not all the time, but sometimes they do. And do couples find they are able to describe themselves and what they are hoping their partner will see in and for them? Yes, they really do by using the conflict-to-connection equation.

So many parents want their partner to understand what *tired* means to them, but until they pause and have some help getting there, they won't be able to understand what that means for themselves. Having this conflict will enable your partner to understand your experience better, and it will also help you understand yourself and what you are going through as well.

A lot of us need compassion from our partners. A lot of us need compassion from ourselves, too. We have been through a lot. We continue to go through a lot, and being gentle with ourselves and each other along the way really can ease some of the exhaustion we feel.

BUT HOW CAN I ACTUALLY SAY ANY OF THIS TO MY PARTNER? SAMPLE SCRIPTS

Tired is a good but imperfect word. You're tired from day-to-day changes, and your and your partner's tired will never be exactly the same. They can't be. And that really is okay as long as both of you understand you may be using the same language but meaning different things. Get into the habit of asking yourself and your partner (as long as that won't further poke the bear of tired in that moment) to go a few layers into the tired.

We cannot know the exact wording that will best suit you and your partner to help move this conflict into the more helpful and productive layers, but here are some sample suggestions to get the conversation started. And it is perfectly normal not only for you to adjust them to make sense for your and your partner's context, but also to practice saying the same ideas but in different ways to see what feels most natural and what seems to deepen the conversation for both you and your partner.

Intentional Expressing

"Sometimes when you say 'I am tired,' I hear you saying you are going to leave me to do everything. I've been thinking a lot lately about how my mom would make dinner for us and then clean up dinner, and all the while my dad would be sitting on the couch because he worked all day and was so tired. My mom worked all day, too, yes, at home with us, and it's been making me angry that they kept going like this. I don't want us to be like that."

"Lately I have been thinking about my body and what the past two years [five years, ten years, or more] have been like for me, even just physically what I have gone through. There have been so many changes. I don't think I fully know what I need to be known about it all, but I think I need to talk about it. It is important for me to feel like you understand that for me as well."

Intentional Listening

"I am tired. I imagine you are tired, too. I wish I knew the full extent of what *tired* is meaning to me right now, and I wish I understood what *tired* is meaning to you. Want to try to talk about it with me?"

"This has all been a lot. Let's walk through these questions and see if we can find some understanding for ourselves and each other."

QUESTIONS FOR REFLECTION

1. What has your past year been like physically?

2. Right now, when you say *tired,* even just to yourself, what emotion feels connected to that? Do you know what that emotion word is about? And do you know something that would help you to feel like you were getting seen in that emotion? (Example: I am tired and it feels a lot like sadness. I am worn down and am feeling used up, and I feel like what would be restorative to me is a morning to sleep in or a lunch out with a friend or a long hug after a good talk with my partner.)

3. What is the most energized you have felt recently? Describe it in as much detail as you possibly can. Can you find ways to do more things like that?

4. Where do you feel most stuck in this conflict? What feels like the most important thing to you in this conflict? How did it come to be that important to you? What feels like it is at stake?

5. Do you feel like you have been avoiding this conflict? Is there anything about this chapter that seemed to resonate with you? Did it stir any feelings or memories? Why might those feelings and memories be coming up now in the season of life and parenting you are currently in?

CHAPTER 10

The "Stop Choosing Your Family over Ours" Conflict

TASHA AND SAM have been together for fifteen years, married for nearly ten, and have three kids. Alani is seven, Letti is four, and Mia is two. They live in Sam's hometown, where most of her family still resides, and Sam works for her aunt's company as the COO. Tasha works as a freelance graphic designer. She does not have a large extended family like Sam, and her parents and one sibling live two hours away. Since Sam's family lives in the area, much of their time is spent with them and with members of the community who have known Sam her whole life.

Tasha loves the energy of a big family, even though it can be overwhelming at times, and having all the uncles, aunts, grandparents, and cousins around feels comforting. Tasha feels in many ways like she won the lottery with how welcoming Sam's family has been to her. She loves that their kids have cousins to play with and have the rootedness of a large community. Tasha and Sam's relationship also benefits from having family so close by. They are able to ask for help with the kids, have regular date nights and even weekends away where they can connect, have time together, and feel completely comfortable about who is watching their kids.

At the same time, Tasha experiences some pressures having Sam's family so close. Her in-laws are wonderful grandparents, but there are times when she feels Sam is more likely to take into consideration how things will impact the larger extended family than their immediate family. Holidays and birthdays are especially fraught with tension for Tasha.

For example, whenever a family member has a birthday, Sam's parents host a special dinner for this person that includes the whole family. It's a long-standing tradition, one that Tasha and Sam have always enjoyed. But this year Tasha's family decided to plan a weekend getaway to celebrate Letti's turning five. Tasha realized that celebrating their middle child's birthday with her parents and sibling meant missing celebrating with Sam's family, but since almost all of their kids' birthdays are spent with Sam's family, she thought it should be a no-brainer that they do this trip with her family instead.

After Tasha's family confirmed and booked the trip, Tasha told the kids and Sam together at dinner. The kids were excited about the trip and started talking about the activities they wanted to do. Sam was surprised, to say the least, and asked for a quick minute to talk with Tasha in the other room.

SAM: I'm confused . . . My family already scheduled a dinner to celebrate Letti's birthday that weekend. Why does the weekend your family wants to celebrate have to be when my family had already planned to celebrate?

TASHA: We always celebrate with your family. Why can't we celebrate one birthday, just once, with just my family?

SAM: Of course we can celebrate with your family. I welcome that, always. I just don't think they have to compete. I think my family will be disappointed to miss a milestone birthday, and we already told my family we could do the party on her actual birthday. I also think it's flaky of us to change plans like this.

Tasha always found Sam's loyalty to her family to be appealing, but at different points in their relationship, it could sometimes take a toll on Tasha—like when their wedding went from being a small, intimate affair into a big ceremony to accommodate Sam's whole family. Tasha didn't realize she had even been holding in some big feelings about Sam's family until this side conversation in the kitchen about Letti's birthday. Neither partner wants to fight, especially with the kids in the next room, so as the tension builds, Sam yields first. "Fine. I'll explain to my parents that this didn't feel like it was going to work out, but at the last minute it came together." They both walk back into the room with the kids, the silence heavy between them.

They each try to behave normally around the other, but both feel frustrated and alone. Tasha finds herself suddenly obsessing about the issues they had around planning their wedding and is completely thrown off by that. She hasn't thought about any of that in years. Sam told her parents, and they said they were happy to reschedule, but Tasha asked Sam not to reschedule and to just let Letti's birthday be celebrated with Tasha's family. Sam now thinks that Tasha is being unreasonable and is set on punishing Sam's family, although for what, Sam's not sure. Neither Sam nor Tasha feels like they can get the other to understand their position. The tension between them continues to grow, as does their resolve that the problem rests firmly on the other's shoulders.

WHY YOU NEED THIS CONFLICT

Very often the conversation around in-laws is one filled with boundary violations and marked by toxicity (see more about this in chapter 14). But some families have wonderful, healthy extended family dynamics, which can be a true lifeline for parents. But these are still relationships that need time and effort put into them and where conflicts will arise from time to time (remember, conflict is simply a signal that indicates something is important). But figuring out how to resolve conflict in already established family systems, all while you and your partner are trying to create your own, typically involves at least some level of discomfort. Each family has its own complex family structure that consist of the following parts:

- **Rules:** "We are optimists in this family, so we avoid all negative emotions."
- **Roles:** "Paul is the black sheep in the family and is always off doing something 'unique' that ends up getting him in trouble."
- **Rituals:** "Every Christmas we go downtown to see the light show with the whole family."
- **Secrets:** "No one knows why Uncle Rob and Aunt Susan stopped talking fifteen years ago, but we just don't mention it."
- **Generational patterns:** "All the men on your mom's side of the family have started their own businesses," or "Women in the family have always pursued higher education."

Understandably, you may find it awkward and stressful to try and integrate into a family system that has been around long before you entered the picture. And because a partnered relationship involves two people, you typically are bringing together two families with their own set of rules, roles, rituals, secrets, and generational patterns. Couples can find balancing out family systems quite challenging, and this can lead to tension and friction between the partner couple.

The most important thing partnered couples have to figure out is how their new nuclear family fits within the larger systems of their families of origin. This process of integrating your new developing family into the already established rules, roles, rituals, secrets, and generational patterns of your families of origin takes effort and often can lead to conflict. Whose family rules do you follow? Do you just do things the way your family always did it? How does that work when your partner wants to do things the way their family has always done it and it differs from how your family operates? Whose rituals do you adopt? What if there are some rituals you don't want to follow? Do you need to keep the family secrets? What if you feel keeping the family secrets is detrimental to your new developing family and your kids?

You can see here, and even have likely felt yourself, the complications that develop with this combining of (or collision of) family systems, but this is exactly why this conflict is important. Partners have to learn how to engage in this conflict so that they both get to make decisions on how they want their own family to operate. No one wants to feel like they don't have any choice (this can be a recipe for resentment), which is what is happening for Tasha. She has suddenly realized she did not make many choices when she and Sam combined families, and feels she is stuck in a world where Sam's family seems to take precedence over the family Sam and Tasha are building. Integrating another's family of origin into your own family will always involve a push-pull effect, but this is a necessary step that leads you to something special: a feeling of belonging to a group of people who accept, love, and support you no matter what and who make you feel safe.

HOW THIS CONFLICT GOES WRONG

Family is formative, foundational, and sacred—even when our growing-up experience was marked with trauma (see chapter 14). We are all a product of our family, so, in some ways, talking about family with our partners can feel vulnerable because in essence we are talking about ourselves, our history, our own story. We are talking about our family rules, roles, rituals, secrets, and generational patterns that made us into the person we are today. So if your partner criticizes or makes fun of your family or compares it to another family, you may feel compelled to defend your family.

This is one way this conflict turns into unhealthy, unproductive communication: when partners start commenting on, criticizing, holding accountable, withdraw from, or just plain make fun of each other's family. Understandably, though not right, the response is to get defensive or hurt each other's feelings. This can be as simple as a partner saying, "Why does your mom always do that?" and their partner bristles and replies, "Well, at least my family doesn't [insert outlandish pattern of behavior here]." Criticism is threatening and sparks our attachment fears that we are not safe, not known, not loved.

Another way this conflict goes wrong is when one partner's family rules, roles, rituals, secrets, or generational patterns have an impact on your children. For example, one family might insist that people hug when leaving one another's presence. Your partner grew up in a family that expected those hugs whether you wanted them or not. Now, as the parent, you and your partner have decided you want your kids to get to make choices about their own bodies, and to whom and whether they want to offer a hug. You and your partner may agree on this completely, but oftentimes addressing these topics head-on can feel hard for the partner whose family rule is being broken. In this case, the fight turns into "So you would rather keep things comfortable for your family at the expense of our kid? You are choosing your family over us."

You may be wondering or asking yourself: Why is it so hard for us to address our own family rules, roles, rituals, secrets, and generational patterns? There could be any number of reasons. If you've always been taught not to engage in a conflict or not to speak up when you disagree, then it's no surprise you don't feel comfortable doing that as an adult, and with your family no less. That hierarchy of power can be difficult to navigate when you have your own family to consider. Maybe you feel afraid of hurting your well-intentioned family, even though logically you know they would want to know if they were upsetting you or your partner. We hear many adults say, "I don't know what it is, but when I go home or start talking to my family, I feel like a little kid again, not the adult I am now." You're already trying to deal with how you interact with your family at this stage in your life; now add in a situation where your partner asks you to "say something to your family about . . ." No wonder you freeze up or avoid the interaction. This response can feel dismissive to the partner that has asked the other to say something, and the partner struggling to say something can feel like their partner doesn't understand why it is so hard. This is an unfortunate pattern that, left unaddressed, can lead to harmful stuck patterns and resentment.

CONFLICT TO CONNECTION: TASHA AND SAM'S SESSION

Sam is noticeably put out by this session; she feels like having the same conversation about her family is pointless. Tasha seems dejected and sad. The couple expressed wanting to work through their conflict, but the overarching feeling of the session is that neither believes anything can change.

SAM: Tasha, I cannot believe that we have gone from talking about a birthday celebration for Letti to how upset you are about our wedding. That was fifteen years ago! You are mad about something that long ago? It feels so ridiculous and nitpicky.

TASHA: Well, of course it would to you, because heaven forbid we should talk negatively or have any uncomfortable feelings about your perfect family.

SAM: I never said my family was perfect, but I guess they are evil for wanting to have traditions that celebrate one another and make Letti feel special.

STEPHEN: I'm going to jump in here and see if we can navigate away from the sarcasm and cutting comments. It feels clear that you both are upset with each other and are currently feeling closed to hearing from the other about why they feel so strongly.

This is a redirection to try and bring both partners into step 1 of intentional expressing and listening. They need to assess and realize they are speaking about a topic that triggers both of them. If they continue down this path, they will keep having a dead-end dialogue.

ERIN: Sam, try to step back for a moment from the intense feelings you're experiencing about Tasha's being upset about your wedding. What do you notice about the feeling you have about her talking negatively about your family?

This question is meant to move Sam into step 2 of intentional expressing: attune.

SAM: It makes me angry. It feels like she is being ungrateful. My family loves us and tries hard to make all of us feel included and like we are part of the family. When Tasha complains, it feels like she is being ungrateful for how my family cares for her and our kids.

ERIN: What does *being ungrateful* mean to you? Is talking about uncomfortable situations not being grateful?

SAM: No, but I just don't understand why it has to be a big deal to Tasha. Why make a big deal about it? It seems unnecessary.

Erin has helped Sam move from being triggered to attuning to what she is feeling when she and Tasha are having this conversation. There is more to explore, but the energy has slowed, and Sam is reflecting on herself rather than being defensive.

STEPHEN: Tasha, why don't you tell us why this is a big deal to you? Obviously, there is something important in what you are saying, and it seems you are struggling to communicate it and Sam is struggling to hear it. Help us out.

Stephen acknowledges that what is happening for Tasha is a big deal to help her assess she is triggered and move into attuning rather than staying in her activated state. She is being invited to intentional expressing.

TASHA: I think one of the things that gets me so upset is what Sam just said. Why does it have to be a big deal? Part of me wants to say, "Can't it be a big deal because I think it is?" Why does her desire not to ruffle feathers or cause a stir with her family have to control how I feel about something?

STEPHEN: I see. So there is a feeling of being controlled by Sam or Sam's family. Can you elaborate?

Now we are asking Tasha to further attune, but also move into step 3 (reflect) so that she can intentionally express why this feels like it's a big deal.

TASHA: I can try. To be clear, Sam and her family are not controlling, but when we get into conversations about her family, it feels like something changes. It's like there is this pull to not rock the boat or do anything that would mess up the positivity of the family. I don't really know what it is, but that is what I feel controlled by, and then I think it makes Sam not listen to me and tell me I'm making a big deal out of something.

ERIN: Tasha, can you tell us a little about Sam's family? What do you like about them?

TASHA: Well, they really are lovely people. You know, we live in the same town Sam grew up in, so all her extended family are there. They have such a warm and welcoming feel to them. I think one of the deepest values they have as a family is to help everyone feel like they belong. I mean, that is why they do their birthday celebration almost every month. They don't want anyone to be left out.

ERIN: Sam, how would you describe your family?

SAM: That's hard. I agree with Tasha that we have always been told that it's important to make people feel welcome and to be welcoming to one another as a family. Family is challenging, and especially since there is a family business that connects a lot of us, I think my parents felt it was important never to let little squabbles become big problems and to work hard to keep the peace for the good of the family.

STEPHEN: Sam, that sounds important: "Never let little squabbles become big problems and to work hard to keep the peace for the good of the family." You know, another way I might say that is "Don't make a big deal out of little things." What does that sound like to you?

SAM: Yeah, maybe so.

TASHA: It sounds spot-on to me!

STEPHEN: How so, Tasha?

TASHA: I never really noticed it, but in what Sam said just now, there is that sense that nothing should be so big or serious that it negatively impacts the family's feeling of togetherness. Honestly, the family is great and there never really are any big blowouts or issues. But I see it in little ways. Like even when Sam wanted to take a particular week off for vacation and her aunt wanted the same week, Sam immediately backed off and didn't say anything, even though she was burned out and felt like she had to get away. It wasn't the end of the world, but Sam said, "There is no reason to make a big deal of this. I'll just wait till the following week."

ERIN: Tasha, how did you feel about seeing Sam do that?

TASHA: I felt bad for Sam. She was so tired and wasn't feeling well from a health standpoint, yet she didn't feel like she could say anything. I wanted to call her aunt and say something myself.

ERIN: But you didn't, and Sam didn't, and this is how it can feel controlling at times?

TASHA: Yeah. Again, I am not trying to say Sam's family is bad. Even her aunt is great. I think she would feel awful if she knew that even happened. I love them. It's just at times I feel like the pressure to hold that family mantra, or however you said it, wins over me and how I might feel about something.

Tasha has just engaged in intentional expressing through assessing, attuning, reflecting, and sharing. In doing so, she has come to name the core issue: sometimes she feels like Sam's family wins over her.

STEPHEN: That sounds important, Tasha—what you just said about sometimes feeling like the family wins over you. How do you end up feeling when that happens?

TASHA: I don't know. Unimportant, left out, in second place.

SAM: I am not picking my family over you, Tasha.

Can you hear the defensiveness in Sam's voice? It's hard to do step 2, suspend defensiveness, when your family's values and reputation feel at stake.

STEPHEN: Sam, what about hearing Tasha say you are letting your family win over her doesn't sit right for you?

SAM: I don't want her to feel that way, and I do feel like I try to consider her all the time. It makes me feel stuck.

STEPHEN: How so?

SAM: Well, honestly, I get what Tasha is saying. I mean, her reminding me about what happened when I wanted that week off gave me a little pause. My aunt would have been happy to let me go, but I didn't say anything. It felt scary or maybe unnecessary.

ERIN: Scary how?

It's now Sam's turn to intentionally express by moving into attuning to her emotions.

SAM: I feel weird saying *scared*, but it is the first thing that came to my mind. I think I love my family and the support we have as a group. I want to keep that and give our kids and Tasha that same feeling, and I don't want it to change.

ERIN: Do you actually think it would have changed if you had asked for the week you wanted for vacation? Did it go poorly to shift Letti's party?

SAM: No, but I was worried it might, and that feels strange because I don't have any experience that would tell me it ever would.

STEPHEN: You know, it's funny how that works sometimes. Because of the goodness of your attachment experience with your family, you're fearful of losing it, so you stress about something that could happen even if there is a stronger chance that it won't.

SAM: I see that. Tasha, I get what you are saying. I am not trying to say what you want or what is important to you is not a big deal. I would want you to think something is important if I felt it was, too. I did not handle Letti's party situation well. I'm sorry.

Sam has moved into step 4 of intentional listening (repair) by taking accountability and acknowledging Tasha's concern.

TASHA: I really appreciate you saying that, Sam. Thank you.

STEPHEN: Tasha, I wonder if you hear how making certain things a "big deal" with Sam's family can feel scary for her?

TASHA: Yeah, I don't think I have ever heard her express that before, but it makes sense.

STEPHEN: So when she is a bit resistant to "a little squabble" mattering, it is not about her not wanting to treat you like you are important. It's about her feeling scared of losing something that has been so good in her life and something she wants for your family.

TASHA: Huh . . . I don't think I have noticed that, but I get it. Sam, I don't think I understood that about you.

SAM: I don't think I understood it about myself.

TASHA: Well, I get why doing something for Letti's birthday still feels so important and just canceling it altogether feels bad for you. I'm sorry I didn't consider that side of it and consult you first on that decision. Can we do the thing with my family, and when we get back, we can be sure to get together with your family?

SAM: That would be wonderful.

Here, Tasha has also reached out to repair with Sam, and in doing so, they can take a different action toward feeling aligned and connected in what used to feel like an unhealthy conflict. This is a perfect example of how conflict can lead to attachment-making interactions.

BUT HOW CAN I ACTUALLY SAY ANY OF THIS TO MY PARTNER? SAMPLE SCRIPTS

Family is complex. Joining families with your partner can be confusing if you are not able to engage the normative conflicts that arise in this process in a way that creates connection. Here are some scripts that can get you and your partner moving through conflict to connection when it comes to family dynamics.

Intentional Expressing: The Partner Being Integrated into a Family

"Hey, I feel like your family is important to you, and there are some things about how your family does things or thinks about the world that I don't really understand. My way of handling that has been to joke about your family, but I don't think that feels good to you and it doesn't seem to move the conversation forward. I do want to understand and don't want you to feel like you have to defend your family against my humor. Can we talk about it?"

"I don't know what it is, but I am noticing that when we talk about your family I start getting tense and feel closed to what you have to say. I imagine that doesn't feel good to you and I don't want to be that way. Can we talk about what is happening for you in these conversations and what is happening for me? I want to try and figure this out."

"I really love your family. I feel like sometimes when we talk about how we want our relationships with them to look, you feel like I don't want to be close with your family. Can you help me understand if there is a way I am communicating that doesn't feel good to you? I want to be able to talk about these things and not feel disconnected."

Intentional Expressing: The Partner That Is Part of the Family

"Can I talk with you about going to my family's this weekend? I feel like we have different expectations about how these visits should go. Can you help me understand what some of the stressful or challenging parts of visiting are? I want to hear what is happening for you."

"I don't know what it is, but I am noticing that when we talk about my family, I start getting tense and feel closed to what you have to say. I imagine that doesn't feel good to you, and I don't want to be that way. Can we talk about what is happening for you in these conversations and what is happening for me? I want to try and figure this out."

QUESTIONS FOR REFLECTION

1. Have you and your partner discussed how, if at all, you would like your families to be a part of your life?

2. What are the established rules, roles, rituals, secrets, and generational patterns of your family of origin? What about for your partner and their family of origin? How do you want these questions to be answered about your family?

3. Do you find yourself ever feeling like you and your partner

have different expectations for the role extended family should play in your family?

4. Where do you feel the most stuck or threatened in this conflict? Does your partner also have the same feelings? What feels like the most important thing to you in this conflict? How did it come to be that important to you? What feels like it is at stake?

5. Do you feel like you have been avoiding this conflict? Is there anything about this chapter that resonates with you? Did it stir any feelings or memories? Why might those feelings and memories be coming up now in the season of life and parenting you are currently in?

CHAPTER 11

The "Your Parenting Is Wrong" Conflict

Keith and Lara have been together for ten years and have been married for close to seven; they have two children. They both work outside of the house full time and have demanding jobs. Both are content in their roles and know each is doing a lot in a day to contribute to their family unit.

For Lara, an important piece of her parenting is to be reflective and self-aware so she is at her personal best and can provide a loving and safe environment for her kids. In college, Lara started going to therapy and found it helped her to understand herself and to make sense of some of the decisions she had ahead of her. She credits therapy with the good, though not perfect, relationship she now has with her parents—one she wants to model for her children. She was also a sociology minor in college and likes researching the latest studies on parenting; she's especially interested in how parenting styles have changed throughout generations and the social context for those styles and changes. She has learned about child development and the impact of childhood on a kid's adult life, and talking with her therapist enables her not to ruminate too much on areas where she feels she may have missed the mark with her kids.

Keith believes in working hard and trying his best, but he doesn't find talking about his childhood brings him much, if any, help or guidance in his day-to-day life. He has an okay relationship with his parents, and he truly believes they did the best they could for him and his siblings. He feels like he turned out all right and doesn't spend much more time thinking about it than that. To him, that's a good thing. He has enough going on right now not to want to get stuck in the past. He doesn't worry about being a good dad. He likes his kids and works hard to give them a good life, and as far as he is concerned, that is an ideal setting to raise a kid in.

Keith and Lara would agree Lara is the primary decision-maker in the house on all parenting issues and anything related to the kids. Although most of the time things run smoothly, there are moments with the kids when Keith and Lara do not agree on how to handle the situation, and they are noticing that it is causing friction in their couple relationship. They both find the distance it is putting between them troubling, but they see the situation very differently.

Keith sees Lara's passion for parenting and for the most part he appreciates her perspective and respects her knowledge on the subject. He doesn't feel that the two of them need to agree on every point of parenting and thinks it may even be good for the kids to see two different perspectives from time to time. For him it doesn't matter that they don't agree on all things parenting, but he does care that it's driving a wedge between him and Lara. He can readily acknowledge that he is less patient with the kids than he would like to be sometimes, but what really upsets him is that when he has had a parenting moment in which he is "anything less than perfect," Lara swoops in and gets angry with him. In his eyes, she makes the whole situation worse than it needs to be.

In Lara's mind, when things are not going well on a parenting level, of course Keith and Lara's relationship would be impacted for the worse. Keith says he thinks they are aligned on all the major things when it comes to parenting, but to Lara, the things they disagree on are quite important. If she had to sum it up, she feels Keith is too hard on the kids. According to Lara, Keith has developmentally unrealistic expectations of them, probably related to his own anxiety. Below is an example of this type of parenting disconnect:

> LARA: It does not calm the kids down when you tell them to calm down. They need you to be with them and help them understand what is happening for them. You being with them is what calms them down.
>
> KEITH: They do not need to be coddled. They need me to help them know how to get through hard things in life. We can't protect them from everything, and we need to help them build resilience.
>
> LARA: Being with them when they are upset is teaching them something. It is teaching them that when they have emotions, they can express them, someone will listen and come close to them, and they do not have to fear difficult things. That's resilience.
>
> KEITH: Nobody did that for me. I had to learn that things happen, and you have to get yourself together and keep moving on. In the real world, no one is going to make everything all better for them.

These kinds of conversations about parenting differences are always frustrating for both Lara and Keith and don't lead to any productive conversation or constructive change. It all comes to a head one weekend after a particularly long workweek for Keith.

Keith had been away traveling for work and returned home Thursday night as the kids were going to sleep. The kids had been excited about his return. From Lara's perspective, he had not been in the door five minutes before he started growing impatient with them. Before long, Keith and Lara were fighting in front of the kids, and the kids went to sleep sad and upset while Lara and Keith wound up their dispute. This was not the reunion any of them had wanted. Their conflict was not just unproductive, but counterproductive.

LARA: You walked in the door and immediately lost your patience with the kids because they were wound up. Did you ever consider that the reason they were wound up was because we foolishly had all been excited to see you?

KEITH: I didn't lose my patience. I was trying to help things move toward bedtime so maybe you and I could have some alone time together. Then you inserted yourself and made a big fuss where there didn't have to be any.

LARA: You think marching around and barking orders at them helps move them toward being calm for bedtime? You think yelling at Luca that it was time to shut his light off when he was crying helped him feel ready to rest? Do you honestly think that helped him go to sleep faster?

KEITH: I didn't yell at anyone. In fact, the only person who yelled was you. Do you honestly think that helped anyone feel more calm?

LARA: You are supposed to be a grown-up and able to regulate yourself without taking your stress out on our kids. Maybe you didn't yell, but you certainly didn't show him any compassion when all he needed was a little comfort and connection with you.

KEITH: But it's completely mature for you to take your stress out on me? And in front of the kids? Luca didn't want to go to sleep, and it was time for bed. He knows he has you wrapped around his little finger and can get you to stop your whole world, including all our bedtimes, any time he cries. He has to learn to do hard things, including going to sleep at night, and honestly you are making it even harder for him. That makes it harder for all of us.

Lara knows Keith is a good dad and cares deeply for their kids, but in these tense moments she feels like he is breaking trust in their relationship. She knows she loses her patience with him and furthers the escalation, but she also wants her kids to know that sometimes how Keith relates to them isn't okay. She wishes she could let him parent as he wants to, but so often when he is around and someone gets upset, it's up to her to make sure they get the attention and repair they need.

Keith trusts Lara as a mom and wishes she would trust him as a dad, too. He doesn't like the feeling he sometimes has that Lara puts herself between him and the kids. He thinks she has endless patience for the kids but next to none for him. Keith supports and trusts her completely, but when the roles are reversed, he feels that she is against him, that he is the bad parent, and that she chooses her relationship with the kids over her relationship with him.

WHY YOU NEED THIS CONFLICT

This conflict often gets categorized as a difference in parenting styles. Remember, our parenting is directly related to our own experiences of being parented and the ways we manage stress. Lara has done a lot of reflective work to understand how her past experiences and her past ways of coping with stress might influence her as a parent. Her goal in this work is to be able to give the healthiest version of herself to her kids and to do so in a regulated state.

The disconnect between Lara and Keith is Keith has not taken the time to reflect on the relationship between his own experience of being parented, his manner of coping with stress, and his parenting techniques. Lara notices Keith being more reactive and irritable with the kids due to stress and a belief that the kids have to learn to do tough things because no one will make life easy for them. Lara feels concerned about this reactivity and belief. Keith is chalking her concern up to parenting differences and saying, "We just see things a little different." But Lara feels like this so-called parenting difference is a result of Keith's not having adequate coping strategies, and her concern is that the kids are paying for it. However, Lara also becomes dysregulated in these interactions and heightens the conflict. She has to get beyond simply saying, "Well, if you didn't react, Keith, I wouldn't get mad," and understand what her own reactivity is about as well. This conflict is about more than parenting differences: it is about the emotional and relational health of each parent and their ability to work together as a healthy parenting unit.

This conflict has to be addressed because we all need to do the work so as to not walk around parenting and partnering from an activated place. What does this mean? Doing the work means understanding how your past experience of parenting and your responses to stress can benefit or harm your family. This can be done by engaging in therapy, by reading helpful research on child development and parenting, and by having open and honest conversations with your partner.

Parents get to choose if how they are currently operating in the world (as a parent, partner, and otherwise) is how they want to continue to operate, or if they would like to change some of their reactions and the ways they have learned to express themselves. It does not mean getting stuck in the past and ruminating about would-haves and could-haves. It means taking an honest look at ourselves and moving forward in our lives with purpose and being on the same team as our partner (not as adversaries).

HOW THIS CONFLICT GOES WRONG

This conflict goes wrong when partners get stuck in the dichotomy of being "too soft" or "too hard" on kids. Lara feels that Keith is too hard on the kids at times; she is stuck cleaning up his mess after he has snapped at the kids or ignored their emotions. Keith believes that Lara coddles the kids and then tries to step in and correct his parenting. He feels that Lara is too soft and that the only way the kids will learn to make it in life is to see that life is not always easy. They are stuck in a useless dichotomy that leaves them both angry and feeling miles apart.

When it comes to parenting styles, there is ample research in the field of interpersonal neurobiology about how parents can create the healthiest environment and attachments with kids. There is no need for a debate about being soft or hard as parents. Neither of these categories are part of the conversation. As we discussed in chapter 1, effective and healthy parenting is all about creating strong attachment bonds with kids through proximity and responsiveness.

Lara and Keith are in conflict because Lara feels that Keith is having attachment-breaking interactions with the kids when he is reactive, and Keith does not agree. The subsequent argument Lara and Keith have then negatively impacts the feeling of connection between Lara and Keith. So the pattern works like this:

1. Keith gets stressed during a parenting task and reacts in a short-tempered fashion, exhibiting anger and irritability, yelling, and ignoring the feelings of the kids.

2. Lara sees this and becomes dysregulated herself—worrying about how the kids are reacting to Keith.

3. Lara lashes out at Keith to get him to stop and calm down. Keith is triggered by feeling like Lara is telling him he is a bad

parent, and he responds with continued frustration and reactivity.

4. The kids are upset, Lara is upset, Keith is upset, and there is a loss of connection in the home and in the couple relationship.

Lara needs Keith to be open-minded and consider how he is currently relating to the kids, where that behavior comes from, if it is going to achieve the outcome he wants it to, and even who he wants to be as a parent. And Keith is asking Lara to do the same but from a partnering perspective. Keith needs Lara to consider her own reactivity and how she can be concerned and even frustrated with Keith but not escalate the situation with her dysregulation—the very thing she is frustrated with Keith for. They need to think about what kind of relationship they want to have as a family and how they want their kids to experience them as parents. They both have to look at how they were parented, how they respond to stress, and how that impacts their parenting and partnership positively and negatively. This way they can choose how they want to parent (their parenting style) and be on the same page as parents and as partners.

CONFLICT TO CONNECTION: KEITH AND LARA'S SESSION

Keith and Lara come into their session feeling anxious about engaging because it feels pointless—they've done this song and dance (albeit in an unhealthy way) and it never ended well.

STEPHEN: If I am hearing this right, would it be fair to put it this way? Keith, you feel like Lara is too easy on or enabling to the kids, and, Lara, you feel like Keith is too harsh and dismissive. Both of you feel like you are not on each other's team.

LARA: Yes, I think Keith wants the kids to just do what he says. When it doesn't happen, he gets frustrated with them, which makes me frustrated with him.

ERIN: That sounds like an exhausting cycle.

LARA: It's the worst on the kids. They are not mini adults. They are figuring out life, and I think the way to help them do that is to come beside them and understand them and then help them make decisions. I feel like being rigid doesn't leave any room for them to be kids.

KEITH: It leaves room for them to get what they want and not have to be challenged and grow.

Because Keith is defensive, he is not able to intentionally listen. He is in an activated/triggered place and is responding out of his stress response system.

ERIN: Keith, Stephen said it seems you feel like Lara is too easy or enabling with the kids. Is that an accurate description?

KEITH: Yeah. She says I'm rigid, but I just have rules and standards. I don't think that is a bad thing. The moment one of the kids cries or seems to get upset, Lara swoops in and solves the problem for them. I want them to know that we care, but that they have to figure some of this stuff out themselves. Life is challenging.

STEPHEN: Lara, would you say that you don't want the kids to be able to solve their own problems or be independent?

LARA: No. Of course I want that for them. I just don't think you get it by being hard on them. I think you get it by helping them feel cared for and having a relationship with them that gives them the confidence to be independent.

STEPHEN: Keith, what do you hear when Lara says this?

KEITH: It sounds nice in theory but entirely impractical in reality. That is not how things work in the real world. I want a good relationship with my kids, too. I think what I am doing is part of having a good relationship. They'll thank me for it later in life.

ERIN: Lara, do you know that Keith wants a good relationship with your kids and that he feels he is trying to accomplish that in how he approaches the kids?

LARA: I wholeheartedly believe Keith wants a good relationship with the kids. I think he has a good relationship with the kids right now. But I also think that his relationship with them is hurt by these moments where his stress gets the best of him and he is harsh.

STEPHEN: You know, a lot of couples think that they develop a parenting philosophy or style as they become parents. But parenting philosophies and styles are formed when we are children. Lara and Keith, believe it or not, you are parenting based on your own childhood experiences.

LARA: That doesn't sound right to me. I would never want to parent like I was parented.

ERIN: What about you, Keith? Do you want to parent your kids like you were parented?

KEITH: I mean, I've never really thought about it, but I think I turned out all right. My home was pretty no-frills, and we had to learn to figure stuff out for ourselves. It wasn't always easy, but I think it helped me make it in life.

The conversation is shifting away from the triggered place, and the focus is moving toward attuning, reflecting, and sharing—all parts of intentional expressing.

STEPHEN: Lara, you said that you would never want to parent your kids like you were parented. What are you afraid of happening if you were to parent your kids like you were parented?

This is an attune and reflect question that invites Lara to intentional expressing.

LARA: Well, my parents didn't listen. They weren't bad people, but they didn't want to hear about what I felt or what I thought. I was supposed to be a good student, play sports, get into a good college, and stay out of trouble. Be obedient and quiet. That's what they wanted for me, and nothing else was important. They didn't want to hear about any of my experiences in school outside of my grades or to help me deal with how difficult middle school was. They didn't talk to me about my first date or what I should expect in terms of consent. I felt ignored. They had other things they were doing.

STEPHEN: So there is motivation for you not to have this same thing happen to your kids. You are going to listen, you are going to ask questions, you are going to pay attention. One of your worst fears might be that they feel ignored.

LARA: One hundred percent.

ERIN: Lara, when you feel that Keith is shutting the kids down or not listening to their feelings, are you aware that part of your "big" reaction to him might be your feeling that the very thing you are afraid of happening as a parent seems to be taking place?

LARA: I think I might be understanding what you are saying, but can you say more?

ERIN: Well, you never wanted your kids to feel ignored or not listened to, and there you are seeing Keith ignore and not listen to your kids, and this makes you really angry.

LARA: Hmm . . . I don't think I would have made that connection, but it does feel right. I just get so mad, it's like I lose my ability to step in while remaining calm.

ERIN: Of course. This is why it's important to understand your own experience of being parented. It impacts how you experience parenting and how you feel about your partner's parenting. Keith, you said you want to parent your kids with rules and standards. This sounds like you feel this is the right way to do things. What are you afraid might happen if you don't parent your kids right?

KEITH: I wouldn't say I'm fearful of anything. I just want the kids to be ready for life.

STEPHEN: What does that mean? To be ready for life?

KEITH: Well, I didn't come from much. My parents had to work hard, and ultimately they did create a good life for our family, but they worked for it. My dad lost his job, my mom had to work some long hours at first, and no one helped them. They had to buckle down and help themselves. Lara and I provide a more stable and secure life for our kids, but I want them to be able to be okay if things get tough and we aren't with them to rescue them from it.

STEPHEN: If they weren't able to be okay, what would that mean?

KEITH: I don't really know. I just know my parents drilled it into me that we had to be able to do hard things and make it. I don't really have an idea in my head about what not making it would be—I just know I don't want that for my kids.

STEPHEN: So, Keith, when you see Lara being soft or when you feel like the kids are not pushing through something hard, you can get frustrated. You are literally watching Lara and the kids not do it right, and this means that things are not going to be okay for them.

KEITH: Yeah. I mean, as I hear you talking, I also get that my feeling things won't be okay is a bit vague. But if I'm honest, I do get anxious and irritated when I feel like Lara is enabling the kids or the kids aren't able to deal with a tough situation.

STEPHEN: If I had to sum up what I am hearing, it seems to me that you get into conflict because you are both seeing something you don't want to happen to your kids happening. Lara, you don't want your kids to feel ignored, and, Keith, you don't want your kids to grow up and not be resilient enough to deal with hard things. Does that sound fair?

LARA/KEITH: Yes.

ERIN: I wonder if you both can see that the source of this conflict stems from your own experiences of being parented. Does that make it clear why it's important to understand these stages of your life and how they are influencing your parenting in the present moment?

KEITH: I can see that. Lara always says stuff like that, but I honestly have not listened to her and just brushed her off.

LARA: And I am seeing that I have been saying that to Keith, but also have not carried this into how my own parenting experience is influencing my responses to Keith.

ERIN: The core of your parenting differences is a desire either not to replicate something you experienced in your childhood or to replicate what you experienced. Neither one of you are talking about parenting. You are talking about things you don't want to happen to your kids if you don't parent right. Fear is driving this conversation and generating the moments that are dividing the two of you.

STEPHEN: That's why it's important to do some reflective work about your childhood experience of being parented. The way to tone down the reactivity of this conflict is to understand what is going on in you and your partner in these moments. Knowing what is really happening in these stressful interactions is the way to space them out more widely, to turn down their intensity, and to shorten the length of them when they do happen.

LARA: I get that. Keith, can you see why I react in such a big way?

KEITH: Yeah. I know your parents, and I honestly feel like they do the same thing to me that they did to you as a kid. It is absolutely frustrating, and I don't want to do that to the kids at all.

LARA: And I know your parents and I can see how you were asked to push through. While in some ways this has really helped you in life, it has also reinforced your belief that no one really wants to hear you "whine."

Here the couple moves to practice intentional listening. They are suspending their defensiveness so they can believe their partner's experience and hear the story behind the actions and behaviors.

KEITH: Okay. So, what does this mean we do?

STEPHEN: What you both did here today was good, and it's important to keep exploring in this direction. Keith, I think it can be helpful for you to keep in mind that when Lara feels you are reactive, it is triggering to her for reasons you now understand better. Knowing this may enable you not to be reactive back and may help you step back, look at what has happened, and be able to talk about it in a different way.

And, Lara, knowing that when Keith is reactive, there is likely something deeper happening for him. Your moving toward him, trying to understand what is going on, and working together to come to an agreement you both like will lead to a conversation about what you want in those moments.

LARA: True. But what do we do about our different perspectives on how to interact with the kids?

Lara is asking a question about repair. Keith and Lara understand each other and some of the stories that are informing their actions and behavior. But they still don't have a way of moving forward, taking action, together.

ERIN: Do more exploring like this. You offered each other so much knowing and kindness when you shared what your experiences were like and just a few of the ways those experiences are shaping your current life. It can be working with a professional, but it doesn't have to be. There are other ways to get into this kind of reflection and discussion.

STEPHEN: I'd like to throw something out there to help this along. This takes intentional and equitable effort from you both. **The sequence goes like this:**

Do your research. Make a plan. Implement your plan. Tweak your plan. Begin again.

What I mean by this is there is plenty of good data about what healthy parenting consists of, parenting that assists kids in becoming all the things you both said you wanted. Both of you, not just one of you, have to dive into that research. Both of you take an hour and research what some of the best books on parenting are (we can give you some recommendations) and then select three you want to look at. Then get the books and have a book club. Both of you read the books and come to the book club ready to discuss what you liked, what you didn't, and what might work for you as a family. Then you need to make a plan about some of the things you would like to implement and enact the plan. Then you assess the plan and make adjustments, and so goes the process.

Keith, I feel like the first part of that plan is going to be the most challenging for you. The intentional and equitable research. Is that an accurate guess?

KEITH: Yeah, I don't feel like I need someone else telling me how to parent.

STEPHEN: No, you don't. But ideally the books and research would help you and Lara talk about some of the ways you were both parented and then together decide what parts of these books you like and don't like. You want to get on the same page with Lara. The way to get on the same page is to develop an idea about how you want to parent *together* rather than trying to get the other one to do it your way. It is hard to articulate what that means unless you talk about it.

KEITH: I don't want to do it, but for us to get off each other's backs and feel like a team, I'll try.

LARA: I would love to give this a try. I do think we will need some help with further facilitation of the conversation, but it is nice to think we are doing this because we want the same thing.

KEITH: It is helpful to reframe the conversation that way.

Lara and Keith are able to repair in that they are both backing off of their dug-in stances and making a plan of action that includes each other and that they both agree to try.

BUT HOW CAN I ACTUALLY SAY ANY OF THIS TO MY PARTNER? SAMPLE SCRIPTS

The plan we outlined for Lara and Keith was very clear and had some measurable steps. However, couples first have to come to the table and agree to do something different. Here are some scripts that can help couples start approaching this conflict in a constructive way.

Intentional Expressing for Either Partner to Use

"I think sometimes when parenting comes up with us that I am not actually all that open-minded. I do have a way I want to parent and a way I think is best, but I would love to be open enough to hear what you think and feel, too. I may not agree with it, but maybe I've never even asked. What are your thoughts?"

"Sometimes I feel like we are adversaries in parenting, and I really want us to be a team. What are your feelings about us as parents? Do you feel like I am there for you? Do you feel you are there for me? Do you feel like we have our own way of parenting, or do you feel like I think it's my way or the highway? Can we talk about finding 'our way'?"

"How do you think we are doing as parents? What do you think our kid would say about me as a parent? What do you think they would say about you? How do you think they would describe us right now? Ultimately, what do we want them to say about who we each were to them as a parent?"

QUESTIONS FOR REFLECTION

1. What was your favorite and least favorite thing about your own parents?

2. What is your favorite thing about yourself and your partner as parents right now? Do you feel like you spend more, less, or equal time encouraging your and your partner's parenting or offering feedback and ways to improve?

3. Do you ever feel that parenting is a barrier to your partnership? Or that your partnership is a barrier to your parenting?

4. What is the most stuck place for you in this conflict? What feels like the most important thing to you in this conflict? How did it come to be that important to you? What feels like it is at stake?

5. Do you feel like you have been avoiding this conflict? Is there anything about this chapter that seemed to resonate with you? Did it stir any feelings or memories? Why might those feelings and memories be coming up now in the season of life, parenting, and partnership you are currently in?

CHAPTER 12

The "A Decision Has to Be Made" Conflict

CHRISSA AND MICHELLE have been together ten years and have three kids—twin three-year-olds, Micah and Miles, and six-month-old Jack. Chrissa has wanted to be a mom her whole life and really hoped she would be able to get pregnant and carry her kids. While Michelle wanted to be a parent, she never felt compelled to carry a child and was more than content to have Chrissa take that on.

Before having kids, Chrissa had worked her way up the corporate ladder in the HR department of a major finance company. She likes her job and is good at it. She is respected in her field and feels capable and confident to solve the never-ending stream of challenges thrown at her day in and day out.

Michelle is a pediatrician, and while the toll of her caseload and family life was always difficult, after the pandemic, Michelle finds work to be even more draining. The practice Michelle works with has lost many healthcare workers, and they have not been able to replace them, so Michelle's workload has grown considerably. Michelle considers looking elsewhere for a better work/life balance, but also feels a responsibility to the team she works with and knows leaving would only further increase the remaining team's load.

When Chrissa and Michelle decided to pursue having kids, they knew they would hire the help they would need when they both returned to work. Chrissa and Michelle both had excellent parental leave packages and were able to take a couple of weeks off together right away after the twins were born. The time together was a welcome relief because the period was intense for everyone in all senses of the word—wonderful and connective for them as a family, but also exhausting. Michelle had a few weeks left of her parental leave but was also feeling the weight of her absence on her colleagues. After much back-and-forth, Chrissa and Michelle decided that overall it was best for Michelle to return to work a few days a week to alleviate some of the stress being gone was causing Michelle and therefore the family. Since this routine worked well for them, they made the same decision again when Jack was born.

Chrissa loves being a parent and finds she is thriving managing all the sweet chaos. She keeps joking that having three kids three and under is nothing compared to the corporate HR shenanigans she is used to dealing with. Chrissa's return to work this time around is a few weeks off still, but she notices she is thinking about it and it feels less positive and more daunting than she expected it would or than it did when she went back to work after the twins.

She pushes the feelings away and instead focuses on their twins and the baby. Chrissa and Michelle faced a few challenges in their relationship during those early months, but felt they were able to communicate about them effectively. In a few instances, they hired help to solve whatever the problem was related to: the messy house now has a weekly professional cleaning, the groceries are now delivered, and the car gets cleaned inside and out weekly as well. As Chrissa says, "Michelle just throws money at the problem," but to Michelle's credit, all the external help has helped. It's expensive and they both agree all these luxuries can't last forever, but they can last for now.

Overall, they are making it and feeling good about how they are doing. They both have been researching child care options but have not come to any final decisions and, at least from Michelle's perspective, haven't really done anything except add more research and data to the conversation rather than reducing the set of options available.

One day they decide they are ready to venture out into the world. They load the twins and Jack into the car and head out for their first meal at a restaurant since becoming a family of five. They arrive and feel more than accomplished—they are proud of their family. Conversation goes off almost without a hitch . . . almost. Toward the end of the meal, Michelle asks how Chrissa is feeling about returning to work and if they should begin to get more serious about finding someone to watch the kids. Michelle is taken aback as Chrissa begins to cry and can't really get any words out. Chrissa obviously has strong feelings about the decision, but she isn't sure why this stirs up such emotion. Michelle doesn't want to press Chrissa, so they load the kids back into the car and go home.

For the next few days, it's back to business as usual, barring the gigantic elephant in the room. Neither one knows exactly where to begin the conversation, but they both know the tension is building and they need to talk. They know they need to talk because whatever happened at the restaurant is clearly important, but also because time is passing and some practical decisions need to be made.

Finally, Chrissa lets Michelle know she is questioning going back to work as they planned she would. Michelle wants to hear her out, but she is having a hard time entertaining this idea. It was not their original plan, it doesn't make any financial sense, and it would throw away everything Chrissa has worked so hard for. Michelle finds that she is having a big reaction to Chrissa's saying this. To Michelle, this feels like an "emotional" decision. She thinks Chrissa should not make such a major decision while her body is coursing with postpartum hormones and she is surrounded by two cute twins and a baby staring up adoringly at her. This is the time to stick to the plan and they can reevaluate along the way.

MICHELLE: You know, Chrissa, this same thing happened last time. When you had to start thinking about going back to work after the twins, you got all sentimental and sad, but eventually you were glad you went back.

CHRISSA: I was sad, but something feels different this time. I was thinking about work today and it all feels so . . . pointless. Just climbing the ladder and moving from one job to another. When I look at our kids, they feel like the single most important thing I could possibly be doing with my time. What could be more important than our prioritizing them?

MICHELLE: You are prioritizing them by giving them a stable future. I love them, too, and believe me, I know work can feel pointless at times when all it does is seem to stress you out more. But we made a plan for our future and the kids, and sticking to it is part of caring for them.

CHRISSA: I know, but sometimes plans change. We might just have to be creative and see if there is another scenario that might work.

MICHELLE: You are so good at your job. It's not pointless at all! I know they are lost without you. Also, I don't want to make you upset, but you tend to make rash and emotional decisions. I don't want to start reinventing the wheel for you to just change your mind three months into some new plan. What we are planning on doing is the best option.

CHRISSA: Well, at least I let my emotions in at all. You just want a "good" plan. What about the relationships with our kids? You are so practical that you won't even allow yourself to adjust if

something changes. You are miserable at work, but since the
plan was for you to stay, you do so, even though it's not a good
fit for you. I don't want to be like that.

MICHELLE: Chrissa, this will pass. Of course it feels hard to think
about going back to work. I felt sad to go back. You'll adjust and
the kids will, too.

Ultimately, both partners just decide to shut things down to avoid
any further tension and keep moving forward with the initial plan.
Both are sharing what they are finding, but neither one is addressing
the something they both know is lurking there. Each day that passes
that they don't talk about it, they grow more scared of what it must
mean.

Chrissa isn't sure if Michelle can really handle what would come
up if Chrissa brings out into the open what she is trying not to think:
how different she feels now; how when she thinks of going back to
work, that work and those tasks seem irrelevant. She knows Michelle
doesn't love her job, either, and doesn't want her to feel she can never
leave if she is the only breadwinner. But Chrissa feels like Michelle is
not hearing her when she says something is shifting within her. She
feels bad about it, but some of her values *have* changed and she is
growing more and more tired of hearing Michelle tell her that things
can (and should) go back to normal. Her resentment is already real,
and it is growing every time this conversation gets shut down or tied
up in a tidy and practical ribbon.

Michelle is angry. Michelle feels like Chrissa is being irrational
and letting her feelings get the best of her. Michelle always wants to
support Chrissa, but also adults have to make difficult decisions
sometimes, especially adults with three little kids they have to plan a
future for. Michelle feels like Chrissa is not being responsible, and
this is a thematic feeling for Michelle. Michelle's parents worked
hard for everything they had and still did not have a lot of money, but

they sacrificed so Michelle could have a better life than they did. She was able to go to medical school and choose a career that would be financially stable for her and her family. She does not believe that she has the privilege of quitting because she doesn't like all aspects of it.

WHY YOU NEED THIS CONFLICT

This couple happens to be fighting over a job, but this conflict could just as easily be about how many kids they should have, whether their kids should go to private school or public, or where they should choose to live. The larger topic is how becoming parents very often creates a shift in who we are as a person and the way our values shake out, or how we express our values now as a parent. As partners, we do not always manage to do this at the same time or in the same way, or to express it in ways that make any sense—to us or to our partner.

Should major life decisions be made amid massive transitions and major life changes? It is commonly understood as good practice that they shouldn't, and maybe it largely makes sense to follow that reasoning. Parents spend a lot of time making plans about how their lives will be and how they will feel after baby arrives, but the reality is that no matter how much planning we do or how many babies we have already welcomed, only after the baby's actual arrival will we know how we will think, feel, and behave. That concept remains true as our kids move into new ages and stages. Despite our best-laid plans, we think, feel, and are different from what we expected we would be as our parenting journey moves through time.

That feeling of "But I wasn't expecting to feel this way!" or "This is not what we discussed or planned!" is a massive shift for many people and can put a strain on the couple's relationship. This mental and emotional shift can come out a lot of different ways, such as:

- "I think I might like to live closer to my family and have help."
- "I want to consider looking at some of our lifestyle habits and how we spend our time."
- "I know we said we would never send our kid to public school, but I really want to consider it; I think it could be great for us all."
- "I know we said we would start trying for another kid around now, but I am not sure I am ready."
- "I feel really alone with your working so many hours; I want you to consider a new job."
- "I know no one wants either one of us to be working more, but our bills and spending are steep and we need to talk about how we can make more money."

However it comes out, the point is, it can feel surprising, scary, and create strong feelings of uncertainty.

These conversations are deeply personal and can evoke a reaction from either partner in these high-stakes arguments. Some partners worry their partner is just being emotional and try to point out the practical flaws in their reasoning. For example, in response to a partner's wanting to move closer to their set of parents, the other partner may say something like "Every time we are anywhere near your family, you turn into what you yourself describe as 'the worst version of yourself.' Are you saying that is what you want our kids to see more of as they are growing up? The worst version of you?" In Chrissa and Michelle's situation, Michelle might say, "Are you saying that a good parent wouldn't want to work? I'm back to work now, so does that make me a bad parent?"

The conversation can also feel personal because the partner that wants a rational, thought-out decision can feel like they are being characterized as emotionless or robotic. Their partner might say things like, "You care more about your plan than you do about me and the kids." One partner feels like they are being dismissed as emotional, and the other feels they are being disparaged as uncaring. Neither actually feels this accurately embodies their partner, but the fear of the unknown and the distance that grows between a couple as they are disconnected on a topic can result in these heightened responses.

While all couples have some shared values, many find that when they become parents, their values seem to become misaligned. This misalignment is scary because values represent the core of who we are as people and shape the decisions we make. As a parenting couple, partners want to feel that their values match because they are intent on creating a life together, and they are trying to create a family that has shared values. The decisions they make are based on these values. So when what one partner's values begin to shift, it can feel like that partner is threatening the future of the family and complicating joint decision-making. It can even feel like a betrayal because very often these things were agreed to, or at least assumed, before kids.

That is why this is a must-have conflict. Changing values influence decisions made about the future direction of the family. The longer these questions of values remain unaddressed, the bigger the gap between the partners seems to be and the scarier the outcome of the conversation becomes.

HOW THIS CONFLICT GOES WRONG

Conversations about values will repeatedly come up over the years as parenting partners' lives and kids develop. Nothing is set in stone, and honestly, that is a key takeaway from this chapter—your values don't necessarily need to change, but as you pass through various stages in your parenting partnership, your conversations must keep up with where you are. Our values are deeply personal, and couples often believe they have signed a pact that read, "We believe this now and always will forever and ever." We're here to tell you, this is not the case! Give yourself permission to change your mind, and in doing so, free your and your family's future of certain expectations.

For us, as is true for many couples, this conversation began with a discussion of child care. As we addressed this first issue, it laid the foundation for us to be able to have such conversations along the way as our kids have grown and we have aged. The initial child care discussion was relatively easy, and we came to a decision we both agreed to—Erin would pause her work in community mental health and get to be a stay-at-home mom.

We thought that was that. Decision made, neat and simple. But the consequences of that decision did not become clear until about a year later. At that point, Stephen had been accepted into and was going to school full time in his medical family therapy PhD program, was working full time as a licensed clinician in a community mental health setting, and was working his hardest at home to be engaged and attentive to his family. He wanted so badly to give all his best energy to his family, but he often found full-time school and full-time work was leaving him a half-engaged dad and partner. He hated it, and Erin hated that part of it, too.

For us, this conversation was very often one about what would help both of us feel less stressed during this stressful period. For Erin, it was moving home to be closer to family, where she could have more help and support while Stephen was gone most of the day. For Stephen, it was being outdoors, which helped him feel some sense of adventure and calm in the midst of his daily drudgery. Unfortunately Erin's mom and the mountains were not even a little bit close to each other. At the end of the day, we had incompatible values.

There were many discussions about it, resulting in a lot of hurt and an abundance of dead ends. Clearly someone would have to sacrifice, to give in. As much as neither one wanted to be the person who had to give up our wants, even more we didn't want to be the person who asked their partner to give up something of who they were. Erin wanted Stephen to get to live the life he had always wanted and to have the kind of family life he had always dreamed of in the mountains. Stephen did not want to keep Erin from her mom, who really did help, and their kids from a grandmother who loved them completely. Both sounded like terrible, awful options.

In all honesty we tried out all the options (sometimes twice): we moved to the mountains for Stephen's PhD fellowship. After the fellowship was completed, we moved back to Erin's mom (actually lived in her house with two little kids for a time!). After that, we moved back to the mountains for a job. We were trying to find the balance we both wanted, but we frequently felt like the other's values were a threat to our personal happiness. We wish we could say that ultimately there's always a perfect solution to the conflict, yet that very rarely happens.

What we had to do was learn how to engage in the conflict and not assume the other's worst or allow our fear to cloud the conversation. The point of this conflict is not to come to perfect agreement— although if you can, that's great! The point is to begin to get comfortable having sometimes difficult and often uncomfortable conversations, to learn to remain connected and aligned even in disagreement. How? By hearing each other out, by not taking someone's change in values personally, by knowing the decisions you make as a couple will sometimes cost each other, and by being open to the ongoing nature of this conversation. The conflict many times is left unresolved, but what is resolved is a couple's commitment to choose to connect in the difference rather than fight because of the difference.

For us, no matter what decision we made, mountains or close to

Erin's mom, one of us did not get what they wanted. However, we did want to stay connected and in alignment, so these decisions were made with mutual consent and awareness of the costs and benefits to each other. We agreed to connect in the conflict.

CONFLICT TO CONNECTION: MICHELLE AND CHRISSA'S SESSION

Michelle and Chrissa come into the session looking tense and concerned. They are only a month or so out from Chrissa's needing to make a final decision about how she is going to handle her job, and neither of them feel like they can make a decision the other would be happy about.

ERIN: So, Michelle and Chrissa, it sounds like you are stuck when it comes to this conversation?

MICHELLE: I wouldn't call it a conversation. It feels like a dead-end argument that doesn't have a nice, tidy resolution.

CHRISSA: Well, it's a dead end because there is only one satisfactory outcome, which is my going back to work and not messing up the grand plan.

MICHELLE: Chrissa, I get that you are having a hard time going back to work. I had a hard time going back, too. It's not like I don't understand. I also feel like we have been here before. You are good at your job. You contribute a lot to this family financially because you have your job. Part of taking care of the kids is not only being with them but giving them a secure future. This is what we have talked about for years. There is a plan. A plan you helped formulate and agreed to. You are acting like I am someone making you go along with the goals and vision *we* set for our family.

ERIN: Michelle, would it be fair to say that you are surprised by Chrissa's stance on going back to work, or actually not wanting to go back?

MICHELLE: I am not surprised that she brought up the question about not going. I am surprised that she seems so serious about it.

This question is asked to bring Michelle into the process of intentional expressing. The goal is to draw her into attuning to her emotional world, which can inform why there is so much energy and intensity around the conflict.

STEPHEN: Chrissa, are you at all surprised by how serious you feel about it?

CHRISSA: Yes, absolutely. I think that is what I have also been trying to say to Michelle. She keeps saying, "You've been here before," but I haven't. That is why this feels so strange and scary. I have not felt this strongly about being with the kids and not wanting to work.

STEPHEN: Michelle, did you know that Chrissa is as surprised as you are about how she is feeling about going back to work?

MICHELLE: I've heard her say it.

Chrissa is upset that Michelle is not believing her experience. Michelle is not able to access intentional listening because she is tuning Chrissa out.

ERIN: Michelle, do you know what feels so surprising to you about Chrissa's feeling like she wants a change?

MICHELLE: I don't know if I really know. Honestly, I think it just makes me feel let down.

ERIN: How so?

MICHELLE: Well, I think one of the things I have loved about Chrissa is that we have been working moms who have had some success in our work and in building a home. I feel proud of us and how we have planned for the future and planned to take care of each other and our kids. It feels good to feel like we are partners in this plan.

Here in Michelle's attuning to her feeling let down, she also reflects on the story that informs her feeling let down. This is how intentional expressing connects step 1, attune, with step 3, reflect.

ERIN: So for you it's not about the logistics of the plan entirely. I'm sure there is some part of you that feels the plan is a good one and does matter, but it's about how the plan says something special about your relationship with Chrissa?

MICHELLE: Yeah, I think she is special, and I think what we are doing is special. Also, my parents worked so hard to provide opportunity for me, and it is something I am proud of them for. I think I see Chrissa and me as carrying on that legacy of working hard together as a couple to give our kids opportunity.

Michelle shares (step 4 of intentional expressing) how the emotions she has attuned to connect to an important story that shapes how she sees the conflict.

STEPHEN: Chrissa, did you know that when Michelle is making a big deal about the plan that it has this kind of deep meaning to her?

CHRISSA: No, I didn't. She is eternally practical, so I am a little surprised there is more to it than just numbers and "what makes sense." She also keeps saying I'm just being emotional, which puts me on the defensive right off the bat. I am saying I feel or believe something and she is basically telling me "No you aren't."

MICHELLE: Well, I do say that you are making emotional decisions, and I get how my saying that can make it sound like I am making a better, nonemotional decision.

Michelle has suspended her defensiveness (step 2) and demonstrated intentional listening.

CHRISSA: I admit I do make decisions with my emotions first, and sometimes that causes problems, but also I very rarely regret the decisions I make. When I believe something or sense something needs to happen, I do it.

STEPHEN: I wonder if you both have noticed that the stuck conversation you started out talking about in the session has shifted a little.

CHRISSA: I can feel that.

MICHELLE: I feel it, too.

STEPHEN: Yeah. If you notice, neither of you has made a decision about what you want to do or even expressed feeling like you know what you need to do. What has happened is you have seen a little deeper below the surface of the conflict.

Today you heard something about the heart of the matter for each other. Chrissa, you're pretty surprised that you feel so strongly. This is not what you thought would happen, but it has, and this helps you know something important is coming up for you. Also, you don't want to be told you don't know what you are doing or that your experience is some harebrained idea motivated by an emotional moment. You want to be taken seriously. Does that sound right?

CHRISSA: Yes.

STEPHEN: Michelle, you were able to realize that the plan means something very special to you, that it's all about what it means about your relationship with Chrissa. The plan is a symbol for how you feel about Chrissa and for what you feel proud about in terms of your relationship and your family. Sound about right?

MICHELLE: That feels so true.

These questions/statements are summative and are meant to help the couple practice intentional listening by believing their partner's experience. By taking each other seriously and listening to the story informing the emotion in the conflict, the conversation moves from a triggered fight to a connective attachment-making interaction.

ERIN: I wonder if you both can hear that those old stereotypes or stuck ways of seeing each other are different here? Chrissa, you said that sometimes Michelle can feel a bit robotic, but her rationale for how she feels is based on something very relational. Michelle, you can characterize Chrissa as emotional and irrational, but she is making a very rational argument. She is saying, "Something feels different. I have never been here before, and I should pay attention to this." This line of thinking seems rational to me. Can you see how part of the conversation about getting unstuck is getting unstuck from some of your typical ways of characterizing each other?

CHRISSA: I totally get that. Michelle, I didn't see that your position is rooted in what you think and how you feel about our relationship. I have totally missed that.

MICHELLE: I can see it, too, Chrissa. You are thinking about your position and not just being emotional. You are experiencing something that feels different and trying to figure it out. I have been saying you are just experiencing the same thing as last time, and that has kept you in a box.

This is the couple repairing (step 4 of intentional listening). They are hold-ing themselves accountable for their actions, forgiving each other, and moving toward different action.

STEPHEN: Chrissa, I am hearing that you don't want to be brushed off by Michelle. Michelle, I hear you saying you don't want to be mischaracterized by Chrissa.

MICHELLE: Yeah, I care about the plan practically, but it also rep-resents a beautiful part of my relationship with Chrissa that I would be sad to see change.

CHRISSA: Yes, I don't like the feeling of being brushed aside be-cause I am being mischaracterized as emotional. I feel like Mi-chelle gets that now, but I also am not sure what we should do or what decision we need to make.

ERIN: True, but I do think you have found some common ground in terms of what you value. Michelle, you said that you value your relationship with Chrissa and are proud of what you have created together. Chrissa, do you feel similar?

CHRISSA: One hundred percent.

ERIN: So I wonder if that can be a guiding principle for you as you try and figure out what you want to do practically. What deci-sion can help you both continue to recognize the value you have of being proud of what you have created as a couple? Is it stick-ing to the plan? Is it developing a new plan that makes you just as proud? Is it a hybrid of the two? What you are talking about is how you want to reflect your shared values and how you can support each other even if there are some differences between the two of you in what that might look like.

MICHELLE: So what you are saying is the manner in which we have the conversation and the spirit of the conversation need to be differ-ent, and this will help us be connected in whatever the outcome is?

ERIN: Exactly.

CHRISSA: I see how that can work.

MICHELLE: Me, too.

We continued to meet with Michelle and Chrissa to help them navigate this conflict (and a few others as they arose), and ultimately Chrissa did decide to stay home. They both decided they could make some serious spending cuts and figure out the finances. If down the road Chrissa did ultimately change her mind or if they needed her to get another job, she always could. It was Chrissa who pointed out that staying home from work was somewhat reversible, but if she went back to work and regretted it, she could never have this time with their kids at this stage back. Once they both felt heard and acknowledged, the decision no longer felt so charged and full of potential resentment. Both were willing to have it not go their way if that's what they both decided ended up being best for their family.

BUT HOW CAN I ACTUALLY SAY ANY OF THIS TO MY PARTNER? SAMPLE SCRIPTS

Values change, and that has an impact on decision-making. Parenting partners have to learn how to talk about changing values in a way that brings connection. Sometimes one of the most challenging things about this conflict is breaking the ice and letting your partner know there has been a change in your values. Here are some scripts that can help the conversation begin.

Intentional Expressing—Either Partner Can Use These Scripts

"There is something I have been feeling. I honestly don't know what it means or if it means anything at all, but I do know it is important and I want to share it with you. I know we said ____, but that isn't sitting right with me at this point. Again, I don't know exactly why, but I was hoping we could talk more about it."

"I feel like you've been trying to tell me something is shifting in you about moving closer to your family. I even think you have tried to talk to me about it, but I don't think I've let you say what you mean. I've been scared to listen, but I want to know you even when it scares me. Can I have another chance?"

"You know how much I love a plan, but I think this current plan for school for the kids isn't working. I want to discuss changing things up, but I worry you are going to hear me say I want everything to be different or just start going around changing everything. Please do not start changing everything! I just want you to hear me, to sit beside me, to be slow and take the real time to talk about this. NO ACTION YET, please."

"I have been looking at our kids and our life and I am not sure we are any longer living a life aligned with our values. I think somewhere along the way we stopped questioning and just kept doing the next thing. But I am not sure I recognize us anymore. I know this is a huge topic. I am not trying to say I'm unhappy, I'm not, but I want us to pause and be intentional about who we are and what we're doing here. Is this something you are willing to talk about?"

QUESTIONS FOR REFLECTION

1. Do I as an individual have established values? Does my partner? Do we as a couple? As a family?

2. Do you and your partner have any decisions that need to be made that feel charged? What are they? What does the decision itself mean to each of you? Are you aware of any deeper meanings for each of you in the decision?

3. What fears do you have thinking about your partner's changing their values? What fears do you have about changing your own?

4. Have you had a conversation about your values before? What were the themes that emerged? Or if you haven't, looking back on it over time, can you see any themes that may have been coming up or may need to emerge now?

5. Do you feel like you have been avoiding this conflict? Is there anything about this chapter that resonated with you? Did it stir any stories about how your and your partner's childhoods may have taught you conflicting values (about the value of money, family, hard work, and time)? Why might those feelings and memories be coming up now in the season of life and the stage of parenting you are currently in?

CHAPTER 13

The "Sex Life? What Sex Life?" Conflict

Alyson and William have been together five years and have a three-year-old, Hank, and a two-year-old, Emmie. They work full time—Alyson from home and William full time at the office. If you asked them, they would say the three years since having kids have been the hardest in their entire relationship. They both love their kids, no question, and know they love each other, but their relationship is feeling strained at the moment. Mostly what they feel is disconnected and chronically irritated with the other. They seem to bicker nonstop. William has noticed that he doesn't try to talk with Alyson and ask her about her day anymore. His feeling is that somehow they would end up fighting about something and spend the rest of the night in separate corners silently seething. So rather than being angry, he figures it is best to minimize his interactions with Alyson. Alyson is aware that she has also pulled back from interacting with William, and while she is grateful to not end her day fighting, it feels just as terrible to end the day isolated in her own home.

One of the biggest areas where Alyson and William feel the distance in their relationship is their sex life. They feel embarrassed to say it, but they rarely have sex, and in a lot of ways the desire has diminished since having kids. When the desire is present, it feels awkward to even approach each other. They are barely talking about any aspect of their lives outside of what needs to be done with the kids, and it feels like a big jump to go from this state of disconnection to getting intimate with each other.

It wasn't always like this, though. Sex used to be a way for them to feel connected, and they would both agree that they liked their sex life before kids. Alyson always had a higher sex drive, and for William it has been surprising to see it diminish so significantly postpartum. In the past, it didn't take much romancing or foreplay to get Alyson in the mood, and now any time William brings up sex, Alyson reacts like he has made some offensive comment. So he hesitates to initiate sex, and since Alyson is not initiating, this important part of how they used to connect has all but vanished. The last time William tried to initiate sex, this is how the interaction went:

ALYSON: Don't forget we have dinner with the Roberts this Saturday.

WILLIAM: I didn't forget. I have the babysitter lined up. I was thinking I could see if the kids could stay over at my mom's house so we could have the whole night and sleep in. Maybe we could even stay at a hotel for a different and fun change.

ALYSON: Your mom just watched the kids, and that seems unnecessary.

WILLIAM: Yes, I know it is unnecessary, but it could also be nice. I think a whole night out could be great for you, for us. A break from the kids and home could be good. You could get out of the house, and we could relax in a bed we don't have to worry about making in the morning.

ALYSON: You mean maybe the reason we aren't having much sex is because I am stressed about making the bed in the morning?

WILLIAM: Much sex? That's generous. And no, I didn't mean that we aren't having sex because of the bed. I just thought it would be nice to have a change of scenery and relax together.

ALYSON: Sure. A change of scenery and a night to relax together would suddenly make all of our problems melt away.

WILLIAM: That's not what I meant.

The content changes for them, but the broader theme remains the same. William is trying to do something to change the environment, which he feels is better than doing nothing. Alyson resents William's efforts because it feels like he is saying, "We aren't having sex because there is something wrong with *you*." So while his intent is to try to move toward Alyson, instead he hurts her feelings.

So many of the fundamentals they knew about their sex life—how they felt in their own bodies; what felt good, what didn't; what aroused them, what turned them off—are different for both of them postpartum. In the three years since they had their kids, they have not reflected on any of these things on their own, and certainly not as a couple. They have been initiating sex in the same old ways they did before they had kids, expecting things to work somewhat the same, but almost nothing about their life is the same as it was before. It stands to reason that sex would and should be addressed in this new season of life, but how can they go about this in a healthy and healing way?

WHY YOU NEED THIS CONFLICT

Sex is vulnerable, intimate, and bonds partners together. There is a circular reality that when there is an emotional, psychological, and spiritual closeness, partners feel a desire to express this through sex. Discussing sex after kids is necessary because sex is an aspect of a relationship that reflects and fosters connection. As we said throughout the book, parenting changes everything, and sex is definitely included. Here are some of the ways sex is impacted by parenting:

- The hormone changes that take place in pregnancy, birth, and postpartum significantly impact the birthing partner's physiology and mood—all of which impact libido. Birthing partners might also feel less secure in their bodies postpartum and not want to be vulnerable by having sex.
- Stress levels increase, which in turn can decrease libido.
- Time is different for parenting partners; namely, there is so little. This loss of time due to caregiving responsibilities impacts a couple's sexual routines. If a couple typically had sex in the evening or morning, these times are now occupied by nighttime routines and early wake-up times.
- The non-birthing partner may have a critical attitude toward their birthing partner's body postpartum, and this may diminish their partner's feeling of safety in being bodily vulnerable by having sex.
- Physical exhaustion is a reality of parenting. Being tired influences desire for sex.

Sex is already a complicated and vulnerable conversation without the overlay of all the ways parenting impacts sex, so it makes sense that talking about sex as parents can feel overwhelming. But this conflict has to be had for parenting partners to stay connected. A healthy sex life requires a healthy couple relationship. A healthy couple relationship requires vulnerability. Vulnerability with your partner is foundational to being able to address sex. That's why it's key for parenting partners to have had at least some of the previous conflicts in this book before addressing this conflict—you are not going to have the intimacy that comes with healthy sex if you do not feel seen and known and understood in at least some of these other areas.

A healthy sex life takes work, though, and very often parenting partners are too tired to tackle the necessary work and it takes a back seat in the relationship. Like the way, way back seat of a minivan kind of back seat. But the work is worth it. The connection and the intimacy gained are often the very fuel we need as individuals, partners, and parents to have a more fulfilled life as a whole.

We acknowledge pursuing sexual health in your relationship involves vulnerability. You have to be vulnerable to wonder, "What would I like sex to look like for us in this new stage of life? What would that look like and feel like?" These are vulnerable things to take the time to ask yourself and even more vulnerable to engage in this conversation with your partner. But addressing these sometimes awkward and/or intimate questions is exactly what moving toward a healthy sex life as parenting partners looks like.

Alyson and William want to feel connected. They have experienced and are experiencing all the changes that come to a sex life post-kids, but they have not talked about any of them. They are afraid that maybe things have changed because their relationship is not as strong. Rather than moving toward each other with curiosity and openness, this fear has caused them to withdraw.

HOW THIS CONFLICT GOES WRONG

Plainly said, this conflict tends to get quite personal very quickly. Intense emotions crop up: feeling unwanted, unattractive, used, taken for granted, anxious, and insecure. We have heard just about every version of this and more, and honestly, we have felt some of these things ourselves.

Like many couples, we experienced the drastic change parenting brings to a parent's sex life. The primary changes involved the lack of time and the deep weariness we both felt. At nighttime, we might both tackle putting the kids to sleep and have grand plans of hanging out afterward that might lead to sex. Then before we knew it, we both had fallen asleep with the kids. Night after night this slowly began to erode the time we had to be together, and since nighttime had been when we typically had sex before kids, sex also slowly disappeared.

As we noticed the infrequency of sex, we didn't really have the mental or physical energy to think creatively about making any adjustments to when and how we had sex. As time went on, the overwhelm of parenting and the general feeling of being disconnected grew for all the reasons it typically does in a parenting partner relationship: mental load, parenting differences, different ways of coping with stress, values changing, and so forth. Couple this feeling of disconnection with fatigue and things began to feel personal. Questions like "Is something wrong between us or with me? Why won't you pursue me anymore? Why do you brush me off when I try to initiate sex?" began to take a toll on our relationship. We began to wonder if the sex life was bad because we didn't feel connected, or if we felt disconnected because our sex life left a lot to be desired. Just like Alyson and William, we began to shy away from each other and from talking about sex because it all felt too difficult to understand and overcome.

For many parents, much of the week is spent feeling misaligned as a couple. So just because it happens to be date night, doesn't mean the connection required for intimacy just shows up. We may want that connection and intimacy to magically appear, but a lot of the time, it doesn't. And the longer it doesn't, the more complicated and hurtful the lack of intimacy is.

CONFLICT TO CONNECTION:
WILLIAM AND ALYSON'S SESSION

William and Alyson come into the session feeling nervous and laughing awkwardly together. They seem to be on edge, and then William relays the story about the interaction he had with Alyson about sex. Alyson calms a bit and gets quiet.

> WILLIAM: I just feel fed up with the whole thing. Alyson sends mixed messages. She says that we never have time together to connect and that she needs a break and so I try and do something to show I'm listening, that I'm thinking about her. Then she goes and says, "That's unnecessary . . . all you want to do is have sex." It makes absolutely no sense.
>
> STEPHEN: Alyson? What was your experience of the fight?
>
> ALYSON: I am fed up, too. I'm fed up with William swooping in with some grand gesture to show me he's listening when nothing changes in the day-to-day. So, yeah, we can have a great weekend, and then Monday rolls around and he's not home, I'm working, I'm parenting, I'm left to do everything and he's confused why I'm not thrilled he planned a night away.

It is clear that the couple is triggered. Step 1, assess, of intentional expressing and listening is meant to help the couple realize they are being triggered and take this as a cue to shift directions in the conversation. Stephen's next question is meant to help the couple make this shift.

> STEPHEN: I can hear the energy behind what you both are saying. This is not where either of you want to be, and in some ways, it feels like you both think the other is being unreasonable. Would that be true?

ALYSON: Yes. I don't understand how William can be surprised by my response to him. It almost feels like he is not living the same life I am on a weekly basis.

WILLIAM: I am living the same life Alyson is, and I don't get why she wants to hunker down in all the bad stuff and wallow in it. We have to try and find something positive to change the feeling of the relationship. It feels like she wants to be stuck, and that makes me want to scream.

ALYSON: I don't want to stay stuck here! But we *are* stuck here, and just having a positive attitude and doing something fun don't change how lonely, missed, and absolutely exhausted I feel. Maybe before we had kids we could just do something exciting and have some great sex and things felt better, but this is not like that. You seem so clueless, and it's been this way since we had the kids. I've been withering for three years, and you want to go out for a night, have fun, have sex, and call it a fix for what is going on between us? It isn't that simple, William. How can you not understand that?

William and Alyson both have shifted toward attuning to the emotions they are feeling related to the conflict.

ERIN: Alyson, you used a powerful word: *withering.* William, what do you hear Alyson saying when she uses that word?

WILLIAM: It sounds scary to me. It is a strong word, and I'm not understanding what Alyson means when she uses it. I don't see how our life is that bad or awful. We have everything we need. Our kids are healthy, and we are stable.

There is a hint of defensiveness in William's voice. In order for him to intentionally listen to Alyson, he will need to suspend his defensiveness and believe the experience she is describing (steps 2 and 3 of intentional listening).

ERIN: It seems like this is what you are talking about, Alyson, correct? You feel like you are screaming something right in William's face and he doesn't seem to be hearing you.

ALYSON: Yes. I have said it over and over.

ERIN: When you say *withering*, Alyson, what do you mean?

ALYSON: I don't even know how to explain it. I love our kids. I love everything about them, but they have sapped me of my energy. I thought pregnancy was tough and uncomfortable the first time, and it almost felt like the second time I began where I left off the first time. Physically, I didn't think I could go one more day pregnant. I began breastfeeding but realized quickly that this was not going to be good for my mental health. Sleep has been a roller coaster. Work has felt like a grind, and I wake up going through the day in a haze of exhaustion and overwhelm. I don't feel like myself anymore. I am withering away.

STEPHEN: Alyson, that is such a vulnerable and honest description. William, have you heard Alyson say things like this before?

WILLIAM: Yes, but I am realizing I really have not been listening.

STEPHEN: What do you mean?

WILLIAM: I think I have been a bit consumed with what having the twins has felt like for me and not looked up to see what is happening with Alyson.

William is suspending his defensiveness, believing Alyson's experience, and this allows him to be open to repair (step 4) with her.

ERIN: William, you used the phrase *looked up*. Where have you been looking?

WILLIAM: Well, just like Alyson said, having the kids has turned our life upside down. I remember we wanted kids, but we weren't planning on having them when we did. It was a bit of a surprise. We had been together for only two years, and it felt like we were both just starting out. Our work was picking up, we were figuring out how to be a committed couple, we were having adventures together. Honestly, life was great. We really enjoyed each other.

Here William is attuning to the emotions that are present for him as he reflects on the story of having kids sooner than expected.

STEPHEN: Was part of this enjoying each other having the kind of sex life you wanted?

WILLIAM: Absolutely. It was just a close, connected, fun, and exciting time in life. Then we found out we were pregnant. Like I said, we were not disappointed. We wanted kids, but it felt like it rushed things or sped things up. It felt like life got serious quick, and some of what we had together got overshadowed by, I don't know, the craziness that was about to happen.

STEPHEN: Alyson, have you ever heard William talk about all of this?

ALYSON: I think I knew it might have felt overwhelming, but maybe that is only because I was feeling some of those things as well. I haven't heard William say much about how he felt about finding out we were having kids.

William is sharing (step 4), and this is allowing Alyson to hear some of the emotions behind his experience. Intentional expressing allows partners to hear the deeper story.

STEPHEN: I think it's interesting as well that William hasn't even made it to the act of having the kids yet. His anxiety started much earlier. William, what happened for you when you thought about the "craziness that was about to happen"?

WILLIAM: Well, I froze. I mean, I didn't stop doing things, but I just felt shocked and then started thinking about everything that I needed to do to get ready for the kids. I started looking at the tasks in front of me.

ERIN: Would you say you put your head down and started moving?

WILLIAM: Yeah. I mean, I started pressing hard at work to try and increase my earnings. I started organizing our life insurance policies. I drilled down on a plan for our savings strategy. I started working out more because I wasn't the healthiest guy and my dad had a heart attack when he was young and I didn't want that to happen and impact Alyson and the kids. I was trying to get myself together because I didn't feel ready. I felt a little immature and unprepared.

STEPHEN: It seems that this is where the pattern of Alyson screaming something and your not hearing it might have started. In the process of your putting your head down for all good reasons, you stopped looking up to see or hear about Alyson's experience.

WILLIAM: I hate to admit it, but I think that is true. Alyson, does that feel true to you?

ALYSON: Yes, it does.

WILLIAM: I feel embarrassed that you have felt like you are withering and I am just standing by not doing anything. I don't know why I feel like I am hearing you say this for the first time, but that felt powerful to hear. When I am able to step back and take a breath, I know that Alyson is not trying to make things hard. She is saying something is going on.

This is a comment that reflects repair (step 4 in intentional listening). He is taking accountability for how his actions have impacted Alyson.

STEPHEN: Alyson, how do you hear what William is saying?

ALYSON: It did feel different to me. I think for the first time in a long time William didn't defend what happened; he just said, "Yeah, that happened." It helps me feel validated. I can feel my insides taking a bit of a sigh of relief. Like, I'm not making this up. This is real.

Alyson is describing what it felt like to have William believe her experience (step 3 of intentional listening).

ERIN: I wonder, Alyson, if you also feel a bit more understanding toward William?

ALYSON: Honestly, I was surprised to hear him say how he felt about finding out about the kids. In a strange way, it feels better to know that he was not paying attention to me because he was paying so much attention to our family, and I am included in that. It still hurts, but it is nice to know he cares so much.

This is a repair statement as well from Alyson. She is forgiving William and expressing understanding for his actions and still acknowledging they hurt her.

WILLIAM: Alyson, I do care. I also get that I have absolutely missed what you have been screaming, and that has hurt you.

ERIN: William, can you see how that hurt can impact how she feels about sex?

WILLIAM: I think so. If she is not feeling close to me and feels like I am ignoring her, it would be hard to want to have sex. That makes sense to me.

ALYSON: Yeah, and why one nice gesture of a hotel doesn't fix my not feeling understood?

WILLIAM: I get it.

ALYSON: I do want to feel close to you, William, and have sex. We did have a great sex life before the kids, and I want to get back to that, too. I don't want you to think that I don't want to have sex.

STEPHEN: So maybe one of the keys to your sex life is for you to feel connected in the chaos of parenting, and, Alyson, for you to feel that William is looking at you rather than looking down?

ALYSON: Yes, that would feel so good.

WILLIAM: I want that, too, Alyson.

BUT HOW CAN I ACTUALLY SAY ANY OF THIS TO MY PARTNER? SAMPLE SCRIPTS

Talking about sex is something every parenting couple should do, with the understanding that the way things were is not the way they are now. Couples have to be flexible and creative in how they navigate their sex life as parents. Also, if couples already feel disconnected due to parenting stress or feeling dismissed, then talking about sex will be more complicated. Here are some scripts to help you and your partner talk about sex and understand how it has changed for you as you parent.

Intentional Expressing for Both Partners

"I know that our sex life has changed a lot since having kids, and it feels like such a challenging topic to even talk about. I do want to be able to talk about it with you and to see if we can understand how to reconnect sexually."

"Can we talk about talking about sex? I am not trying to bring up sex and move in that direction right now. I do notice that when sex comes up, it seems to create a lot of tension and miscommunication. Do you know what is happening for you when we discuss sex?"

"I am wondering if you are feeling a little distant or disconnected? I know that when we don't have sex, that usually means that we are not feeling as close as we want. Is there something going on that I am missing?"

"You are really important to me, and so is our relationship. I feel like we are not connecting, and it seems that our communication is struggling. Also, it feels like since we are not feeling connected, we are not having sex, either. Can we talk about it or try and get some outside help to help us talk about it?"

QUESTIONS FOR REFLECTION

1. Have you talked with a doctor to rule out physical and psychological needs that need medical attention and might be impacting your sex life?

2. Does sex feel different for you and your partner now that you have a child? If so, can you be very clear and explicit about what the changes are as you see them? Just remember to be specific and not to throw blame, but just to share your experience.

3. Is there anything that your body may have stored and is holding on to from past significant events that is preventing you from being intimate? This could be related to past abuse, past pregnancies, past illness, and so forth.

4. How do you want your sex life to look and feel? Have you shared your hopes with your partner? Do you know what your partner wants your sex life to feel like now after kids?

5. Do you feel like you have been avoiding this conflict? Is there anything about this chapter that resonated with you?

CHAPTER 14

The "I Hate Your Family" Conflict

DAN AND VANESSA have been together for five years. Their daughter, Isabella, is eighteen months old. Becoming parents has mostly been a great experience, but it has stirred up the hornet's nest that is Vanessa's relationship with her mother-in-law, Angela.

Vanessa and Angela have had a difficult relationship from what seemed like the very first time they met. Vanessa's own parents divorced when she was young, and she and her sister lived with their mom and saw their dad very little. Dan's parents are married, but Dan has always joked that it's just because his dad has learned how to tune his mom out. Dan has told Vanessa some version of the same thing throughout their relationship when Angela has said hurtful things to Vanessa or to Dan. They will leave an event where Vanessa has lashed out, and Dan will say, "Angela was just being Angela," which Vanessa feels is just a way to downplay how unkind she is. Vanessa will say to Dan, "I hate that you let her talk to you that way. She has no business telling you what you should be doing at work or how you should be doing it." Dan usually replies with some version of "It really doesn't bother me. She doesn't know what she's talking about. I just let it go in one ear and out the other. You should, too."

The first time Angela said something directly to Vanessa, it was a passing comment about how Vanessa should consider a new vocation that might be more "family friendly." Vanessa said very calmly, "I like my job. It's important to me. I am not interested in looking for a different one." Tension immediately filled the house, and shortly afterward, Vanessa asked Dan if they could leave. They did, but these kinds of interactions crop up in some form or fashion each time they are around Angela, and the conversation between Dan and Vanessa after the event never seems to improve.

If it were up to Vanessa, she and Dan would see Angela very little. According to Dan, out of respect for Vanessa, they already see his parents less than the rest of his siblings do. Dan sees it as disrespectful to his own family that Vanessa wants nothing to do with his parents when they know Vanessa's own mother is over all the time. He likes his mother-in-law, but feels they are sending mixed signals to his parents. The arrival of Isabella only intensified the already strained dynamics between Vanessa and Angela, and as a result between Dan and Vanessa.

Vanessa feels like Angela is judging her for every decision she makes as a parent, and Dan is growing tired of listening to Vanessa's frustration about that, because he feels like his mom hasn't said a word about their parenting and he thinks Vanessa is assuming the worst. Vanessa points out to Dan that Angela has a lot to say about everyone's parenting. Angela isn't quiet about talking about this or that cousin who did something she deems outrageous: "They named their baby a nickname and not a real name!" She'll even issue a diatribe at dinner about a mother she saw at the supermarket. "She was looking at her phone the entire time she shopped. I feel so sad for that woman's children." Vanessa's response to this statement was: "For all we know, that woman may have been checking her grocery list," to which Dan shot Vanessa a dirty look. He really wishes Vanessa would tune Angela out. Vanessa doesn't feel it's a stretch to say Angela is also judging her as a mom and has no doubt she is the topic of her mother-in-law's conversations with her lady friends all too often. Vanessa wonders just what kinds of things Angela says about Dan and her when they aren't around. As anxious as Vanessa was when she was forced to be around Angela before having Isabella, now she really doesn't want Angela's negativity around Isabella and she certainly isn't happy to be the recipient of Angela's snide comments and criticism.

Tension between Dan and Vanessa reached a breaking point after a recent birthday party at Dan's sister's house. Vanessa steered clear of Angela and made sure to feed Isabella in a different room because feeding Isabella is one of the sticking points where she feels like Angela is judging her. She was proud of her and Dan for working out a plan and holding to it, but when they got into the car to leave, the conversation turned south.

VANESSA: I saw you talking to your mom for a while. What were you two talking about?

DAN: Oh, yeah, it was fine. She asked what the plan was for day care. I was just telling her what we have been talking about.

VANESSA: You can't be serious, Dan. She is toxic! She is going to use this against me, against us.

DAN: What are you talking about? I hate when you say that. What does *toxic* even *mean* when you are talking about a human? The conversation was harmless. She was just letting me know she was available to watch her a few days a week for us if we wanted. Don't worry—I know how you feel about her and we obviously won't do that.

VANESSA: I cannot believe you talked with her about this.

DAN: What was I supposed to say? "I'm sorry, Mom, Vanessa wouldn't want me to talk with you about our child." That would have been even worse. Also, we never talked about not talking to her about day care. I didn't say anything that would upset you. This shouldn't be a problem.

VANESSA: The problem is that you don't see this is a problem!

DAN: The problem is that you are making this a problem!

Dan admits that Angela does and will say hurtful things, but he has learned to tune them out as his dad advised: "Grow a thick skin." He wants Vanessa to be happy, but he doesn't want that to mean he doesn't get to be around his family anymore. More and more he feels like Vanessa is asking him to choose his family or her, which angers and upsets him. He knows he is growing angry about the dynamic because he cannot tolerate hearing Vanessa bring up his mother without having a big reaction. He feels like Vanessa tries to make even little things into big things. And he is feeling more and more exhausted by this steady stream of her finding a new reason to hate his mom. Most likely unbeknownst to Dan, this dynamic can leave him feeling controlled by Vanessa's feelings about his mom. He is reacting strongly to feeling controlled, and this reaction negatively impacts his communication with Vanessa.

Vanessa, although most likely outside of her awareness, is also feeling controlled. When she tries to address how Angela talks to her, Dan tells her to ignore Angela, not to make a big deal about it or take it personally. Vanessa doesn't think she can talk with Dan about her feelings concerning Angela and that she is required to approach the relationship like Dan. This feels dismissive and controlling. Vanessa is getting from Dan what he learned he had to do to get along with his mom—any attempt at a conversation is viewed as a confrontation, and hoping to be heard is futile.

WHY YOU NEED THIS CONFLICT
···

So, what exactly is a toxic relationship anyway? Well, the short answer to this is that it is one in which you do not trust the other person and in which you do not feel able to relax in their presence. You often do not feel like your wants and needs will be respected. These relational dynamics are generally driven by the "toxic person" repeatedly ignoring boundaries that have been set or requested due to their belief or desire to have their own needs met above others or their inability to see the importance of others' needs. Extended family, in-laws, our own parents, our partner's close friend—the who matters less than the wear and tear on a couple (and the entire family) when the couple disagrees on the impact that person has on their family or ways to deal with it.

We intentionally used Dan and Angela's relatively mild story here because very often it is these seemingly insignificant interactions that pile up and can break a couple down. Take, for example, a sister-in-law who offers unwanted feedback on very sensitive topics to you like how to feed your baby, how long your baby should be sleeping, or what you should do about child care "since you insist you have to go back." It can be your own mother repeatedly telling you "breast is best" when you have told her over and over it was not a healthy decision for you anymore. When you try to tell your partner about these examples, your partner can miss the importance of them, because, after all, they are not some glaring abuse or trauma. More often than not, couples agree about the major things, but these "minor" things can erode a relationship.

You need this conflict because if you or your partner feels belittled, intimidated, or dismissed, or as though your opinion is not taken into consideration, this must be addressed and handled in a healthy manner or it will lead to resentment and disconnection.

Dan and Vanessa need this conflict about Angela so they can come to consensus about how to move forward in interacting with her. They need to talk about how to be in relationship with Angela, but also they need to talk about engaging in this conflict. Dan genuinely believes any conflict is pointless and will produce a hurtful outcome. If you consider his context and the messages he received about conflict, it's easy to see how he came to that conclusion. Vanessa is not Angela, though, and Vanessa needs Dan to know that conflict with her is not pointless and does not have to lead to stuck communication. It is the very avoidance of this conflict that is leading to a hurtful outcome.

HOW THIS CONFLICT GOES WRONG

Merging families is a big deal, and each new stage in the couple relationship (like becoming parents) very often yields new areas that need attention in the larger extended family system. As discussed in chapter 10, what emerges varies widely, but often things that just used to irritate you (for example, a family member who talks openly about your weight each time they see you, or a cousin who drinks too much at every family occasion) turn into situations in which you as a couple need a game plan about how to approach the situation now that you have a baby or kids to take into consideration.

We often discuss toxic relationships with couples. Sometimes the situation is very clear, and the couple agrees without question that boundaries are needed and what those will be. Sometimes the situation is murky and boundaries are not so easy to agree on. This is often the biggest, most damaging place this conflict goes wrong because what ends up happening is one partner feels they must prove to their own partner that the person in question feels unsafe, and the situation is maddening and damaging. Meanwhile, the other partner feels like they are being asked to turn their back on someone who is important to them, even if that person is difficult to be around.

Sometimes couples feel they cannot be around a former friend or family member any longer and need, for the sake of their family, to cut that person off completely. We have been here, and it is a very painful outcome and not one that we nor anyone we have ever spoken to took lightly. Since that is a very serious and unwanted outcome for a relationship, that is what is very often feared and what a partner can become so reactive about. When partners bring up a concern about a toxic relationship, they usually do not know exactly what they are looking for beyond an expression from their partner that they believe them and will stand with them. When that is not present immediately (or to the extent they were looking for), this conflict gets worse and fast.

When partners feel they have to prove that someone makes them feel unsafe, they can and often do hyperfocus on that person, pointing out each and every last thing that person did at any given moment (that is what nervous systems do to stay safe when threatened!). For the partner who does not feel the threat, or at least not in the same way, their partner's hyperfocus can actually generate hypoarousal in their nervous system: "No, no, no, hold on here. Let's relax and move on." This conflict goes wrong because they keep going further and further to an extreme to try to make their partner see their place of fear. The longer the threatened partner feels unsafe and unheeded, the more it makes them distrust their partner. What most partners are looking for when there is a toxic relationship is fairly simple. (Notice we said simple, not easy.) Most often what a partner wants is:

1. To be believed that what they are feeling and sensing is real to them. It does not have to be real to both partners for it to be real to one of them.

2. Clear boundaries around the person who doesn't feel completely trustworthy, which would lead to both partners being able to stop the tug-of-war between hyperfocus and hypoarousal.

Boundaries can feel scary to implement, especially when someone has been in relationship with people who press and press and press relationally. This is the tough part for Dan; he does not have an experience of setting boundaries with Angela that feels doable and safe. When Vanessa asks him to set boundaries with Angela, he feels uncomfortable and scared, like what she is asking him to do is impossible. Vanessa fears that she won't be believed and will have to continue to ignore her experience in order for Dan to feel more comfortable. This is the stuck place for Dan and Vanessa. They both feel threatened by each other's need in the context of their relationship with Angela, and they can't see a way toward connection.

CONFLICT TO CONNECTION: VANESSA AND DAN'S SESSION

Dan and Vanessa begin the session looking anxious. They both have come into the session hopeful this could help, but also very aware of how often this conversation has ended poorly.

VANESSA: Dan's mom, Angela, just has this way of weaseling herself into our life and our decisions. When we had Isabella, she made some comment about my needing to get a more "family friendly" job, and then Dan started talking to her about what our plans are for day care and she was trying to elbow her way into taking care of Isabella.

DAN: She was not trying to muscle her way in. I was just answering a question about what we were doing. I really don't get what the big deal is. You are so sensitive about her.

VANESSA: I'm sensitive because she is nosy and opinionated and judgmental. She doesn't need to have an opinion about what I do for work. The fact that she thinks she has that right and then keeps making comments about it when I am not around makes me feel like I can't trust her with anything.

DAN: Vanessa, you care too much. The way you handle Mom is just to ignore her. She doesn't have to get to you unless you let her. I don't want her to watch Isabella, and I don't feel like she has to even if she asks about our day care plan. She can think and say whatever she wants. It doesn't impact me.

VANESSA: That's the problem. I'm telling you it impacts me, and you don't care. I don't think avoiding the whole situation is a good tactic. You might have avoided conflict with your mom your whole life, but that doesn't mean this is a healthy thing to do. It's like she is controlling our whole relationship. You care more about not upsetting your mom than you care about how I feel and what is going to be best for Isabella.

ERIN: Dan, do you care more about not upsetting your mom?

DAN: No, but it's complicated. My mom is a lot to deal with, and she does try to make things her business that are not her business. She has done it my whole life, and the best thing to do is to pay it no attention.

ERIN: Can you also see how that strategy is not working for Vanessa? In the end it's not working for you, either, because you and Vanessa are sitting here with us.

This is a question that is meant to start the process of attuning (step 2 of intentional expressing). Dan has stated his mom is a lot to deal with, and Erin is asking Dan to tune into what this feels like for him and then subsequently how it might feel for Vanessa. We expand on the question below.

STEPHEN: Dan, what is the deal with your mom? What makes her complicated?

DAN: I remember when I was a teenager and would get upset with her for coming into my room and snooping around. I would tell her I didn't like it, that I felt like she wasn't giving me any space for myself, and she would get angry and then start pouting. She would start saying things like "I'm just trying to show some interest in my son's life, and he keeps telling me to go away." It was confusing and she wouldn't stop unless I tried to make it better by apologizing or just letting her say her piece.

STEPHEN: So you also know what it feels like to have your mom push her way into your life in a way you don't like.

DAN: Yeah.

If we help Dan see that he's had a similar experience with his mom, perhaps he can believe Vanessa's experience and not be defensive.

STEPHEN: And you have the feeling that your mom's way of being is intractable and you have to be the one to make the adjustment if you still want to be in relationship with her. It's either you "put up with your mom" or you don't have a relationship with her.

DAN: Sort of. I do feel like trying to confront her would drastically impact my relationship with her. I would just see her less or she would be more difficult to be around. I guess there is a chance that she would just cut me off, but that doesn't seem likely.

ERIN: Dan, your relationship with your mom seems important to you. Would you mind elaborating on that?

DAN: Well, she's my mom. Also, all the family events and stuff are at her place, so if I want to see my other family, then I have to see her, too. I appreciate my family and want Isabella to know them and feel a part of the family like I did and still do.

ERIN: Vanessa, apart from Dan's mom, do you want to be a part of Dan's family? Do you want Isabella to experience Dan's family?

VANESSA: Yes. I love Dan's family. His uncles and aunts and cousins are all so much fun to be around. It's just that his mom can make those experiences feel stressful and tense for me. I like seeing his family, but I also feel on guard when we go to his mom's house. I am just waiting for the next comment she is going to make that makes me feel angry or makes me feel bad about myself—either as a parent or as Dan's partner.

STEPHEN: Vanessa, Dan's tactic has been to ignore his mom. It seems he is asking you to employ the same tactic. What about this request feels wrong or hurtful?

Now we shift to helping Vanessa intentionally express through attuning, reflecting, and sharing.

VANESSA: Well, it hurts because I am trying to tell Dan something feels awful for me and he keeps telling me it feels this way *because* of me. It's like he doesn't believe me and I am the problem. The problem is the way his mom interacts with people. Everyone tiptoes around her. It feels unfair that she has that much power and that I am being told it's my fault. It seems so backwards and wrong to ignore. I feel controlled and I feel like I am being told how I feel does not matter.

STEPHEN: Dan, can you see how the avoiding tactic communicates to Vanessa that she is the problem and that she needs to let your mom control the situation?

DAN: Yeah, I can see that. I don't think I have ever really thought about how the whole family, me included, are being controlled by my mom's way of interacting. We are all just trying to not make waves around her.

Dan is practicing intentional listening. His statement is part of repair (step 4). He is taking accountability for how his tendency to ignore his mom makes Vanessa feel controlled.

STEPHEN: But something about making waves feels important.

DAN: I guess it feels scary to press the issue. The few times I have seen this happen, it has not gone well. She makes a big scene, starts talking about it with everyone, and she plays the victim card, saying, "I'm so misunderstood." She pushes you into feeling you have to fix it. Honestly, just thinking about this makes me feel a little sick to my stomach.

ERIN: Hmm, you actually realize what it feels like to have your mom turn things up if you are her target?

DAN: It feels awful.

ERIN: That is what Vanessa is trying to tell you. She feels awful around your mom, and she wants you to support her and help steer this relationship in a way that can change this feeling. For her, avoidance perpetuates the awful feeling. Honestly, I don't hear you saying anything different about how avoidance makes you feel. You are just more practiced in ignoring the awful feeling. It seems like this might have worked for you, but Vanessa is trying to tell you this doesn't work for her or your family.

Vanessa, can you hear the difficulty Dan is experiencing thinking about trying to shift out of avoiding his mom? It's not that he doesn't care about you, it's that he doesn't like how it feels to have to engage his mom. It's hard to jump in and start setting boundaries with her. He has tried, others have tried, and it's been bad.

VANESSA: I can see that.

Vanessa is practicing intentional listening by suspending her defensiveness and believing Dan's experience.

DAN: I can see that you are trying to tell me you feel awful. I get it. It does feel bad. I feel stuck. I don't know what to do. It's kind of how I have felt my whole life with my mom.

VANESSA: I feel stuck, too. I don't want to make things worse for you. I just want our family—you, me, and Isabella—not to get stuck in being controlled by your mom's moods, interactions, and opinions.

STEPHEN: Dan, what do you think about what Vanessa just said? She doesn't want your family to repeat this pattern of being controlled by one person.

DAN: That makes sense. I don't want that, either.

STEPHEN: So right there! That's the starting point. Do you both see it?

VANESSA: See what?

STEPHEN: At the start of this conversation, you felt like you wanted different things in terms of the relationship with Dan's mom. The common ground is that you both don't want to feel controlled by your mom's style of relating. What you are trying to agree on is how to interact with your mom in a way that doesn't feel controlling, which is something you both want.

DAN: I can see that. We both don't like being controlled by Mom and we want that to stop.

VANESSA: That is good to hear. I think I didn't know Dan felt controlled. It just seemed like he didn't care.

ERIN: It feels clear that he cares, it's just he doesn't know what else to do.

DAN: Exactly.

STEPHEN: So where we are now is that you both can see you don't want to be controlled by your mom's style of relating and you have to come to some kind of collaboration about how to do this in a way that feels good to you both. Granted, it won't be perfect, but this is a bit different than feeling that you want different things.

DAN: I can see that. I need to give a little on my "avoid" approach, and Vanessa doesn't have to make it sound like I need to cut off my mom.

VANESSA: Yes, and I don't want you to cut things off with your mom. I want to be clear about how we interact with her and what she gets to know about our lives. I want your help in that area.

DAN: I get it. I can do that.

Dan and Vanessa have moved into repair and are trying to develop a different plan of action.

BUT HOW CAN I ACTUALLY SAY ANY OF THIS TO MY PARTNER? SAMPLE SCRIPTS

Some partners weren't allowed to put up a boundary in dealing with their loved ones. Other partners may have felt like they needed a boundary every second of the day. Nervous systems try to keep us safe, but that does not mean we got to choose how our nervous system reacted. Some of us freeze when we wish we could act. Some of us act when we wish we could flee. Just because we developed one way of reacting to our family and environment does not mean we can't learn a new one. It is not easy, but it is possible and worth it so that you get your own choice back.

Boundaries do not have to be negative. In fact, boundaries can be good! Boundaries can be the thing that allow you and your partner to safely be in relationship with challenging people (or when necessary, make the choice to no longer be in that relationship). They also allow you and your partner to feel safe with each other. They also give you the opportunity to raise your kids to express what feels safe and unsafe to them and help them know how to take care of themselves in those situations, an experience many of us unfortunately did not have as a kid. We can't know the exact wording that will best suit you and your partner, but here are some sample suggestions to engage in healthy conflict and get the conversation started.

Intentional Expressing for Both Partners

"I feel uncomfortable sometimes around Uncle Rob when he has been drinking. I'd like to discuss how we are going to handle being around him now that we will be taking Charlie to his house for Sunday dinners. When would be a good time for you to discuss that before Sunday?"

"I want our kids to feel empowered to say no to the physical touch of another, no matter who that person is. I know your grandmother is not trying to upset Kelvin, but to me, making Kelvin let her hug him even when he is clearly not wanting to feels like we are sending him the wrong message. I really believe we can stop this dynamic for him without making some massive ordeal around it in front of the whole family."

"I know the trip with your friends is coming up, and I was hoping we could talk about our expectations before we go into it so we can both enjoy it."

"I know when we have tried to talk about this before, you have heard me say I don't want your parents to meet our kid. And I want to start with I am not saying that. What I am wanting us to discuss is what is going to be the best way for your parents to meet our kid in a way that can feel good to us all. I was thinking we could meet them out at that place they love so I would know how long to expect things to be and they would know we thought about what they would like. What does that sound like for you?"

QUESTIONS FOR REFLECTION

1. Are there any people in your life currently where you feel like you have a toxic or tricky relationship? Does your partner?

2. What does the word *boundaries* mean to you? What did they look like or feel like in your family growing up? What about for your partner?

3. Can you think of a time growing up where you saw your parents enforce a boundary where it did not go well? Can you think of a time in your childhood where you tried to enforce a boundary and it went well? What happened?

4. What are some ways you and your partner push each other to the extremes when talking about your own or your partner's family? Can you identify some specific ways you are contributing to that polarization and take responsibility for your part in that?

5. Do you feel like you have been avoiding this conflict? Is there anything about this chapter that resonated with you? Did it stir any stories about how your and your partner's childhoods may have taught conflicting ideas about boundaries and what to do and how to approach relationships that do not feel healthy for

you? Do you know how you want your own children to approach tricky people? Have you considered that what you may want for your kids may be different from what you feel you have had to do in relationships? And can you see any areas where you may want something for your kid and not be extending the same message to your partner?

CHAPTER 15

The "Why Can't You Just Get over It?" Conflict

TRIP AND JUN have been together for five years and have two kids—Zara, who is three, and Ren, who is one. They both work full time outside of the home, and Jun's mom takes care of the kids during the day. Trip and Jun's pregnancy and birth experience with Zara went smoothly, but Jun's pregnancy with Ren was very stressful. Jun experienced regular spotting throughout her pregnancy, which made both Trip and her anxious, because they had experienced pregnancy loss previously.

Trip and Jun responded to Jun's spotting differently.

JUN: Trip, I think talking about my anxiety and fears about this situation is actually going to help me feel less stressed.

TRIP: I don't want to be a part of generating more worry, Jun. Talking about what might happen is just worrying about a future that is not real. I don't want to get worked up with you about this.

JUN: How can you not see that I'm not trying to work myself up? This is real. We could lose this pregnancy. We have lost one before. That's not some fake reality. I'm talking about something that has happened and could happen again.

TRIP: When we lost our first pregnancy, you wanted to talk about it all the time, and all it did was make things worse. You got more and more depressed, and it's like our life stopped moving anywhere. You were so sad for so long. I don't get why you are trying to go back there.

JUN: I *made myself* depressed? You were about as caring and supportive to me when we lost our pregnancy as you are being now. So I guess I'm the fool for thinking it would be any different.

Trip and Jun never resolved their differences about Jun's pregnancy with Ren, and in some ways, Trip felt that having a healthy baby vindicated him and his approach to their pregnancy scare. He would say to Jun, "I knew it would be okay." Jun got even more furious with Trip and his continued dismissiveness toward her. What she also noticed is that she felt angry with him not only about her pregnancy with Ren but also about their past pregnancy loss.

Jun realized that after their pregnancy loss she wanted badly to talk with Trip about the experience, but he seemed to ignore her attempts to talk. She felt that he kept telling her to move on and get better. He didn't say this directly, not at the time, but he would say things like "We can try again" or "I know this is hard, but just sitting around talking about it is only going to make it worse." In all of these comments, Jun heard Trip saying, "Stop feeling. Hurry up and get over this."

Eventually after the pregnancy loss, Jun did feel like she had to move on because Trip wouldn't engage with her. She had a few friends who had experienced pregnancy loss and felt safe to express herself with them. So she moved on, disregarding her own feelings about wanting to discuss this with Trip, and pushed forward, focusing on being pregnant again. When she and Trip got pregnant with Ren and they made it safely through the pregnancy, they were thrilled to have him. It felt like maybe things were okay. Their life moved on. They had two healthy kids and were grateful for their family.

Jun would say that she and Trip have a good relationship now, yet at times Jun's anger boils up and she finds herself thinking again about how lonely she felt after their pregnancy loss and throughout the pregnancy with Ren. Typically it happens when Jun feels she is stressed or overwhelmed with parenting and work and reaches out to Trip for help or understanding.

Jun: You know, Trip, you never change. Ever since our pregnancy loss, you refuse to listen to me when I am trying to tell you something is important to me.

Trip: Oh no, not this again. Are you going to hold that against me forever?

Jun: Well, how about we just go back to this past year, when we had Ren and you did the same thing, or last week, when I was trying to tell you I feel like I am getting crushed by parenting and work and you told me I was blowing things out of proportion?

Trip: Jun, you always do this. It's like you have an unending file of all the stuff I've done wrong, and in any fight, you flip through it and give me a history of how I am nothing but uncaring. How am I supposed to ever compete with that?

Jun: It's not a competition, Trip. How about you actually pay attention to what I am saying and take me seriously?

This is where Jun and Trip get stuck. The past keeps coming up, and the same pattern of Trip's feeling blamed and Jun's feeling dismissed cycles through the couple's relationship.

WHY YOU NEED THIS CONFLICT

Resentment is nasty. No one wants to feel it, and no one wants to feel it directed at them. Resentment starts with an experience of not being acknowledged, seen, heard, believed, and engaged in your experience.

Often the resentments that couples come to us with are about sleep, time with friends, working out, being on the phone, taking forever in the bathroom, and work-life imbalance, to name a few. Couples think these are "silly" things to fight about and can't figure out why these trivial things keep coming up. Couples also have resentment about "bigger" things like the pregnancy loss Jun and Trip can't stop fighting about. The "bigger" things couples come in with are: processing addiction now that a partner is in recovery; trying to "get over" their partner having an affair; how poorly the engagement went (often feels like a sign the partner didn't care to get it right); if they are married, the ring given comes up (commonly it feels like a demonstration of how little the partner knows them); a partner who has ADHD, depression, or a chronic illness, to name just a few (no one wants to resent their partner for these things but it is very common).

You need this conflict because there is not a couple in the world that does not deal with resentment in their relationship. It might sound negative to say that resentment is a part of every relationship, but this is just realistic. No partner can perfectly understand the experience of their partner every time. No partner can always be available and in the mood to lend an understanding ear to their partner. No partner is flawlessly selfless to the degree that they never feel bothered by their partner's need to be seen, heard, and engaged.

Mistakes happen. Your partner comes to you with something personal, important, and vulnerable. They try to tell you about it, and you blow it off or you miss how important it is to them. Maybe your partner doesn't say anything about what happened—they just quietly move on. Or maybe your partner does say something to you about their feelings being hurt and you get defensive and blow them off. Whatever the case, these things happen, and when they keep happening or when they happen regarding a monumental event or experience, it builds up.

Resentment is like the cholesterol of a relationship. Often you are not aware of it and everything seems fine until the pathways to the heart of a relationship (love, kindness, patience, the benefit of the doubt, playfulness, respect, humor, curiosity) are blocked and the lifeblood of your relationship cannot flow between you and your partner. You and your partner will find your relationship is in critical condition. Resentment that has hardened impacts every facet of a parenting partner relationship. Thus it's no longer about the pregnancy loss or the missed anniversary or the lack of support during pregnancy. It suddenly becomes about every detail of the relationship.

HOW THIS CONFLICT GOES WRONG

This conflict turns into an unhelpful stuck argument when partners don't take the time to listen to each other. This happens because anger and defensiveness are what couples generally express when the conflict is based on resentment. Anger and defensiveness are like two earplugs that shut out the opportunity to connect. What they block partners from hearing is the deep hurt below the surface of resentment.

We experienced the reality of resentment in our relationship around the ever-present and contentious topic of sleep. Historically, all our kids have preferred to be put to sleep by Erin. When the kids were infants, this was because she nursed them to sleep, and as they progressed through the toddler years, their preference for Erin in this regard continued to hold true.

What this meant for Erin is that there were many nights where she lost time that she might have had to herself, while Stephen got extended periods of time to himself in the evening hours. On the off chance that Erin wouldn't fall asleep with the kids and could have an opportunity to have some time for herself or to hang out with Stephen, she still found herself going back into the bedroom multiple times to soothe the kids if they started to stir or needed to nurse. The long and short of it is that Erin, who already felt taxed and like she was bearing a lot of the parenting load, felt like she was also left to carry out the nighttime routine with the kids.

When Erin tried to address her exhaustion and frustration with being the sole parent for the nighttime routine, Stephen was not very receptive. Conversations would go something like this. Erin would say, "I am feeling really frustrated with the assumption that I am the one that is going to do the nighttime routine. I wish you would try and jump in and help." Then Stephen would retort, "I'm not sure what I could do. My going in would only upset them further." Erin would maintain that she was not trying to blame Stephen, but that she was asking him to try and be creative in thinking about how he could be part of the nighttime routine so that she did not feel so alone and exhausted in the process.

What happened over time as we had this repeated conversation is that Erin started to feel that Stephen was not acknowledging, seeing, hearing, believing, or engaging her in the conversation. Not only that, he was still getting more time to himself when the kids were asleep. As this continued to happen, Erin's resentment began to grow. Soon the conflict was not just about sleep but about all the other ways that Erin had been feeling Stephen was not listening to her. So a fight about sleep could also turn into a fight about things that had happened related to pregnancy, the postpartum period, work, or extended family dynamics.

As Erin felt more dismissed, her resentment grew and colored how she saw the relationship. She expressed more anger at Stephen, and he became more defensive. What we each missed was the hurt and loneliness each of us was feeling in this conflict. (Stephen was also feeling hurt because the manner in which Erin expressed her anger was not always kind or fair.) This conflict went wrong and goes wrong when couples get stuck expressing their anger and defensiveness and not intentionally listening.

CONFLICT TO CONNECTION: TRIP AND JUN'S SESSION

Jun and Trip find themselves feeling like they are in a good place, then suddenly all it takes is for one tiny thing to happen and they are launched into a seemingly never-ending cycle of old hurts being revisited and felt all over again.

> ERIN: So, Jun, if I am understanding the story you are telling us, there have been some important moments where you have felt deeply sad and you have tried to tell Trip and he has not acknowledged your experience.
>
> JUN: Not just not acknowledged my experience. He very clearly told me that what I am feeling is only making it worse, and in a sense he has told me I am wrong for how I feel.
>
> TRIP: Hang on. I haven't told you you're wrong. I have said that continuing to sit and focus on feeling sad doesn't feel like it is going to help you feel better or our relationship be any better. I am not saying what you are feeling is wrong.

Trip defends and does not believe the experience Jun is sharing. He is not intentionally listening.

JUN: How can you not hear that what you are saying communicates to me that what I am feeling is wrong? What is so bad about having strong feelings about something, and who says there needs to be a time limit on it?

STEPHEN: Is this little sound bite how the conversation typically goes? Jun, you express some frustration, some—dare I say?—anger, and, Trip, you defend what you have said and try to tone the conversation down?

JUN: Trip isn't toning the conversation down. He's trying to tone *me* down!

STEPHEN: Hmm . . . Jun, what do you mean by that?

Before Jun gets fully triggered, we ask a question to shift the conversation toward intentional expressing. Stephen is asking her to attune (step 2) to the emotion she is feeling.

JUN: I feel like Trip thinks I'm too much. I mean, it goes all the way back to our pregnancy loss. That was one of the most devastating times in my life, and I was falling apart with grief. It was so dark, so painful emotionally, physically, and psychologically. It was awful, and what I remember Trip doing was telling me to stop making myself sad or making it worse by talking about it all the time. He didn't want to hear how I felt, and I'm just so sick of feeling like I can't express myself.

Jun reflects (step 3) on some of the stories that are informing her emotions.

STEPHEN: Trip, do you want to tone Jun down?

TRIP: No, I mean, I just don't understand why we have to wallow in the bad stuff. The pregnancy loss was bad. The pregnancy with Ren was scary. When hard things happen, I would rather have some hope and try and enjoy something each day rather than go down a dark hole and stay there. Jun gets stuck, and who knows if she is going to come back from her sadness and grief?

STEPHEN: So you *do* try and tone her down.

TRIP: I mean, hearing you say it so bluntly sounds awful, but yeah, I guess I do.

ERIN: What sounds awful about it, Trip?

TRIP: Well, it sounds terrible to be trying to tone a person down, and I never want to tone Jun down. Especially not her.

ERIN: How come you especially don't want to tone Jun down?

TRIP: It just sounds controlling, which I don't want to be. But also, it's Jun. Jun is someone I respect, and I want to hear from her. I like her ideas, I like talking to her, I like her. I don't want her to feel toned down.

STEPHEN: I wonder, Trip, if you can see that you are toning her down even though you don't want to.

TRIP: Yes, I can.

Trip has suspended his defensiveness, believed Jun's experience, and even begun repair by taking accountability for toning Jun down. He is intentionally listening.

ERIN: Jun. How are you hearing what Trip is saying?

JUN: Well, it ticks me off. I have been aching just trying to tell him how scared and sad and hard all of this has been. All of it. From the moment we first got pregnant to now has been so hard. I have loved it and yet I have felt like I barely have made it through. He says he wants to hear from me, but he doesn't want to hear that stuff. He just wants to hear things that aren't hard. So I don't care that he says he wants to hear from me. He doesn't show it in a single thing he does.

Jun is in an activated place and defensive.

ERIN: Jun, Trip has really hurt you, hasn't he?

JUN: So much, he has hurt me so much.

STEPHEN: Trip, I imagine that is hard for you to hear.

TRIP: Yeah, I feel awful and I don't know how to change what has happened.

STEPHEN: I'm curious about something, Trip. You said that you didn't feel focusing on all the bad stuff is helpful because it felt like going into a dark hole, and then you said something that stuck out to me: "Who knows if she is going to come back from her sadness and grief?" What did you mean by that?

This is looking to have Trip intentionally express through attuning to the emotions, reflecting on the story that shapes the emotion, and sharing with Jun. The hope is Jun will hear the deeper story and be able to suspend her defensiveness and move toward repair through intentional listening.

TRIP: Like Jun was saying, the pregnancy loss was really devastating. It is one of the saddest things we have ever experienced as a couple, and Jun was so not herself. Her heart, mind, and body were confused and undergoing so much turmoil. It was really hard to see her struggling, and I think I started to worry that maybe she wouldn't be able to come back to herself. That maybe I would lose her in some way like we lost the pregnancy. I don't really know. I just felt scared and I was sad about the pregnancy, but I was also really concerned for Jun.

STEPHEN: Jun, did you know that Trip was worried for you?

JUN: Not really. I mean, I know he was sad and was concerned for me, but I don't think I knew he was afraid I might not come back to myself.

TRIP: I was so worried, Jun. I just wanted you to be okay and I knew you weren't and I felt helpless.

ERIN: So maybe one of the things you did was try and get Jun as far away from the bad feelings and grief that seemed to be the root of the problem. You tried to refocus her attention away from the bad stuff to pull her out of the dark hole.

TRIP: I don't think I have ever thought about it like that, but that feels right. It just felt like a bad idea to keep talking about how sad she was and how painful the pregnancy loss was. I felt panicky about it all.

Through Trip's intentional expressing, a deeper story has come out that helps Jun see that Trip is not wanting to tone her down because her experience is not important, but due to his own fear of losing her.

STEPHEN: And this is where the pattern of resentment started. We could call it the tone-it-down pattern.

JUN: It definitely feels like that is when it started for me. I think that what happened with Ren activated the pattern in an intense way similar to the pregnancy loss. I want to talk about it and I feel Trip trying to silence me.

TRIP: I can see that. I think the pregnancy loss has cast a longer shadow on our relationship than I thought or maybe I knew. It was just so scary that I ignored it.

ERIN: Which means you ignored Jun, too, though that wasn't the intended result. As you said, the intended result was to pull her out of a black hole.

STEPHEN: The long shadow that seems to have been cast on your relationship is the shadow of resentment. Jun, you were really hurt by how Trip ignored you after the pregnancy loss. The wound has been so deep that as other moments have taken place in your relationship where you feel ignored or toned down, it has opened up that first one even more. So things have stacked up and your resentment has grown toward Trip.

JUN: That sounds right.

STEPHEN: We have heard a bit more of the story, but we have also gone a bit deeper into the motivating forces. Trip, your defensiveness is a direct result of your fear—fear that Jun will get lost in her sadness and not come back. In order to prevent this, you tell her she should stop being so sad, and when she says you're wrong, you defend your position because you don't want her to be lost to a dark hole. What does that sound like to you?

TRIP: I'm tracking. Sounds accurate.

STEPHEN: Jun, you are just flat-out angry. Angry that Trip has not heard you. Your anger is not bad or unwarranted. But your anger is getting in the way of your future happiness. Today your anger has helped us all see that something very important is going on and that there needs to be some kind of change. Would you agree with that, Trip?

TRIP: I am most certainly hearing that something important is being said and that something needs to change.

STEPHEN: Your anger has been helpful, Jun, but your anger is not just saying something is important and needs to change. It is also saying you are hurt. I think you have expressed a little bit today what that hurt feels like. I'm sure there is much more to it and much more we need to hear about. Do you feel that Trip has listened in a different way today?

JUN: Yes. I think it's because you are both here, but I don't feel like he has been defensive or tried to tell me to tone things down. In fact I feel like I understand him a little more and understand why he had been defensive and tried to tone me down. I don't like it, and it feels very hard to move on from, but I do feel like he heard me differently and I heard him differently.

Jun is doing a good job of suspending her defensiveness and believing Trip's experience. She admits that this is hard, but intentional listening is helping her grasp the fuller story of what has been taking place.

ERIN: Trip, how do you think you heard Jun differently?

TRIP: I think just hearing myself say I wanted to tone her down felt sobering to me. It felt wrong, and then thinking about the pregnancy loss and how scary it was, I think I realized I was scared and I shut Jun down. I ignored what was happening for her and then hearing her say how grief-stricken she has been and how sad and how Ren's pregnancy brought a lot of this back up . . . I don't know. I can see how she has been hurting and I have not been listening and how that has added to her hurt. It just feels clearer to me.

This is Trip repairing and seeking resolution.

ERIN: Jun, what is it like to hear Trip say that?

JUN: I appreciate it so much. It also makes me angry that it has taken so long for this to happen. Why did it have to take so long?

STEPHEN: And this is the tough part. You both have a choice here. Jun, you can choose to forgive Trip or not. Trip, I think there is a part of this where you have to choose to forgive yourself for missing Jun and being part of her hurt.

JUN: None of that sounds easy. I don't even know if it is possible.

STEPHEN: You're right—it might not be possible, but there's still a chance it could be. Forgiveness does not mean you forget what happened. That is part of the story. But there is also a part of the story that you didn't know. You didn't know that Trip's dismissal of your experience and his subsequent defense of dismissing you was done out of fear and worry for you. This doesn't mean it's okay that Trip did this, but it does expand the story. It expands it from "Trip hurt me" to "Trip hurt me, but he also was desperately worried about me and cares for me." The choice to forgive here is which part of the story you choose to focus on and let win. You can let the hurt part win, or you can let the part that says Trip cares for you win. And honestly, there will be times when you struggle to not focus on the hurt and angry side. Again, that is why forgiveness is a choice and is work.

JUN: I get it. I feel like I have to think through all this and figure out what I'm feeling.

STEPHEN: Of course you do. Trip, I think choosing to forgive in your case looks like not getting lost in the mistake but moving toward the action you wish you had taken. I think you did that a bit today by acknowledging that you hurt Jun and not trying to defend what happened but doing the very thing she says she wants from you: to acknowledge, see, hear, believe, and engage her in her experience.

TRIP: Absolutely. I can see how being defensive is not forgiving myself and just trying to cover my tail. Jun, I missed it. I missed you. I messed up and I want to understand, if you feel willing to offer me that chance.

JUN: I really appreciate you saying that, Trip. I want to be willing. Right now I just have to take a breath and figure out what I am feeling.

TRIP: I get it.

Trip and Jun have moved into working for repair—accountability, forgiveness, and different action. This hopefully can shift the pregnancy loss story from an attachment-breaking interaction into an attachment-making interaction.

STEPHEN: Resentment takes some undoing and some time to work through, but the process is straightforward. I think one way to envision the rest of our time working together is addressing resentment head-on by not getting lost in anger and defensiveness but rather by understanding what choosing to forgive means practically.

BUT HOW CAN I ACTUALLY SAY ANY OF THIS TO MY PARTNER? SAMPLE SCRIPTS

Resentment will ruin your parenting partner relationship. The pervasive nature of resentment will move into every facet of your interactions with your partner and create constant disconnection; but you can move from conflict to connection, and these scripts can help start the process.

Intentional Expressing—Partner Feeling Resentful

"I am noticing that I am feeling angry toward you. Are you noticing this? I don't want to feel angry. Can we talk about what is going on?"

"I have been thinking and I am noticing that I am feeling a lot of resentment toward you. I know that probably doesn't feel good to hear and that your automatic response might be to defend yourself. I don't want to feel this way and I don't want to blame you. I do want to talk with you about how I am feeling and some hurt I am feeling. Do you think you would be able to have this conversation with me?"

Intentional Expressing—Partner the Resentment Is Directed Toward

"I can tell that you are really angry with me. I am not understanding what I did or said that has activated your anger, but I would like to understand. I don't want to make you feel this way. Would you be able to talk about it with me?"

"You said that you are feeling some resentment toward me. Honestly, I don't like hearing this, but I do want to understand what has been going on. I think I might have some resentment built up myself. I want to have this conversation with you."

QUESTIONS FOR REFLECTION

1. What are some of the key areas where you feel resentment in your relationship? Do you agree that all relationships develop some level of resentment?

2. Are you more apt to be the one expressing anger about resentment or being defensive when your partner expresses anger?

3. Do you believe that forgiveness is a choice?

4. When you consider expressing how you have been hurt in your relationship, what do you notice happens for you? Do you get scared? Do you get numb? Do you get angry? Do you find yourself avoiding your feelings?

5. Do you feel like you have been avoiding this conflict? Is there anything about this chapter that seemed to resonate with you? Did it stir any feelings or memories? Why might those feelings and memories be coming up now in the season of life, parenting, and partnership you are currently in?

Where Do We Go from Here?

PARENTING PLACES A couple's relationship in a unique context of wonder, adventure, chaos, and stress. The stress can quickly and easily create a feeling of disconnection between partners and result in conflict. We wrote a book about the importance of engaging in conflict so that you can move toward connection in your parenting partner relationship and stop having unhealthy conflict. So you can enjoy the beautiful moments, laugh together, and cherish each other along the way. Using the conflict-to-connection equation, you and your partner can discover how conflict is an opportunity for connection.

To be very clear and fair to this process, we want you to think about how old you are. That is how long you have been practicing the protective strategies you currently have in place. You are not going to be able to just flip the script on these overnight. It will take practice and patience, just like a lot of parenting really, but it will not take nearly as long as you might think to start feeling the transformative nature of these tools in your daily life.

We suggest that when you feel a little change in a good direction, have a full-blown celebration! Seriously, mark it in any way that feels helpful to you. Just as you might give funny names to your conflicts, like the "dinosaur-pants disaster," you might also give names to when the conflict went great. It could be as silly as "We successfully engaged the strawberries-in-the-car-seat fiasco!" As couples, we spend a lot (a lot!) of time focusing on what is not going well, so making a point to celebrate when you have done something you like or are really proud of is an important skill for a good relationship but also to model for your kids.

Sometimes in trying to utilize the conflict-to-connection equation, you and your partner are not going to do it perfectly. You are going to say the snarky comment or check out on your phone rather than engage with your partner. It is going to happen. We hope less and less often, but it will. To the best of your ability, be curious and compassionate even when it feels all wrong. Repairing the rupture as quickly as possible is important for keeping the momentum going toward a new way of relating and building trust in each other.

In the eighteen years we have been practicing the conflict-to-connection equation, we can honestly say that the frequency, intensity, and duration of our conflicts have qualitatively changed. We have also been given the honor of being invited into the worlds of thousands of parenting partners doing the work to engage in conflict to find connection and have seen it work for them, too. When we do have conflict, we trust that the other is for us and that the intention of the conflict is a movement toward genuine mutual understanding and repair. We hope you feel a sense of this as you engage in healthy conflict with your parenting partner.

Additional Resources

A QUICK GUIDE TO HOW TO ENGAGE IN CONFLICT IN FRONT OF OUR KIDS

Should we have conflict in front of our kids? The short answer is yes. Yes, you should address tension when it is present. Kids are aware of the tension, and addressing it gives them the language to understand what they are feeling. But if the conflict has turned unhealthy in front of your kids, there are some things to keep in mind:

1. Remain calm and respectful.

2. Pay extra attention to your body language and the words you use (fewer words is best).

3. Stay on task and don't bring up old arguments.

4. Do not bring your kids into it (triangulation). An example of

what not to say is: "Don't you remember when Daddy did this same thing last week?"

5. Make certain they know there has been repair.

SAMPLE SCRIPTS FOR ADDRESSING
THE CONFLICT WITH OUR KIDS

If you trust you and your partner to have conflict and can keep it to an abbreviated version, there shouldn't be any reason you can't work the equation in front of your kids. Model the conflict-to-connection equation for them when you can; it's an invaluable life skill for them to learn. Short and sweet when kids are around is best, but if you and your partner are still practicing how to make all this run smoothly, here are some ideas for addressing the stressed or tense dynamic without having an intense argument in front of your kids (they definitely do not need to see that).

You know your kid best, so modify to what seems best for your kid's age and stage. These are ideas to help get you started thinking about what works best for you and your family.

1. "There is probably more to say on all of this later, but for now this is probably a good place to pause."

2. "I can tell something here is important and I want to understand. I also think we are struggling to communicate right now. Can we revisit this tonight?"

3. "I am not ready to talk more about this right now."

4. "That did not feel right to me. I need to think more about it. Then can we come back to this later?"

5. "We are really misunderstanding each other right now, aren't we? I want you to know that's not my intention. Could we pause and try again tonight?"

6. "I am really missing something very important to you, I can tell. That is not my intention. Should we try again later? Maybe tomorrow during our lunch hours?"

SAMPLE SCRIPTS TO ADDRESS THE REPAIR WITH OUR KIDS

"Mom and I were frustrated, but remember how we told you we would work it out? We did! We worked to understand what was frustrating each of us. We hope you know you can talk with us when you are frustrated and we will work it out, too."

"Dad and I disagreed about the best way to handle that situation. But did you hear that? We were able to tell each other what we were thinking and feeling about it and came up with a solution we both feel good about."

"I hurt Mommy's feelings earlier. I am so thankful she knew she could come and tell me about it. We want to know when we have hurt your feelings, too."

"Daddy and I worked really hard to understand each other and are so glad to know we both will take the time to really listen to each other."

"We had a plan that was working, and then we realized it wasn't working anymore. We have come up with a new plan we think will work great for all of us."

"Mama and I were having a hard time saying what we were feeling. Sometimes it is hard to know what to say in the moment, and sometimes it is hard to understand what someone is saying, especially when it is really important to them. But it is worth trying to know what feels important to the people we love. We want to know about what's important to you, too. Even if we do not always understand the first or second or even the third time, we will keep trying."

Bibliography

Massimo Ammaniti and Vittorio Gallese. *The Birth of Intersubjectivity: Psychodynamics, Neurobiology, and the Self.* New York: W. W. Norton, 2014.

Daniel A. Hughes. *Attachment-Focused Parenting: Effective Strategies to Care for Children.* New York: W. W. Norton, 2009.

Daniel A. Hughes and Jonathan Baylin. *Brain-Based Parenting: The Neuroscience of Caregiving for Healthy Attachment.* New York: W. W. Norton, 2012.

Susan M. Johnson. *The Practice of Emotionally Focused Couple Therapy: Creating Connection,* 3rd ed. New York: Routledge, Taylor & Francis Group, 2020.

Daniel J. Siegel. *The Developing Mind: How Relationships and the Brain Interact to Shape Who We Are,* 3rd ed. New York: Guilford Press, 2020.

Daniel J. Siegel. *The Mindful Therapist: A Clinician's Guide to Mindsight and Neural Integration.* New York: W. W. Norton, 2010.

Michael White and David Epston. *Narrative Means to Therapeutic Ends.* New York: W. W. Norton, 1990.

Acknowledgments

W E ARE PARENTING partners ourselves, and we know firsthand how challenging and how profoundly beautiful these years are for families. We wrote this book because it is the book we wished we'd had to help us navigate these fights, and we sincerely hope they will be the help you need. We hope in these pages you find deeper connection to yourself and to your partner. We are grateful beyond words to the people who have helped us along our journey and in writing this book.

First, we want to acknowledge how grateful we are for our family. Writing a book is a lot! We have been supported and loved through this process by our brothers and sisters, aunts and uncles, and all our nieces! Luke and Megan, we love you and thank you for loving us. Elisa, Caleb, Esther, and Clark, being able to parent side by side with you has been not just a lifeline at times, but a true joy. You have stabilized us and you have celebrated with us. Having shared roots with you and your families is one of our greatest privileges in life.

We want to thank Rachelle Gardner for helping us get our start and introducing us to Michelle Howry. Michelle, from our very first meeting you made this book better and helped us make it into one we ourselves grow more excited about by the day. It would not be what it is without you, thank you! We want to thank Ashley Di Dio for her editing of this book, and the rest of the team at Putnam who have helped to refine this book into what it is today: copyeditor Nancy Inglis, proofreaders Kathleen Go and Lisanne Kaufmann, production editor Brittany Bergman, production manager Erin Byrne, senior managing editor Emily Mileham, managing editor Maija Baldauf, creative director Anthony Ramondo, cover designer Sanny Chiu, publicists Ashley Hewlett and Jazmin Miller, and marketer Molly Pieper. Thank you all for your work on *Too Tired to Fight*!

We want to thank our community through social media and our private practice clients. We thank you for how you have supported and encouraged us and the ideas we present in this book. We are honored and humbled to be invited into your stories.

We want to offer a sincere thank-you to our kids. This has taken more time than you wanted it to, and all along the way you have been patient and encouraging. Great news, it's finished! We hope you always know what a gift you are to us and how being able to be your parents is an indescribable joy.

Index